Education and the Supreme Court

EDUCATION

UNIVERSITY OF ILLINOIS PRESS · URBANA, 1955

by Clark Spurlock

COURT

and the

SUPREME

DEDICATED

to

R. R. REICHART

Professor in History and

Philosophy of Education

Oregon State College

and to

THOSE OTHERS

WHOM I CALL TEACHER

PREFACE

This volume is intended to provide Supreme Court opinions bearing on education in a form readily useful to teachers and laymen. The cases involved have been assigned their constitutional context and are cast against the general historical background of their times. Then, because the Justices, more than most public servants, have had to give reasons for their actions at the moment of performance, and because many of the Court opinions which include these reasons have become notable documents in the history of American education, the Court is extensively quoted. It may be discovered that the Court's impressive building in Washington has grown close to affairs in and about our neighborhood schools.

This effort had its inception in material originally included in a doctoral dissertation submitted to the School of Education at Oregon State College. The whole undertaking would not have reached the present point without the assistance of many people. Among them, Mr. Theodore Grams of the Portland Extension Center library proved a remarkably helpful member of a notably helpful profession.

CLARK SPURLOCK

Portland, Oregon

January, 1955

vii

CONTENTS

PART THREE

QUESTIONS ON RIGHTS OF PERSONS RAISED
UNDER THE FOURTEENTH (AND FIFTH) AMENDMENT

x

LIST OF EDUCATION CASES TREATED

SOME ADDITIONAL EDUCATION CASES

(Cited but not reviewed in detail)

INTRODUCTION

On the first Monday of next October, the most powerful judicial tribunal in the world will meet at Washington in regular annual session. Thence, until the following June, it will resume its role as an arbiter of American political and social development. The Supreme Court has been committed to this role since it began to exercise the power of judicial review and, it should be remembered, this power of judicial review is the outstanding fact in American jurisprudence. From the exercise of this power, Supreme Court decisions which bear clear social implications have lately included an increasing number which affect education.

Education, although affected by the decisions, is not, however, mentioned in the Constitution and is never, therefore, directly at issue before the Supreme Court. For the founding fathers, seeking to adjust the differing ideologies entangled in the colonial heritages and in American sectionalism, responded to the matter of education as they did to many others. They simply relegated it to the individual states and to the future through the expedient of making no reference to it in the original document. Nor has it been mentioned in any of the amendments.

Consequently, public education resides as a function of the state and local governments. Federal control can be exercised only through: (1) Such general federal power as that emanating from the guarantee

of religious freedom contained in the First Amendment as extended
to the states by the Fourteenth[1], and (2) through judicial review of
state and federal law. Many federal statutes, from the Ordinance of
1787 through the Morrill Act of 1862 and down to the G.I. Bill of
Rights and the current subsidies for programs of research, have made
the federal government, in words once used by Ellwood P. Cubberley,
"an interested, benevolent spectator in the growth of state school
systems" (12, p. 739).

Thus, the appearance of education before the Court remains always incidental—but not necessarily of secondary significance—to
cases adjudicated within the Court's prescribed purview.

Indeed, as the Supreme Court has grown under certain of its strong
personalities and through the exigencies of history toward its present
stature, its decisions have increasingly involved education. By 1948,
Mr. Justice Jackson, speaking in the *McCollum* case (102, p. 478),
remarked that the Court exhibited tendencies to become the national
school board. This tendency became most noticeable during the second quarter of the present century, when more education cases were
argued before the Court than in all its previous history. The twenty-
five years that witnessed this acceleration also saw the cultural complexities within the nation increasing. At the same time the political
process was becoming increasingly centralized. Both the cultural complexities and the political process may have become thereby the more
sensitive to action by the Court, and the Court may have been made
the more sensitive by them. Most of the Supreme Court's decisions
affecting education during the whole period between 1789 and 1954
have turned upon the questions of: (1) State or federal power and
function, (2) Civil rights under the First and Fifth Amendments,
(3) "Due process of law" and "equal protection of the laws" under
the Fourteenth Amendment.

The foregoing classification should demonstrate both the oblique
nature of the relationship between education and the Court and the
diversity of the involvement. This may be amplified, with an indication of the chronology and accelerated frequency of contests, by
Table I.

The succeeding chapters will review the decisions in thirty-seven of
the forty-five cases shown in Table I. Though not discussed in detail,
the other eight cases shown by the table are mentioned in connection
with related cases which are viewed as more significant and which
are reviewed at length.

---

[1]These amendments and other constitutional provisions bearing on education
will be found in Appendix A.

TABLE I

SUPREME COURT DECISIONS AFFECTING EDUCATION

25-year Periods	No. of Decisions	Principal Constitutional Bases of Decisions:*			
		State or Federal Powers & Function	1st Amendment	5th & 14th Amendment Non-Race	Race
(1789) - 1800					
1801 - 1825	1	1			
1826 - 1850	1		1		
1851 - 1875	5	5			
1876 - 1900	2	1			1
1901 - 1925	9	3	1	4	1
1926 - 1950	19	5	7	1	6
1951 - (1954)	8		6		2
	45	15	15	5	10

*Some decisions involved more than the single basis indicated. Eight cases which are not treated in detail in this study are included in the table. The table is an over-simplification in many ways, and it is intended only as an indication of chronology and of the types of questions.

THE SUBJECT

The subject of this book is the effect of these decisions, and particularly the more significant of them, upon the students, their parents, and the teachers and administrators of the schools of the United States.

Obviously there may be differences of opinion as to the selection of cases which did affect education, or of how much they affected it. For example, it might legitimately be held that a great many decisions in taxation contests have affected the financial support of education and thereby the curriculum and instruction. Likewise, to take an extreme, opinions rendered on questions of state laws for inspection of foodstuffs may affect education by virtue of some incidental influence upon school lunch programs. Therefore, the selection to be included here is no doubt an arbitrary one.

By glancing first at those matters which seem prevalent in school problems, especially during the last quarter-century, three problem areas appeared, and the focus was brought upon: (1) Conflicts in which schools were involved with questions touching on the separation of church and state, and with the guarantee of freedom of speech. (2) Conflicts over segregation by race in schools. (3) Conflicts between individual rights and the requirements of the state. The third classification appears to underlie the other two; for here, with the conflicts most notably arising where parents' assertion of their rights to educate their children in a manner of their own choosing has clashed with local or national authority, the battle has frequently related to the first classification by being fought between religious beliefs and the requirements of the state as these requirements are furthered in public schools. Church and state both know that it is in the schools that the battle over convictions may be won. And the state, in its concern for convictions on political ideology, has imposed loyalty tests and oaths which have brought clashes with teachers. Likewise, Negro parents in asserting their rights to non-discriminatory treatment of their children have clashed with states which insist on the requirement that segregated public schools be maintained. Here, too, though not in the constitutional sense, men's minds and convictions are involved.

Next, a closer and longer look at Supreme Court decisions from the viewpoint of both educational and historical development under the Constitution revealed two general types of cases in which: (1) A school or a school system has been involved in conflicts between state and federal power and function under our system of dual government. (2) Acts of schools or school officials have been brought into conflict with the rights of individuals. Again the essential problem of the individual and the state appears in the second type. The first type, while not directly involving rights associated with human individuality, does include certain decisions which have affected the structure and support of our schools; moreover, these cases are useful to reveal and clarify the position of our school systems and school matters in the dual government established under our Constitution.

Hence these two types, which also comprehend the three problem areas noted previously, governed the selection of cases to be offered. Included in this study, then, are substantially all the cases relating to education and schools which pursuit of these matters through indexes and annotations of Supreme Court decisions reveal.

The selected cases will be presented by examining the questions and the contests within the framework of the prevailing constitutional and social context. This review will be accompanied by limited analyses of the decisions and by some comment upon consequences and implications. However, the nature of our federal system of government can make a particular decision by the Court have less effect beyond the specific circumstances or outside the state in which the case arose than would sometimes be supposed. In some cases the general effect of decisions rendered recently is largely conjectural. In other cases the Court does appear to have spoken clearly and with a certain finality in a mandate of nationwide application.

Therefore, as seems necessary, greater or lesser comment is included with the decisions to be treated. Moreover, neither the decision nor the comment on a single case may reveal the whole story until the issue has reached the Court in several of its possible aspects.

PURPOSE

The purpose here is to present Supreme Court decisions touching upon education in a form that will be readily useful to school administrators, school boards, teachers, and publicists. There is, of course, no dearth of information on the subject, but the educator who pursues a particular phase of the topic may often find that the information and materials sought can be assembled only with difficulty, and that they may then prove either too highly specific or too generalized to suit his demands. The following chapters seek to provide context for the Court's decisions, which are then presented very largely in the words of the Court itself.

Anyone concerned with education may be served in greater or lesser degree by a single work which is focused at the point where the highest judicial adjustments have been applied to the struggles by which the American public and their teachers have sought to establish their educational principles or their individual rights. Both the public and the educators may discover or sharpen two broad concepts: (1) That long-standing procedures with respect to the schools may well prove to be illegal upon challenge, and (2) that in certain directions the educators and legislators may possess more freedom of action than they have permitted themselves.

SOURCES AND CITATIONS

Materials from the press and from social and constitutional histories of the United States are used to supplement the Court reports, which are, of course, the chief source.

Those portions of the Court's decisions which are relevant to education and to broad constitutional development are quoted, usually in large parts and frequently at substantially the original length. Yet, to have reproduced all of the original in each of the decisions would have made this book longer than it need be to serve its purpose. Such material as, for example, the Court's statements on procedural matters, has been eliminated. Because education always arrives before the Court as incidental to the question at issue, the decision may include material which is largely extraneous to educational interest. Again, such material has been eliminated except as it contributes significantly to the constitutional framework for future contests over the same type of question. Obviously any material treated in this fashion becomes in some degree an interpretation as well as a special test of competence and good faith. Two criteria have been applied: (1) Is all the material relevant to education or to the problems prevailing for and about schools included, and (2) is the material giving development to the relevant constitutional points included? These two are, of course, actually but emphases within a single criterion. Accordingly, then, some of the cases to follow may appear to emphasize the Constitution while the others emphasize education, but all of them contribute to both.

An apparent inconsistency in citations of the Court's decisions results from a practice prior to 1875 of citing Supreme Court *Reports* by the name of the court reporter who prepared them and from a practice beginning with the 1875 volume (cited as 91 U. S.) of numbering the volumes consecutively. There are two unofficial publications of Supreme Court decisions: *United States Supreme Court Reporter* (cited as Sup. Ct.); and *United States Supreme Court Reports, Lawyers' Edition* (cited as L. Ed.). Most of the material quoted hereafter is from the *United States Supreme Court Reporter*. Three liberties have been taken in quoting the sources: (1) Where the original shows asterisks in ellipses, the dotted form has been substituted, (2) Where the words "affirmed" of "reversed" are separated by lines and spaces from the body of the decision in the original, the words have been brought to the juxtaposition expected in common usage, and (3) Where the typographical symbol for "section" or "sections" appears in the original the words have been spelled out.

The education cases have been classified and divided into three parts according to the categories shown in Table I. The basis for the Court's decision in a given case was not, of course, so discrete as such a simplified classification might indicate. Nor, indeed, are all the assignments entirely accurate in the strict constitutional sense. Therefore constitutional points upon which a decision actually turned are shown just preceeding the title for each case. It should be noted that, because the Court and Constitution change, decisions which once turned upon certain points alone might today turn upon others. Where this appears to be clearly so, the point made applicable by later circumstances is similarly shown, but in parenthesis. An example is the case of *Pierce v. Society of Sisters* in 1925 (128). There, the question bore religious connotations, but because the First Amendment's religious clause had not yet been extended to the states by the Court's interpretation of the Fourteenth Amendment, the question was decided under the latter amendment's "due process of law" clause alone.

Within each of the chapters to follow, the cases will be found in the chronological order of their decision, except for very similar cases which break the order slightly by being brought together. The bracketed numbers preceding the title in the heading of each case are arbitrary case numbers for this work.

A section designed to show briefly how cases reach the Supreme Court, and how the court then deals with them, is included as Appendix B. An abridged version of the Constitution of the United States is shown as Appendix A. Provisions which have had a bearing upon the "education cases" are thus more easily found for reference.

SOME SIMPLE CONCEPTS TO USE IN CONSIDERING COURT DECISIONS

Readers of Court decisions and opinions on education may find it helpful if they will:

(1) Remember that, just as an individual is presumed to be innocent until adjudged guilty, laws and regulations and rules governing administrative practice are presumed constitutional until declared otherwise.

(2) Take note of the principle that the concern of courts is with the reasonableness of the law, not with the wisdom of the law, and that the determination of reasonableness is entirely at the court's discretion. Since the two terms are as ambiguous to jurists as they are to laymen, different courts or different times may see a question entertained that would not be acceptable to other courts or other times. Moreover, and particularly for courts of last resort, there may be no guide in this matter except the court's own convictions as to what may be necessary and proper—that is, desirable.

(3) Hold no expectation that the courts will necessarily make definition of the point at issue, e.g., "due process of law." They may, in fact, expressly refuse definition in order to avert constraint in a similar contest later. Thus, future cases can be decided upon their merits rather than upon precedent—except for those precedents which buttress the action which seems reasonable at the time.

(4) Keep in mind the legal theory that schools are primarily for the protection of the state through their basic function of providing an informed and competent citizenry.

(5) Note that schooling, even though compulsory for a certain age classification of citizens, may be viewed by courts as a privilege or a duty rather than a fundamental right, but that an individual citizen does possess the right to substantial equality of opportunity within the framework of the privilege granted or of the duty imposed.

(6) Construe the language of court decisions according to common

usage. Most court opinions are relatively free from technical terms and from common words with special meanings. Read the opinions "whole" and for intent. Usually, as would be expected, they are clearer than the law involved.

PART ONE

QUESTIONS OF STATE AND FEDERAL POWERS AND FUNCTION

Which means that schools or school people were involved in cases which included the question of federal as against state control.

1

EDUCATION IN OUR DUAL SYSTEM OF GOVERNMENT

Perhaps the most distinctive accomplishments in American culture have been practical developments: First the enduring federal system of government and secondly the system of education whereby young Americans of modest economic and social status can progress from primary grades on through the university in tax-supported schools. These two, our governmental system and our "ladder system" of education, however imperfect, may also be the most notable American contributions to Western civilization. Although both were revolutionary contributions, neither resulted from a single generation's experience, nor indeed were the two contributions initiated by the same generation.

The federal Constitution resulted from at least a quarter-century of deep preoccupation with government. The sharply rising debate over the problem of the colonial position within the British imperial organization following the end of the French and Indian War in 1763 first clearly centered American political thought. Then, after a dozen years, as increasingly defiant American theories and actions were countered by increasingly pointed assertions of Parliament's sovereignty, the Americans turned their unrest into armed rebellion. The British countered at last with an offer of something like dominion status, an offer which failed less because it was too little than because it was too late. American independence became a fact, but the blessing of independence was served by the Articles of Confederation, which proved so imperfect and inflexible that debate over government was revived for additional years. Then in 1787, the Constitutional Convention constructed an enduring framework within which the debate was successfully confined. The crux of the Convention's success was its distribution of powers between the central and the state governments, with all powers resting upon popular sovereignty. Although neither a republic nor a democracy was at the time historically unique, they had hardly been adjusted to the problems of vast area, disparate cultural heritages and divergent sectional interests until American federalists devoted themselves to the task.

The resulting federal system defies simple definition. To attempt a brief one in terms of division of powers is but to evoke the question of the possible division of sovereignty—a concept which, in itself, is perhaps as knotty as any in all the social sciences. Professor Andrew C. McLaughlin has dealt with such over-simple definitions of the American federal system and has turned to a "vaguer" but "preferable" definition, noting that it possesses meaning only if considered in the context of subsequent American history. He said:

. . . the United States is a federal state, because it is a complex or composite system of political organization; it has the quality of diversification, not of concentration or complete consolidation. The central government on the one hand and each state on the other have their respective spheres of legal authority. The United States differs from a mere league of totally sovereign states and from a totally unitary state. . . . (26, p. 5)

There, in the area between the two spheres, between those powers expressly or implicitly assigned to the federal government and those reserved to the states, is the locus for the indefinitive points upon which federal action, state action, and concurrent action must frequently be balanced, hence providing much of the scope for adjustment by the Supreme Court. Such adjustments or court opinions thereupon become "case law," supplementing statute law and restricting or extending the Constitution in two ways: (1) By interpretation of constitutional and statute law, and (2) by the application of common law principles. The latter are invoked to deal with a specific combination of circumstances not covered by legislation but demanding a determination of rights by the judiciary, whose decision must, therefore, find its basis somewhere within general principles and traditions.

Hence the Supreme Court of the United States in the formative decades of the republic and particularly in its thirty-four years (1801-35) under John Marshall, had, as McLaughlin puts it, a "unique opportunity":

. . . [For Marshall] was called upon to construe the fundamental law of a nation, to lay down principles which were to be of supreme consequence in securing national stability and national development. No other justice in the course of past ages had such an opportunity and such responsibilities. The Constitution he was called upon to interpret and apply was the Constitution, moreover, of a federal, not of a unitary or centralized state; in consequence, judicial problems were novel. . . . (26, p. 299)

Among the novelties have been the problems arising from the system of education developed by Americans and, also, from the effect of the federal Constitution, which, though remaining ever silent about education, did include provisions which came to have a profound influence upon education.

The key of such provisions was the Tenth Amendment, which, by virtue of the fact that education had not been mentioned in the Constitution, reserved it, along with all other matters not delegated to the federal government, as within the powers of the states. Every state constitution directs the legislature to establish and maintain a a system of free public schools. (10, pp. 35-36)

The second of the provisions is a general emanation from the Bill of Rights, or from all the first eight amendments, by which local custodians of the revolutionary heritage sought to limit the possibility that the federal government might arrogate to itself too much power, particularly through the usurpation of traditional liberties. This second provision was destined to become, ultimately, a restraint upon the states as well. For, although the Fourteenth Amendment was adopted in the reconstruction era that followed confirmation of the federal government as a national government (as a result of the Civil War), it was not until after World War I that the Supreme Court was persuaded to such interpretation of a clause in the amendment that the process of applying the restrictions of the first eight to the states was begun. Thenceforth, all states have been increasingly restrained by the Bill of Rights, even though the consequence may be an apparent limitation of power in those fields, including education, which are otherwise constitutionally reserved to the states.

Since contests in this and other areas must be decided by the courts whose function it is to interpret legislative enactments as well as constitutional provisions, and since more than one interpretation is frequently possible, the power of the courts in directing the course of law is obvious. Thus, the power to direct the course of law involving education becomes a power to direct education itself—if not in philosophy and goal, at least in the degree and manner of day by day achievement. (22, p. 15) The interaction between education and the Court is diagrammed as follows.

HOW THE SUPREME COURT MAY AFFECT EDUCATION

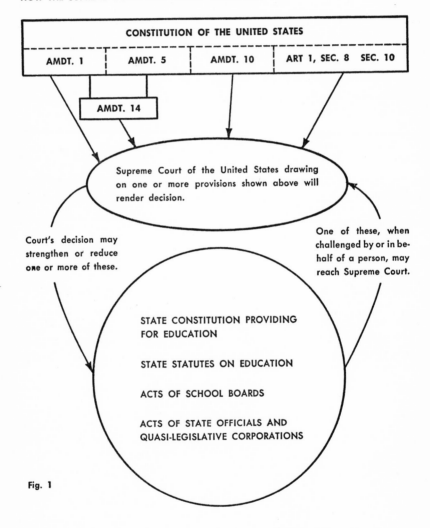

Fig. 1

American educational, as well as political, thought and practice, was destined to be changed in consequence of the quarter century of disturbance centering around the American Revolution. But whereas by 1787 the new political design had achieved formal structure in the work of the Federal Convention, more than a long generation was to pass before the design of the future structure of education in the United States might be discerned, and then only in a preliminary sketch against the background afforded by the so-called rise of the common man. (17, pp. 231-80)

Men of the generation of the American Revolution, as sons of the age of science, reason, and the enlightenment, had, of course, given impetus in America to the forces of that age. Thought had become perceptibly scientific and, at the same time, sufficiently secularized to permit separation of church and state. A rearrangement of social classes had become manifest in the advance of the middle class and to some degree in moderate grip by common men upon the instrument of political power. The capstone of the age was the theory of progress.

Yet this dynamic, optimistic, humanistic theory, which might have been expected to direct its focus upon education as the means by which mankind might be improved until his institutions reached perfection, had that effect upon only a few thinkers of the time. Most of the American revolutionaries appear to have been satisfied, by virtue of their own indubitable eminence, with the old system that had produced them. This system proves, in a sense, no system at all when viewed within the context of the divergent responses to education developed or borrowed by quite disparate sections and ideologies in colonial America. Any attempt at the time to weld American education into a "national, rational, republican" system, "free for all at the expense of all" would have been fraught with dissension. Moreover, many of the revolutionaries of 1776 had become, in a degree, the conservatives of 1787. The republican document produced by the Constitutional Convention was, no doubt, radical to the eyes of crowned heads in Europe, but it represented, nevertheless, American conservatism's effort to consolidate the gains of a revolution showing signs of getting out of hand. So, at the Federal Convention, the formula sought, both in general and in detail, was the formula to end dissension. Circumstances neither in the convention hall nor abroad in the nation encouraged reasonable men to raise issues that might be avoided. Accordingly, those who might have desired a national program of education may have envisioned adequate opportunity within the scope of the authority granted Congress to promote the general welfare. But, most likely, the failure of the Constitution to mention education represents no compromise nor any intent to make education an express function of state governments. As commentators have said, it probably represents nothing more than the then prevailing view of education as a private, or a religious, or a philanthropic function. (17, p. 240)

At any rate, it was clearly the common man of a later generation who, profiting from the clash of agrarianism and rising capitalism and taking the words of his revolutionary fathers in literal creed, gave dramatic content to democracy and broadened its dogma to include a public school system free to all on equal terms.

The *Dartmouth College* case, the first "education case" to reach the Supreme Court of the United States, was decided in 1819 during the period when the republican concept of education struggled for acceptance. The "turning point toward a public school system" was still more than fifteen years away. Efforts had, however, been devoted to making existing schools, particularly at the college level, more responsive to public will. (17, pp. 251-53)

The decision was rendered at a time when the gains of the American Revolution had found additional consolidation in the surge of American nationalism following the second war with England.

The *Dartmouth College* case follows. As with other cases to come after, the circumstances through which this case was developed and the questions which it raised are outlined. The decision of the Court is then quoted in part, but extensively, and certain of the consequences for education and for constitutional development are indicated briefly.

2

CHALLENGES OF POWERS
OF STATE LEGISLATURES

ART. 1—LEGISLATIVE DEPARTMENT
Sec. 10—Powers Denied to the States

[1] THE DARTMOUTH COLLEGE CHARTER

TRUSTEES OF DARTMOUTH COLLEGE
V. WOODWARD
4 Wheat. 518 (U. S. 1819)

The Supreme Court of the United States held that a charter granted to a private college is in the nature of a contract and cannot be revoked or altered by a state legislature without the consent of those to whom it was granted.

Dartmouth, a Congregational college, was founded in the Colony of New Hampshire during the religious revival known as the Great Awakening and was granted a charter by the English Crown in 1769. (14, pp. 213-15; and 17, pp. 253-54) Authority over the school was vested in a self-perpetuating board of twelve trustees subject only to such state control as the state (colonial) governor might exercise as an ex officio member.

By the period of the War of 1812 the first president had been succeeded by his son, John Wheelock, and he had come to differences,

17

at first personal, then sectarian, with the board. This division became a breach with sharp political implications when Wheelock associated himself with the Presbyterians and Republicans (Jeffersonian Democrats), while the board remained adamantly Congregationalist and Federalist. The board removed Wheelock from the presidency in 1815, but the Republicans captured the state government in the following year's election and proceeded to reorganize the college in order to bring it under state control. To that end, the legislature expanded the board of trustees to twenty-one members, appointed by the governor and council, and at the same time subordinated it to a new body of twenty-five overseers, composed of state officials and appointees of the governor. A schedule of reports and inspections of the school was provided, and the name was changed to Dartmouth University.[2]

The College trustees refused to comply with the provisions of the legislation. The University trustees then occupied the buildings and elected Wheelock the University president. Thereupon, the College trustees located other space, and after drawing away many of the members of the faculty and most of the students, continued operations. The legal battle was shortly joined by the College through action to recover the seal, records, and accounts held by the secretary and treasurer, Woodward, who remained with Wheelock at the University. The success of this recovery action would turn upon the constitutionality of the New Hampshire legislature's statute of 1816 altering the charter.

The Court of Appeals of New Hampshire heard the case in 1817. It accepted the argument that the College had become a public institution, was therefore subject to state control, and the charter properly subject to legislative modification.

The College then appealed on a writ of error to the Supreme Court of the United States in 1818. Daniel Webster, an alumnus of Dartmouth, was its chief counsel. As in his argument before the state court, Webster made but small issue of the contract clause in the Constitution in arguing the case at Washington, but chose rather to build upon the more general point of necessity in protecting vested rights.[3] Chief Justice John Marshall, who for seventeen years had been

---

[2]Efforts were made to secure state control over all the former colonial colleges except Brown, Princeton, and Rutgers. In addition to Dartmouth, Columbia and Pennsylvania were actually converted for a time. Harvard, Yale, and William and Mary allowed state representation on their governing bodies (47, p. 64).

[3]In words that the traditional schoolboy was once alleged to know, Webster is supposed to have said to Marshall: "Sir, you may destroy this little institution; it is weak; it is in your hands! . . . It is, sir, as I have said, a small college,—

staunchly establishing his reputation as "the Federalist in a Republican Government," sympathized with Webster's argument, but apparently concluded that a stronger one resting on a more specific point could be made for the Federalist position. This stronger argument was embodied in his decision giving complete victory to the College. The decision was for some reason uncommonly delayed until the opening of the 1819 session. The Court then held the College to be a private institution and its charter of incorporation to be inviolable since the charter was a contract within the meaning of the Constitution of the United States.

Chief Justice Marshall's opinion said, in part:[4]

This Court can be insensible neither to the magnitude nor delicacy of this question. The validity of a legislative act is to be examined; and the opinion of the highest law tribunal of a state is to be revised: an opinion which carries with it intrinsic evidence of the diligence, of the ability, and the integrity with which it was formed. On more than one occasion this Court has expressed the cautious circumspection with which it approaches the consideration of such questions; and has declared that, in no doubtful case, would it pronounce a legislative act to be contrary to the Constitution. But the American people have said, in the Constitution of the United States, that "no State shall pass any bill of attainder, ex post facto law, or law impairing the obligation of contracts." In the same instrument they have also said "that the judicial power shall extend to all cases in law and equity arising under the Constitution." On the judges of this Court, then, is imposed the high and solemn duty of protecting, from even legislative violation, those contracts which the Constitution of our country has placed beyond legislative control; and, however irksome the task may be, this is a duty from which we dare not shrink. . . .

It can require no argument to prove that the circumstances of this case constitute a contract. An application is made to the Crown for a charter to encorporate a religious and literary institution. In the application it is stated that large contributions have been made for the object, which will be conferred on the corporation as soon as it shall be created. The charter is granted, and on its faith the property is conveyed. Surely in this transaction every ingredient of a complete and legitimate contract is to be found.

The points for consideration are,

1. Is this contract protected by the Constitution of the United States?

2. Is it impaired by the acts under which the defendant holds?

1. On the first point it has been argued that the word "contract", in its broadest sense, would comprehend the political relations between the government and its citizens, would extend to offices held within a state for state

---

and yet there are those who love it." This appears to have been given currency some thirty years after the case was argued. (25, p. 230) It is not in the record examined.

[4]Separate concurring opinions were delivered by Justice Washington and Justice Story. A dissent was registered by Justice Duval.

purposes, and to many of those laws concerning civil institutions, which must change with circumstances, and be modified by ordinary legislation; which deeply concern the public, and which, to preserve good government, the public judgment must control. That even marriage is a contract, and its obligations are affected by the laws respecting divorces. That the clause in the Constitution, if construed in its greatest latitude, would prohibit these laws. Taken in its broad, unlimited sense, the clause would be an unprofitable and vexatious interference with the internal concerns of a state, would unnecessarily and unwisely embarrass its legislation, and render immutable those civil institutions which are established for purposes of internal government, and which, to subserve those purposes, ought to vary with varying circumstances. That as the framers of the Constitution could never have intended to insert in that instrument a provision so unnecessary, so mischievous, and so repugnant to its general spirit, the term "contract" must be understood in a more limited sense. That it must be understood as intended to guard against a power of at least doubtful utility, the abuse of which had been extensively felt, and to restrain the legislature in future from violating the right to property. That anterior to the formation of the Constitution, a course of legislation had prevailed in many, if not in all, of the states, which weakened the confidence of man in man, and embarrassed all transactions between individuals, by dispensing with a faithful performance of engagements. To correct this mischief, by restraining the power which produced it, the state legislatures were forbidden "to pass any law impairing the obligation of contracts", that is, of contracts respecting property, under which some individual could claim a right to something beneficial to himself; and that since the clause in the Constitution must in construction receive some limitation, it may be confined, and ought to be confined, to cases of this description; to cases within the mischief it was intended to remedy.

The general correctness of these observations cannot be controverted. That the framers of the Constitution did not intend to restrain the states in the regulation of their civil institutions, adopted for internal government, and that the instrument that they have given us is not to be so construed, may be admitted. The provision of the Constitution never has been understood to embrace other contracts than those which respect property or some object of value, and confer rights which may be asserted in a court of justice. It never has been understood to restrict the general right of the legislature to legislate on the subject of divorces. Those acts enable some tribunal, not to impair a marriage contract, but to liberate one of the parties because it has been broken by the other. When any state legislature shall pass an act annulling all marriage contracts, or allowing either party to annul it without the consent of the other, it will be time enough to inquire whether such an act be constitutional.

The parties in this case differ less on general principles, less on the true construction of the Constitution in the abstract, than on the application of those principles to this case, and on the true construction of the charter of 1769. This is the point on which the cause essentially depends. If the act of incorporation be a grant of political power, if it create a civil institution to be employed in the administration of the government, or if the funds of the college be public property, or if the state of New Hampshire, as a government, be alone interested in its transactions, the subject is one in which the legislature of the state may act according to its own judgment, unrestrained by any limitation of its power imposed by the Constitution of the United States.

But if this be a private eleemosynary institution, endowed with a capacity to take property for objects unconnected with government, whose funds are bestowed by individuals on the faith of the charter; if the donors have stipulated for the future disposition and management of those funds in the manner prescribed by themselves; there may be more difficulty in the case, although neither the persons who have made these stipulations, nor those for whose benefit they were made, should be parties to the cause. Those who are no longer interested in the property may yet retain such an interest in the preservation of their own arrangements as to have a right to insist that those arrangements shall be held sacred. Or, if they have themselves disappeared, it becomes a subject of serious and anxious inquiry whether those whom they have legally empowered to represent them forever may not assert all the rights which they possessed while in being; whether, if they be without personal representatives in the eye of the law as to stand in their place, not only as respects the government of the college, but also as respects the maintenance of the college charter.

It becomes then the duty of the Court most seriously to examine this charter, and to ascertain its true character. . . .

A corporation is an artificial being, invisible, intangible, and existing only in contemplation of law. Being the mere creature of law, it possesses only those properties which the charter of its creation confers upon it, either expressly or as incidental to its very existence. These are such as are supposed best calculated to effect the object for which it was created. Among the most important are immortality, and, if the expression may be allowed, individuality; properties, by which a perpetual succession of many persons are considered as the same, and may act as a single individual. They enable a corporation to manage its own affairs, and to hold property without the perplexing intricacies, the hazardous and endless necessity, of perpetual conveyances for the purpose of transmitting it from hand to hand. It is chiefly for the purpose of clothing bodies of men in succession with these qualities and capacities that corporations were invented and are in use. By these means a perpetual succession of individuals are capable of acting for the promotion of the particular object, like one immortal being. . . .

From this review of the charter, it appears that Dartmouth College is an eleemosynary institution, incorporated for the purpose of perpetuating the application of the bounty of the donors to the specified objects of that bounty, that its trustees or governors were originally named by the founder, and invested with the power of perpetuating themselves; that they are not public officers, nor is it a civil institution, participating in the administration of government; but a charity school, or a seminary of education, incorporated for the preservation of its property, and the perpetual application of that property to the objects of its creation. . . .

According to the theory of the British constitution, their Parliament is omnipotent. To annul corporate rights might give a shock to public opinion, which that government has chosen to avoid; but its power is not questioned. Had Parliament, immediately after the emanation of this charter and the execution of those conveyances which followed it, annulled the instrument, so that the living donors would have witnessed the disappointment of their hopes, the perfidy of the transaction would have been universally acknowledged. Yet then, as now, the donors would have had no interest in the property; then, as now, those who might be students would have had no rights to be violated; then, as now, it might be said that the trustees, in whom the rights of all were combined, possessed no private, individual, beneficial interest in the property confided to their protection. Yet the contract would at that time have been deemed sacred by all. What has since occurred to strip it of its inviolability? Circumstances have not changed it. In reason, in justice, and in law, it is now what it was in 1769.

This is plainly a contract to which the donors, the trustees, and the Crown (to whose right and obligations New Hampshire succeeds) were the original parties. It is a contract made on a valuable consideration. It is a contract for the security and disposition of property. It is a contract on the faith of which real and personal estate has been conveyed to the corporation. It is then a contract within the letter of the Constitution, and within its spirit also, unless the fact that the property is invested by the donors in trustees for the promotion of religion and education, for the benefit of persons who are perpetually changing, though the objects remain the same, shall create a particular exception, taking this case out of the prohibition contained in the Constitution.

It is more than possible that the preservation of rights of this description was not particularly in view of the framers of the Constitution when the clause under consideration was introduced into that instrument. It is probable that interferences of more frequent recurrence, to which the temptation was stronger and of which the mischief was more extensive, constituted the great motive for imposing this restriction on the state legislatures. But although a particular and a rare case may not in itself be of sufficient magnitude to induce a rule, yet it must be governed by the rule, when established, unless some plain and strong reason for excluding it can be given. It is not enough to say that this particular case was not in the mind of the convention when the article was framed, nor of the American people when it was adopted. It is necessary to go farther, and to say that, had this particular case been suggested, the language would have been so varied as to exclude it, or it would have been made a special exception. The case, being within the words of the rule, must be within its operation likewise, unless there be something in the literal construction so obviously absurd, or mischievous, or repugnant to the general spirit of the instrument as to justify those who expound the Constitution in making it an exception.

On what safe and intelligible ground can this exception stand? There is no expression in the Constitution, no sentiment delivered by its contemporaneous expounders which would justify us in making it. In the absence of all authority of this kind, is there, in the nature and reason of the case itself, that which would sustain a construction of the Constitution, not warranted by its words? Are contracts of this description of a character to excite so little interest that we must exclude them from the provisions of the Constitution, as being unworthy of the attention of those who framed the instrument? Or does public policy so imperiously demand their remaining exposed to legislative alteration, as to compel us, or rather permit us to say, that these words, which were introduced to give stability to contracts, and which in their plain import comprehend this contract, must yet be so construed, as to exclude it?

Almost all eleemosynary corporations, those which are created for the promotion of religion, of charity, or of education are of the same character. The law of this case is the law of all. . . .

The opinion of the Court, after mature deliberation, is, that this is a contract, the obligation of which cannot be impaired without violating the Constitution of the United States. This opinion appears to us to be equally supported by reason and by the former decisions of this Court.

2. We next proceed to the inquiry whether its obligation has been impaired by those acts of the legislature of New Hampshire to which the special verdict refers.

From the review of this charter which has been taken it appears that the whole power of governing the college, of appointing and removing tutors, of fixing their salaries, of directing the course of study to be pursued by the students, and of filling up vacancies created in their own body, was vested in the trustees. On the part of the Crown it was expressly stipulated that this corporation, thus constituted, should continue forever; and that the number of trustees should forever consist of twelve, and no more. By this contract the Crown was bound, and could have made no violent alteration in its essential terms without impairing its obligation.

By the revolution the duties as well as the powers of government devolved on the people of New Hampshire. It is admitted that among the latter was comprehended the transcendent power of Parliament, as well as that of the executive department. It is too clear to require the support of argument that all contracts and rights respecting property remained unchanged by the Revolution. The obligations, then, which were created by the charter to Dartmouth College were the same in the new that they had been in the old government. The power of the government was also the same. A repeal of this charter at any time prior to the adoption of the present Constitution of the United States would have been an extraordinary and unprecedented act of power, but one which could have been contested only by the restrictions upon the legislature to be found in the constitution of the state. But the Constitution of the United States has imposed this additional limitation, that the legislature of a state shall pass no act "impairing the obligation of contracts."

It has been already stated that the act "to amend the charter and enlarge and improve the corporation of Dartmouth College" increased the number of trustees to twenty-one, gives the appointment of the additional members to the executive of the state, and creates a board of overseers, to consist of twenty-five persons, of whom twenty-one are also appointed by the executive of New Hampshire, who have power to inspect and control the most important acts of the trustees.

On the effect of this law two opinions cannot be entertained. Between acting directly and acting through the agency of trustees and overseers no essential difference is perceived. The whole power of governing the college is transformed from trustees appointed according to the will of the founder, expressed in the charter, to the executive of New Hampshire. The management and application of the funds of this eleemosynary institution, which are placed by the donors in the hands of trustees named in the charter, and empowered to perpetuate themselves, are placed by this act under the control of the government of the state. The will of the state is substituted for the will of the donors in every essential operation of the college. This is not an immaterial change. The founders of the college contracted, not merely for the perpetual application of funds which they gave to the objects for which those funds were given; they contracted also to secure that application by the constitution of the corporation. They contracted for a system which, as far as human foresight can provide, retain forever the government of the literary institution they had formed, in the hands of persons approved by themselves. This system is totally changed. The charter of 1769 exists no longer. It is reorganized; and reorganized in such a manner as to convert a literary institution, molded according to the will of its founders and placed under the control of private literary men, into a machine entirely subservient to the will of government. This may be for the advantage of this college in particular, and may be for the advantage of literature in general; but it is not according to the will of the donors, and is subversive of that contract on the faith of which their property was given.

In the view which has been taken of this interesting case, the Court has confined itself to the rights possessed by the trustees, as the assignees and representatives of the donors and founders, for the benefit of religion and literature. Yet it is not clear that the trustees ought to be considered as destitute of such beneficial interest in themselves as the law may respect. In addition to their being the legal owners of the property, and to their having a freehold right in the powers confided to them, the charter itself countenances the idea that trustees may also be tutors with salaries. The first president was one of the original trustees; and the charter provides, that in case of vacancy in that office, "the senior professor or tutor, being one of the trustees shall make choice of, and appoint a president." According to the tenor of the charter, then, the trustees might, without impropriety, appoint a president and other professors from their own body. This is a power not entirely unconnected with an interest. Even if the proposition of the counsel for the defendant were sustained; if it were admitted that those contracts only are protected by the Constitution, a beneficial interest in which is vested in the party who appears in court to assert that interest; yet it is by no means clear that the trustees of Dartmouth College have no beneficial interest in themselves.

But the Court has deemed it unnecessary to investigate this particular point, being of opinion, on general principles that in these private eleemosynary institutions, the body corporate, as possessing the whole legal and equitable interest, and completely representing the donors, for the purpose of executing the trust, has rights which are protected by the Constitution.

It results from this opinion, that the acts of the legislature of New Hampshire, which are stated in the special verdict found in this cause, are repugnant to the Constitution of the United States; and that the judgment on this special verdict ought to have been for the plaintiffs. The judgment of the state court must therefore be reversed. (149, pp. 625-54)

COMMENT

The decision in this case broadened an earlier one in *Fletcher v. Peck* (82) wherein it was held that a contract involving state lands and attended by fraud, having once been made by the state could not be rescinded by unilateral action of the state after the land had passed into the hands of innocent parties. The two decisions together confirmed the Federalist doctrine of the sancitity of private property and the irrevocable nature of a contract.

Robert Eugene Cushman, professor of government at Cornell University, in writing specifically of the decision in the *Dartmouth* case summarizes certain of the effects. He says:

> The doctrine in this case, that a corporate charter is a contract which may not be impaired by legislative enactment, has been most bitterly criticized as making it possible for corrupt and ignorant legislatures irrevocably to grant away privileges and rights contrary to the public interest and welfare. There can be no doubt that it did create opportunities for legislative corruption. At the same time it put the public upon its guard with reference to corporate grants and it emphasized the importance of good faith at a time when public opinion seemed willing to sponsor interference with promises. In an economic sense the decision was of great importance in giving to those who invested money in corporate enterprises assurance that the corporations would be free from legislative interference, and it thus encouraged the expansion of business enterprise in the fields of railroad construction, insurance, commerce and industry. . . . (14, p. 215)

The same commentator goes on to point out that two subsequent decisions of the court modified the breadth of the two earlier decisions on contract. Chief Justice Robert B. Taney in the *Proprietors of the Charles River Bridge v. Proprietors of the Warren Bridge* (131), "held that the terms of a charter contract must be strictly construed and that no rights or privileges may be granted away by the public by mere implication." (14, p. 215) While John Marshall was Chief Justice, the Court, in *Ogden v. Saunders* (121), had decided, again in Cushman's words:

> . . . that the obligation of a contract . . . consists not merely in the promise or agreement between the parties but also in the law applicable to the subject which is in existence when the contract is made. This rule makes it possible for the states to pass general laws reserving the right to amend or repeal corporate charters under certain circumstances. . . . (14, p. 215)

It should be observed that the foregoing doctrines and the constitutional clause concerning impairment of "the obligation of contracts" from which they were derived have become, to a degree, outmoded. Present day contests between governmental powers and private rights turn largely upon the concept of "due process of law" (48, pp. 971-80), i.e., reasonable law, as the Court sees it.

The first resort to this new concept appears to be in Taney's decision in the Dred Scott case (138), but, (as will be shown in Parts Two and Three), only long after the Fifth Amendment had been buttressed by the Fourteenth following the Civil War was common resort made to it. (48, p. 974)

The effect of the *Dartmouth* case upon education in the United States has been variously interpreted. Professor Cubberley in his *Public Education in the United States* presented what seems to have become the traditional analysis when he said:

. . . The effect of this decision manifested itself in two different ways. On the one hand it guaranteed the perpetuity of endowments and the great period of private and denominational effort now followed. . . . (12, p. 272)

Figures and opinion are cited in support of the foregoing. (12, pp. 270, 272) They are not questioned here. It is, however, suggested that the fact of "the great period of private and denominational effort" following the *Dartmouth* decision derived from other powerful impulsion than the coincidental assurance of security for endowments. (47, pp. 55-129; 133-83) The next two decades witnessed the clear beginnings of industrial capitalism and fluid fortune in the United States. Much of the American mind was active in the spirit of the New England Renaissance and in the spirit of the humanitarian revolt. The prolific pioneer, working at the "American multiplication table" was busy peopling the land, and Americans were filling the valleys of the Ohio and the Mississipi in one of the greatest population growths and movements of the Western World. The "civilization," the local cultural differences, went with them on the move. So, it may be conjectured, with these influences prevailing, there would have been a marked extension of the prevailing denominational and private schools without Chief Justice Marshall's helpful decision.

Professor Cubberley said as his second point: "On the other hand, since the states could not change charters and transform old establishments, they began to turn to the creation of state universities of their own." (12, p. 272) Professors Newton Edwards and Herman A. Richey of the University of Chicago express a contrary belief. They say:

It has often been stated that the states, prevented by the Dartmouth College decision from transforming private colleges into state institutions, turned with renewed effort to the establishment of state universities. Tewksbury has presented evidence and a most convincing argument that, on the contrary, the decision contributed in no small measure to checking the development of state universities for at least a half a century. . . . (17, p. 254)

Effects of the *Dartmouth College* decision are diagrammed on the following page.

A question related to that decided above by Chief Justice Marshall has subsequently involved schools before the Court. In essence, this question is again one of revocable privilege versus "contract," but specifically in the matter of tax exemptions. In this connection, the following appears among annotations prepared by the Library of Congress:

LIMITS OF THE DARTMOUTH DECISION   4 Wheat. (U.S. 1819)

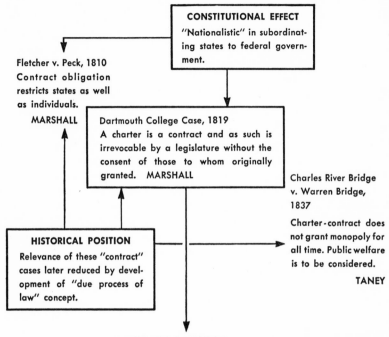

CONSTITUTIONAL EFFECT
"Nationalistic" in subordinating states to federal government.

Fletcher v. Peck, 1810
Contract obligation
restricts states as well
as individuals.
MARSHALL

Dartmouth College Case, 1819
A charter is a contract and as such is irrevocable by a legislature without the consent of those to whom originally granted.   MARSHALL

Charles River Bridge
v. Warren Bridge,
1837

Charter-contract does
not grant monopoly for
all time. Public welfare
is to be considered.
TANEY

HISTORICAL POSITION
Relevance of these "contract"
cases later reduced by development of "due process of
law" concept.

EFFECTS ON EDUCATION:

1. Provided security to corporations and endowments. Doubtful that it stimulated private and denominational schools
2. Also doubtful that it stimulated establishment of state universities subject to legislative control

EFFECT ON ECONOMY:

1. Assured investors that corporations were free from legislative tampering, thus gave security to business enterprise

Fig. 2

. . . the legislature of a state "may exempt particular parcels of property or the property of particular persons or corporations from taxation, either for a specified period or perpetually, or may limit the amount or rate of taxation, to which the property shall be subjected", and such an exemption is frequently a contract within the sense of the Constitution. Indeed this is always so when the immunity is conferred upon a corporation by the clear terms of its charter. When, on the other hand an immunity of this sort springs from general law, its precise nature is more open to doubt. . . . (48, p. 342)

Justice Davis' decision in *Washington University v. Rouse* (156) in 1869 is illustrative of the above commentary which also says:

. . .exemptions from taxation have in certain cases been treated as gratuities repealable at will, even when conferred by specific legislative enactments. This would seem always to be the case when the beneficiaries were already in existence when the exemption was created and did nothing of a more positive nature to qualify for it than to continue in existence. . . . (48, p. 342)

Justice Day's decision in *Seton Hall College v. South Orange* (139) in 1916 illustrates this point. Similarly, a number of decisions, including that by Justice Clifford in the *Pennsylvania College Cases* (125) as early as 1872, had established that the states might reserve the right to "amend, alter, and repeal" corporate charters by general law, with the result that the reservation became applicable to all charters subsequently granted. The case of Northwestern University, *University v. People* (152), where the state sought to introduce a reservation at a later date, may also be mentioned. Here the Court held that an Illinois statute of 1855 which provided that all the property of Northwestern University should be forever free from taxation had established a contractual obligation which neither a new state constitution in 1870 nor new legislation under it had affected by provisions designed to limit this exemption to lands and other property occupied or in immediate use by the University.

The *Berea College* case (58) of 1908, discussed in detail in a later chapter, demonstrated that although reservations may be properly made for purposes of amending, altering or repealing corporate charters, such reservations must be applied reasonably and consistently.

The case next to be detailed deals with a different matter. It sustains state authorities in a specific application of funds for school purposes.

AMDT. 10—RESERVED STATE POWERS
THE TAXING POWER

[2]   COLLECTION AND APPROPRIATION OF SCHOOL FUNDS

SPRINGFIELD TOWNSHIP V. QUICK
22 How. 56 (U. S. 1859)

The Supreme Court of the United States upheld a state which had refused to apportion state funds to schools receiving township aid from a federal grant of land until other state schools had achieved a parity with the schools benefiting from the grant.

This is the Court's first decision on a case rising from practices of public school authorities, and it is the only decision affecting apportionment of public school funds.

Neither the *Dartmouth College* case nor the *Girard College* case, the two other decisions most frequently cited as affecting education during the first century under the Constitution, involved schools which exclusively reflected a differentiating American culture as this one appears to do.

Here was a case which could hardly have risen prior to the establishment in the old Northwest of that cultural feature—free, public, secularized schools in part supported by a "permanent endowment" of abundant land—which was to become typically American by the end of the nineteenth century.

Among the manifold problems facing the newly independent Americans in their efforts to form a central government less makeshift than the Continental Congress, was the question of the western lands held by certain of the states. Claim to these lands rested upon royal dispensations which in many cases had been either ambiguous or contradictory as to boundaries. Maryland, enjoying no western claim, remained adamantly outside the Confederation until New York led the states possessing claims in ceding them to the central government. (28, vol. 1, pp. 259-60) As has often been remarked, this immense area of some 400,000 square miles provided the new nation with a community of property and a centralizing problem which militated strongly for greater unity.

Connecticut, in making her cession, retained a Western Reserve for the support of her schools, and may have thereby directed the attention of Congress to the potentiality of the lands for such use.

Congress (of the Confederation) first enunciated a policy for the western cessions in the "Land Ordinance" of 1785. Among other features of this act, the New England system of townships surveyed six miles square was included. Section sixteen of every township was reserved for the support of township schools. (24, pp. 138-39)

This enactment made no provision for government of the region, but the famous Ordinance of 1787 did. Its provisions created a situation by which this nation was disposed for an orderly expansion westward, new states joining in equal political status with the old, so that the "clash of metropolis and colony" which sundered the mother empire did not happen here[5]. (3, vol. 1, pp. 510-513)

But the general land policies, and particularly the solutions with respect to land disposal, were not quickly, easily, or systematically established under either the Confederation or the Constitution. How-

---

[5]The Ordinance of 1787 has been called the most significant legislation, next to the Constitution of 1789, which has ever been enacted by Americans. The same has been said of the Fourteenth Amendment.

ever that may be, liberal federal land grants in behalf of education were not forgotten in the process of the fantastically prodigal grants made by Congress to road, canal, and railroad enterprise during the nineteenth century.

The provisions under which Ohio was admitted to the union in 1803 established the pattern for school land grants to states. Section sixteen in each township was set aside to provide the state a fund for common schools[6]. (13, p. 18) Congress had not however, promulgated terms or a policy for the utilization of the lands thus granted. The need for such shortly arose, and within the year Congress gave Ohio authority to lease the school lands, but lessees were not attracted (46, p. 86), undoubtedly because of the competition from plentiful land available to ownership rather than to mere tenure. Consequently, but only after some twenty years, Congress responded to a plea from Ohio and in 1826 granted the state the right to sell the school lands, provided that: (1) The township involved should consent and (2) the proceeds be used for a school fund. The foregoing congressional acts for Ohio were repeated for other states of the old Northwest as they entered the Union.

Thus, when Indiana was admitted in 1816, section sixteen in each township received in a grant to the territory in 1806 was confirmed to the state for school support, and, as the case of *Springfield Township v. Quick* shows, Congress had in 1828 permitted the sale of Indiana school land upon the same conditions as those given above for Ohio.

The mode of distributing proceeds from the sales of such lands gave rise to the Indiana case which reached the Supreme Court. The state legislature, acting under article eight of Indiana's new constitution of 1851, had approved various school laws, particularly the acts of June 14, 1852, and March 5, 1855, in seeking to establish a consolidated school fund. Against the legislature's efforts Springfield Township complained and asserted its "power and right to the exclusive control" of its school section and the proceeds, and charged that the legislature had undertaken:

. . . to distribute generally over the state the proceeds of the 16th section of each township reserved by Congress to the inhabitants of the respective townships in which the sections are situated, for the use of schools therein . . . . (143, p. 257)

---

[6]The Act of 1848 making Oregon a territory first granted two sections in each township for school support. (5, pp. 699, 701) California was the first to be admitted as a state with this doubled bounty. Certain later states received a quadrupled benefit. Of the states admitted since Ohio, only Texas, Maine, and West Virginia have received no such grants. (17, p. 239)

The court's decision was to indicate that this statement of effect of the questioned legislation did not represent the whole truth.

The township had initiated legal action by petitioning the county court to enjoin the auditor, Quick, from distributing school funds in accordance with the law of 1855. This law required that townships maintaining schools from the proceeds of their own school lands should not receive additional funds, largely tax moneys, until other schools were on a parity with them. The injunction was granted. The county officers then appealed to the state supreme court, and the lower court was reversed. Thereupon the township appealed to the Supreme Court of the United States.

In defense the state contended that the action of its county officials had in no way violated the terms of the act of Congress making the grant. Moreover, argued the state, it is:

. . . a well settled principle that the power of a State to levy taxes, to create a revenue for any specified object, is an incident of sovereignty, and only restricted by constitutional inhibitions; . . . The Constitution of the State being silent as to the mode of distributing the common school fund, that burden was necessarily cast upon the legislature. In the exercise of this necessary incidental power, that body directs that all the funds raised to constitute a common school revenue be so distributed, taking into consideration the congressional township fund, as to insure an equality of educational facilities throughout the State. . . . (143, p. 259)

In a brief decision, the Court sustained the Indiana legislation in question.

Justice Catron wrote the opinion of the Court. He said, in part:

. . . The Acts of the Legislature equalize the amount that shall be appropriated for the education of each scholar throughout the State, taking into the estimate the moneys derived from the proceeds of the 16th section, with the proviso, that the whole of the proceeds shall be expended in the township. If it be more than an equal portion to each scholar elsewhere furnished by the state fund—still, the township has the benefit of the excess, but received nothing from the treasury; and if it be less, then the deficiency is made up, so as to equalize according to the general provision.

. . . And our opinion is, that expending the proceeds of the 16th section for the exclusive use of schools "in the township" where the section exists, is a compliance with the legislation of Congress on the subject; nor is the state bound to provide any additional fund for a township receiving the bounty of Congress, no matter to what extent other parts of the State are supplied from the Treasury.

The law is a perfectly just one; but if it were otherwise, and the school fund was distributed partially, nevertheless those receiving the bounty from Congress have no right to call on this court to interfere with the power exercised by the State Legislature in laying and collecting taxes, and in appropriating them for educational purposes, at its discretion. . . . (143, pp. 259-260)

COMMENT

In a portion of the decision not quoted the Court did, however, warn the legislature that it would not approve attempts through subterfuge to alter established procedures for the distribution of the funds. In issuing this warning the Court referred to the case of *Trustees for Vincennes University v. State of Indiana* (148) which it had decided in 1852. That case had arisen when the legislature attempted to defeat, through lesiglative artifice, a trust based on land. This attempt the Court had refused to sanction because the act establishing the original trust was found to have established a contract.

The decision in the present case, since the state was sustained, did not contain such explicit expression of the Court's reluctance to interfere with the educational policies of a state as appear in some later cases, expecially in *Meyer v. Nebraska* (113) where the action of the state in restricting the teaching of foreign languages was, nevertheless, held valid.

For states enjoying the congressional grants of school lands, the decision confirmed the right to withhold additional funds derived from tax moneys and other sources from those schools benefiting directly from the grants, until such time as equality of educational opportunity had been established in the state. Thus, a possible disparity and complication was removed from the administration of consolidated funds for school support and equalization. The Indiana law sustained by the Court embraces a fundamental concept in the school law of the states.

3

CHALLENGES OF POWERS
OF CONGRESS

ART. I—LEGISLATIVE DEPT.
Sec.   8—Powers of Congress
Cl.   3—Regulate Commerce

[3] INSTRUCTION BY CORRESPONDENCE AS INTERSTATE COMMERCE

INTERNATIONAL TEXT-BOOK CO. V. PIGG

217 U. S. 91, 30 Sup. Ct. 481 (1910)

The Supreme Court of the United States held that communication or the transmission of intelligence and instruction by mail, and contracts relating to the transportation of such, is commerce among the states under the terms of the federal Constitution, and is not to be unnecessarily obstructed or encumbered by the states.

The Court's opinion in this case quotes Chief Justice Marshall's words from his 1824 decision in *Gibbons v. Ogden* (88) wherein he said: "Commerce, undoubtedly, is traffic; but it is something more; it is *intercourse*." Although the great Chief Justice qualified this by using the word "commercial" with the word "intercourse" later in the same opinion, he had, nevertheless, asserted an idea which, after a century of history, was to stand with the qualification stripped away by the Court.

Although determination of exactly what comprises interstate commerce in concrete cases remains troublesome, a commentator can now say:

> Today "commerce" in the sense of the Constitution, and hence "interstate commerce" when it is carried on across State lines, covers every species of movement of persons and things, whether for profit or not; every species of communication, every species of transmission of intelligence, whether for commercial purposes or otherwise. . . . (48, pp. 119-20)

This case of *International Text-Book Co. v. Pigg* contributed substantially to the result just described. As in the "telegraph cases" which the Court cites here, and as in the "radio case" (79) decided more than two decades later, techniques and processes unknown to the framers of the commerce clause were involved.

Instruction by correspondence, the method used by the school concerned, may have appeared in earliest organized form in Germany in 1856. The method spread over England and the United States during the 1870's. With the opening of the new University of Chicago in 1892 and the inclusion of a correspondence department as an integral part of the university, the correspondence instruction achieved a certain respectability. (5, pp. 9-30)

Commercial correspondence schools shared in filling the demand for home study courses, and the publicity and salesmen used by such schools popularized the method.

The present case arose consequent to the activity of the International Text-Book Company, a Pennsylvania corporation which dealt in correspondence courses. In 1905, a salesman for the company secured from a Mr. Pigg, in Kansas, an agreement to pay the company $84.00 for a course in commercial law. After Mr. Pigg had failed to remit $79.60 of the principal, the company sued in a Topeka court to recover that amount with the interest due, under the contract made for the course. (105, pp. 481-82)

Mr. Pigg did not deny making the contract, nor that he owed the amount mentioned, but he did contend that "by reason of the company's *failure to comply with certain provisions of the statutes of Kansas*, it was not entitled to maintain this action in a court *of Kansas*." (105, p. 482) The refuge thus sought lay in a Kansas statute which required any corporation doing business in the state for profit to submit a detailed annual report of the condition of the corporation. Failure to comply would bring forfeiture of the "right or authority" to do business in the state. (105, p. 483)

The company maintained that its business was interstate in nature, hence the state statute did not govern because its operation materially or directly burdened the business of the company. (105, p. 483)

The Kansas supreme court affirmed the judgments of two lower state courts in favor of Mr. Pigg and in defense of the statute (105, p. 481). The case was taken by the correspondence course company to the Supreme Court of the United States.

Mr. Justice Harlan delivered the opinion of the Court, and said in part:

. . . It is true that the business in which the International Text-Book Company is engaged is of a somewhat exceptional character, but, in our judgment, it was, in its essential characteristics, commerce among the states within the meaning of the Constitution of the United States. It involved, as already suggested, regular and practically continuous intercourse between the Text-Book Company, located in Pennsylvania, and its scholars and agents in Kansas and other states. The intercourse was conducted by means of correspondence through the mails with such agents and scholars. While this mode of imparting and acquiring an education may not be such as is commonly adopted in this country, it is a lawful mode to accomplish the valuable purpose the parties have in view. More than that; this mode—looking at the contracts between the Text-Book Company and its scholars—involved the transportation from the state where the school is located to the state in which the scholar resides, of books, apparatus, and papers, useful or necessary in the particular course of study the scholar is pursuing, and in respect of which he is entitled, from time to time, by virtue of his contract, to information and direction. Intercourse of that kind, between parties in different states,—particularly when it is in execution of a valid contract between them—is as much intercourse in the constitutional sense, as intercourse by means of the telegraph,— "a new species of commerce," to use the words of this court in Pensacola Teleg. Co. v. Western U. Teleg. Co. 96 U. S. 1, 9, 24 L. ed. 708, 710. In the great case of Gibbons v. Ogden, 9 Wheat. 1, 189, 6 L. ed. 23, 68, this court, speaking by Chief Justice Marshall said: "Commerce, undoubtedly, is traffic; but it is something more; it is *intercourse*." Referring to the constitutional power of Congress to regulate commerce among the states and with foreign countries this court said in the Pensacola case, just cited, that "it is not only the right, but the duty, of Congress, to see to it that *intercourse* among the states and *the transmission of intelligence* are not obstructed or unnecessarily encumbered by state legislation." This principle has never been modified by any subsequent decision of this court. . . . (105, pp. 484-85)

COMMENT

The effect which this decision may have had in freeing commercial correspondence schools from encumbrances by the states is not known. The proliferation of correspondence schools a decade later appears to have ensued from the increased demand for more education which followed World War I. Many commercial correspondence schools continue to fill educational needs scarcely met by university extension services. Hence, the better correspondence schools are a valuable adjunct to the public school systems.

Similar transmission of intelligence or instruction by motion picture films, by radio and by television appears destined for increasing importance among educational methods or materials. While films are most feasible for group instruction, radio and television serve a modified form of correspondence study in reaching from schools to individuals. Radio, in the 1933 case of *Federal Radio Commission v. Nelson Bros.* (79) has, like correspondence study, when it is carried on across state lines, been held by the Court to fall within the protection of the congressional power over commerce and, therefore, beyond unwarranted interference by the states. Since, in addition to the *Pensacola Telegraph* case cited by the Court in the *International Textbook* decision, another, in 1918 (159), resulted in a similar holding, television would presumably be viewed in the same light. No case involving motion picture films appears to have been tested precisely upon this point, although in 1915, in the case of *Mutual Film Corporation v. Hodges* (119) Kansas was sustained in its statute forbidding motion pictures to be exhibited in the state unless first certified by the State Superintendent of Instruction as being moral and instructive. However, so far as censorship over motion pictures and radio is concerned, the Court has lately taken the position that both "are included in the press whose freedom is guaranteed by the First Amendment" (151). This matter appears in *Burstyn v. Wilson* (65), which is presented in a later chapter.

ART. I—LEGISLATIVE DEPT.
Sec. 8—Powers of Congress
Cl. 1—Taxation
Cl. 3—Regulate Commerce

[4] FEDERAL TAXATION OF STATE EDUCATIONAL INTERESTS— TARIFF ON IMPORTS

UNIVERSITY OF ILLINOIS V. UNITED STATES
289 U. S. 48, 53 Sup. Ct. 509 (1933)

The Supreme Court of the United States held that although a state university may further state functions by the use of imported scientific equipment, and although our governmental system is federal or dual, the state is not rendered independent of federal power and the authority of Congress in the matter of foreign commerce and import duties.

Under our Constitution the congressional power to levy taxes knows but one exception: exports from a state may not be taxed. There are, however, two qualifications: direct taxes must be based on apportionment in accordance with the census and indirect taxes must be uniform in geographical application. (48, p. 105)

This power was established obviously and primarily to raise revenue, but early in the nation's history, over the protests of strict-constructionists, a protective tariff was passed, and such legislation has existed almost continually since that time. In addition, Congress has used its taxing power to limit or to destroy the availability of goods. For example, in a 1902 provision, only lately modified, a tax of ten cents a pound was laid on all margarine colored to resemble butter, and in 1914 an earlier tax on smoking opium was raised to $300 a pound. (14, p. 384)

"The only checks upon the rate of taxation are political checks," and quite burdensome taxes can be imposed on ordinary sources if the fiscal need warrants. The Supreme Court has nevertheless held that some taxes which appear to be penalties rather than taxes are unconstitutional. (14, pp. 384-85) The purposes for which Congress may levy taxes are, therefore, subject to challenge.

Another question, one with which the Court has dealt periodically since the case of *McCulloch v. Maryland* in 1819 (111) develops from our dual system. Since federal and state governments each possess the power of taxation, the question arises as to what extent one government may tax the other or affect the other by exercising the taxing power. In the 1819 case just cited, Chief Justice Marshall established federal immunity from state taxation. Then, in 1871 in *Collector v. Day* (71) the Court ruled specifically that the salary of a state officer was not subject to federal income tax, and at the same time laid down a general rule that Congress may not impose a tax which impairs the sovereignty of the states. Although a retreat from the decision in *Collector v. Day* began shortly after the turn of the century and its specific holding on the income tax was expressly overruled in *Graves v. O'Keefe* in 1930 (94), the general rule against a tax which impairs the sovereignty of the states is regarded as still "retaining some vitality" (48, p. 106) but as having declined within the present century.

Today the intergovernmental tax immunity doctrines, according to Professor Cushman, are much as follows:

1. The federal or state government, together with its functions, property, instrumentalities and processes—anything reasonably regarded as an attribute of sovereignty—is absolutely immune from any tax levied by the other government.

2. However, this immunity is limited in matters where a state engages in a business enterprise, in contrast to a function traditionally governmental in nature.

3. Such immunity does not extend to persons who merely have business or other relations with the government, unless such persons can show that

to tax them is to impose a direct and substantial burden on the government itself. (14, pp. 377-78)

The present case, *University of Illinois v. United States*, arose from the state's contention that because it used articles imported by one of its instrumentalities, the federal import duties did not apply. In holding the contrary the Court pointed out that control of imports was not a traditional part of the sovereignty of a state within the United States. The first of Professor Cushman's points just quoted received additional substance thereby. His second point was likewise given increased substance by the Court in *Allen v. Regents* (54), the case to be discussed next.

In the present case the Court describes the circumstances of the challenge made by Illinois in the following words:

The University of Illinois imported scientific apparatus for use in one of its educational dep'ts. Customs duties were exacted at the rates prescribed by the Tariff Act of 1922, c. 356, 42 Stat. 858. The University paid under protest, insisting that an instrumentality of the state of Illinois, and discharging a governmental function it was entitled to import the articles duty free. At the hearing of the protest, the Customs Court decided in favor of the Government (59 Treas. Dec. 747), and the Court of Customs and Patent Appeals affirmed the decision. (61 Treas. Dec. 1334) (153, p. 509)

Following this judgment by the Court of Customs and Patent Appeals the case was taken on certiorari to the Supreme Court.

Chief Justice Hughes delivered the unanimous decision. He said, in part:

. . . The principle invoked by the petitioner, of the immunity of state instrumentalities from federal taxation, has its inherent limitations . . . It is a principle implied from the necessity of maintaining our dual system of government. . . . Springing from that necessity it does not extend beyond it. Protecting the functions of government in its proper province, the implication ceases when the boundary of that province is reached. The fact that the state in the performance of state functions may use imported articles does not mean that the importation is a function of the state government independent of federal power. The control of importation does not rest with the state but with the Congress. In international relations and with respect to foreign intercourse and trade the people of the United States act through a single government with unified and adequate national power. There is thus no violation of the principle which petitioner invokes, for there is no encroachment of the power of the state as none exists with respect to the subject over which the federal power has been exerted. To permit the states and their instrumentalities to import commodities for their own use, regardless of the requirements imposed by the Congress, would undermine, if not destroy, the single control which it was one of the dominant purposes of the Constitution to create. It is for the Congress to decide to what extent, if at all, the states and their instrumentalities shall be relieved of the payment of duties on imported articles.

The contention of the petitioner finds no support in the history of tariff acts or in departmental practice. It is not necessary to review this practical construction. It is sufficient to say that only in recent years has any question been raised by state officials as to the authority of Congress to impose duties upon their imports.

In view of these conclusions, we find unnecessary to consider the questions raised with respect to the particular functions of the petitioner and its right to invoke the principle for which it contends. . . . (153, pp. 510-11)

COMMENT

By this decision the Court showed that the immunity of state instrumentalities from federal taxation, while implied from our dual system of government and made necessary in maintaining the system, does not extend beyond the requirements of such necessity. More specifically, although the University of Illinois was engaged in education, a function of states rather than of the federal government, this fact in no degree operated to limit the taxing power of Congress or to alter the exclusive control of the national government over commerce with foreign nations.

In the next case a state sought to include within the scope of its educational function an enterprise more sustained but less traditional than the importation of scientific apparatus.

ART. I—LEGISLATIVE DEPT.
Sec.   8—Powers of Congress
Cl.   1—Taxation

[5] FEDERAL TAXATION OF STATE EDUCATIONAL INTERESTS— EXCISE ON GATE RECEIPTS

ALLEN V. REGENTS OF UNIVERSITY
SYSTEM OF GEORGIA
304 U. S. 439, 58 Sup. Ct. 980 (1938)

The Supreme Court of the United States sustained a federal excise tax on admissions to athletic contests sponsored by a state agency in the guise of a university, notwithstanding that the net proceeds were used to further the state's educational program.

Five years after the case of the *University of Illinois v. United States* (153) was decided, another state university appeared before the Court to argue the question of intergovernmental tax immunity. Georgia university authorities felt that because the proceeds from athletic contests were used to further the state's program of education, the federal excise tax on admissions unconstitutionally burdened the state in fulfillment of its educational functions.

The authorities took this view in the face of Supreme Court decisions which held that when a state embarked upon a business not ordinarily a function of government the state lost its tax immunity so far as that business was concerned. These decisions, several of which are cited by the Court in the present opinion, dealt largely with cases in which states had gone into the liquor business. In a case in 1905 the Court held the agents of South Carolina were subject to the federal liquor tax because the dispensing of alcoholic beverages was not an ordinary function of government in 1787. (48, p. 107) In a similar case for Ohio in 1934 the rule established for South Carolina "was reaffirmed and applied to the liquor monopolies set up in a dozen or more states after the repeal of national prohibition." (14, p. 377) The Georgia university authorities did not deny that their athletic contests constituted a business that would ordinarily be taxable, but they did appear to feel that because the athletic contests were a part of the state's educational program as well as one of its income-producing sources, the Court might distinguish the enterprise from the liquor business and hold it within the state's area of tax immunity. The school authorities also made a point of the burden imposed upon the state in being required to collect the federal excise tax.

The Regents of the University System of Georgia accordingly refused to comply with the terms of the Revenue Acts of 1926 and 1932. Thereupon the Collector of Internal Revenue sought to compel them to do so in the District Court, but his suit was dismissed. The case was twice reviewed by the Circuit Court of Appeals before being taken to the Supreme Court on a writ of certiorari. (54, p. 981)

There, the opinion of a divided Court was delivered by Justice Roberts. Justice Black and Justice Stone concurred, Justice Butler and Justice McReynolds dissented. The majority opinion said, in part:

. . . For present purposes we assume the truth of the following propositions put forward by the respondent: That it is a public instrumentality of the State government carrying out a part of the State's program of public education; that public education is a governmental function; that the holding of athletic contests is an integral part of the program of public education conducted by Georgia; that the means by which the State carries out that program are for determination by the State authorities, and their determination is not subject to review by any branch of the federal government; that a state activity does not cease to be governmental because it produces some income; that the tax is imposed directly on the State activity and directly burdens that activity; that the burden of collecting the tax is placed immediately on the State agency. The petitioner stoutly combats many of these propositions. We have no occasion to pass upon their validity since, even if all are accepted, we think the tax was lawfully imposed and the re-

spondent was obligated to collect, return and pay it to the United States. . . .
[The court then reviews in two paragraphs the size and extent of the business enterprise involved.]

It is evident that these exhibition enterprises are comparatively large and are the means of procuring substantial aid for the schools' programs of athletics and physical education. In final analysis the question we must decide is whether, by electing to support a governmental activity through the conduct of a business comparable in all essentials to those usually conducted by private owners, a state may withdraw the business from the field of federal taxation.

When a state embarks in a business which would normally be taxable, the fact that in so doing it is exercising a governmental power does not render the activity immune from federal taxation. In South Carolina v. United States, 199 U. S. 437, 26 S. Ct. 110, 50 L. ed. 261, 4 Ann. Cas. 737, it appeared that South Carolina had established dispensaries for the sale of liquor and prohibited sale by other than official dispensers. It was held that the United States could require the dispensers to take licenses and pay license taxes under the internal revenue laws applicable to dealers in intoxicating liquors, and this notwithstanding the State had established the dispensary system in the valid exercise of her police power. In Ohio v. Helvering, 292 U. S. 360, 54 S. Ct. 725, 78 L. Ed. 1307, it was shown that Ohio, in the exercise of the same power, had created a monopoly of the distribution and sale of intoxicating liquors through stores owned, managed, and controlled exclusively by the State. It was sought to enjoin the Commissioner of Internal Revenue and his subordinates from enforcing against the State, her officers, agents, and employees, penalties for the nonpayment of federal excises on the sale of liquor. Relief was denied and the views expressed in the South Carolina case were reaffirmed. In Helvering v. Powers, 293 U. S. 214, 55 S. Ct. 171, 79 L. Ed. 291, the court found that Massachusetts, in the exercise of the police power, had appointed a board of trustees to operate a street railway company's properties for a limited time. It was held that, though the trustees were state officers, their salaries were subject to federal income tax because the State could not withdraw sources of revenue from the federal taxing power by engaging in a business which went beyond usual governmental functions and to which, by reason of its nature, the federial taxing power would normaly extetd.

The legislation considered in South Carolina v. United States, supra, provided for a division of the profits of the dispensary system between the State treasury and cities and counties. Thus the enterprise contributed directly to the sustenance of every governmental activity of the State. In the present instance, instead of covering the proceed or profits of the exhibitions onto the State treasury, the plan in actual operation appropriates these monies in ease of what the State deems its governmental obligation to support a system of public education. The difference in method is not significant. The important fact is that the State, in order to raise funds for public purposes, has embarked in a business having the incidents of similar enterprises usually prosecuted for private gain. If it be conceded that the education of its prospective citizens is an essential governmental function of Georgia, as necessary to the preservation of the State as is the maintenance of its executive, legislative, and judicial branches, it does not follow that if the State elects to provide the funds for any of these purposes by conducting a business, the application of the avails in aid of necessary governmental functions withdraws the business from the field of federal taxation.

Under the test laid down in Helvering v. Gerhardt, 304 U. S. 405, 58 S. Ct. 969, 82 L. Ed. —, decided this day, however essential a system of public education to the existence of the State, the conduct of exhibitions for admissions paid by the public is not such a function of state government as to be free from the burden of non-discriminatory tax laid on all admissions to public exhibitions for which an admission fee is charged.

The opinion in South Carolina v. United States, supra, at pages 454-457, 26 S. Ct. 110, points out the destruction of the federal power to tax which might result from a contrary decision.

Moreover the immunity implied from the dual sovereignty recognized by the Constitution does not extend to business enterprises conducted by the States for gain. As was said in South Carolina v. United States, supra, at page 457, 26 S. Ct. at page 115; "Looking, therefore, at the Constitution in the light of the conditions surrounding at the time of its adoption, it is obvious that the framers, in granting full power over license taxes to the national government, meant that that power should be complete; and never thought that the states, by extending their functions, could practically destroy it." . . . (54, pp. 980-81)

COMMENT

This case, together with the preceding, showed that a state could not expect from the Supreme Court any greater immunity from federal taxation in nontraditional parts of its educational function than could be expected for other functions not ordinarily associated with state sovereignty. Pleas for special consideration of education are profitably addressed only to Congress. It is there that the taxing power is exercised.

Pleas were addressed to Congress and after sixteen years they were successful. On April 1, 1954, a release from the United States Treasury Department, Internal Revenue Service, cited Public Law No. 324, approved March 31, 1954. The release included the following:

The new law . . . provides for exemption from tax for admissions to athletic games and exhibitions, including wrestling and boxing matches between educational institutions provided they are held during the regular athletic season for the particular activity involved, and provided that the proceeds inure exclusively to the benefit of the participating educational institutions. However, admissions to post season games, such as bowl games, continue to be subject to tax.

As a result of this legislation the Court will not need to look on state liquor stores and state college football games from an identical constitutional viewpoint.

4

TEACHER CONTRACTS— PUBLIC OFFICES

ART. I—LEGISLATIVE DEPT.
Sec. 10—Powers Denied to the States
Cl. 1—Obligation of Contracts
AMDT. 14—RIGHTS OF CITIZENS
Sec. 1—Due process of Law

[6] **TEACHER TENURE, STATUTORY**

PHELPS V. BOARD OF EDUCATION
300 U. S. 319, 57 Sup. Ct. 483 (1937)

The Supreme Court of the United States upheld a New Jersey statute and school board action taken under it to reduce all salaries of its employees, notwithstanding tenure status, as being no violation of any rights previously granted by the legislature. The Court determined that the tenure status of teachers in New Jersey, although in aspects contractual, was essentially statutory and hence subject to the will of the legislature.

In this case and the two immediately following, public school teachers contested actions of school authorities as denials of contractual rights. Their contention rested ultimately upon that same constitutional point concerning obligation of contracts as had the decision in the *Dartmouth College* case (149). But here, of course, no corporate charter was involved. The teachers, as occupants of public office, insisted that the terms under which they held such office had created rights which the legislature could not impair. In two of the cases the teachers were destined to disappointment in their contention, but in one case the teachers' view was sustained. The difference in decision turned upon differences in the statutes with which the teachers were involved. Those decisions have added very substantially to the case law on this point of contractual rights pertaining to public offices. (48, pp. 340-41)

Public offices do not establish a contractual obligation, "whether as to tenure, salary, or duties, all of which remain, so far as the Constitution of the United States is concerned, subject to legislative modification or outright repeal." (48, p. 340) Thus, under the Constitution, despite a contrary principle in common law, "there can be no such thing in this country as property in office." (48, p. 340) However—and this was the view of the teachers—after services in public office "have once been rendered, there arises an implied contract that they shall be compensated at the rate which was in force at the time they were rendered." (48, pp. 340-41)

Tenure laws for teachers, and their retirement laws as well, have generally risen by a rationale somewhat similar to that which brought the Civil Service into the political field. Teacher tenure laws have been justified, for two reasons: (1) The welfare of the schools, and (2) the welfare of the teacher as a person.

Except for a single case decided more than a half a century earlier the *Phelps* case and the *Brand* case appear to be the first in which public school teachers asserted contractual rights before the Supreme Court. The earlier case, *Head v. University of Missouri* (98), decided in 1874, resulted from dismissal after four years service of a professor-librarian who held a six-year contract, "subject to law." The qualifying phrase led the Court to hold the contract to be one which the proper authorities could terminate without the consent of the professor.

The *Phelps* case was raised by a teacher of the West New York, New Jersey public schools who had achieved tenure status. The state had enacted a comprehensive school law in 1903 by which local school boards were empowered to regulate the employment of school personnel and the "terms and tenure of such employment, promotion, and dismissal, salaries and their time and mode of payment, and to change and repeal such rules and regulations from time to time." In 1909 this general school law was modified by legislation of which the following portion is relevant:

. . . The service of all teachers, principals, supervising principals of the public schools in any district of this state shall be during good behavior and efficiency, after the expiration of a period of employment of three consecutive years in that district, unless a shorter period is fixed by the employing board. . . . No principal or teacher shall be dismissed or subjected to reduction of salary in said school district except for inefficiency, incapacity, conduct unbecoming a teacher or other just cause, and after a written charge . . . shall have been preferred. . . . (127, p. 484)

In 1933, the New Jersey Legislature, alluding to the depressed economic conditions, passed an act enabling each school board "to fix and determine salaries to be paid officers and employees" for the ensuing fiscal year, "notwithstanding any such person be under tenure." The West New York school board availed itself of the foregoing authorization and resolved to reduce salaries of teachers and principals by a graded percentage of their existing salaries, and the salaries of clerks to a specified figure. (127, p. 484)

Certain school personnel of the district appealed to the school authorities, first at the local level, then at the state level, requesting that the order be rescinded. An adverse decision by the State Board of Education caused the school employees to petition for certiorari from the Supreme Court of the United States on the point of state violation of Article I, Sections 10 and 1 of the federal Constitution. The writ was issued, and after a hearing, the New Jersey Court of Errors and Appeals affirmed the action by the school board upon the opinion of the Supreme Court of the United States. (127, p. 484)

Justice Roberts reviewed the above facts in rendering the opinion of the Court, which held, in part:

The position of the appellants is that by virtue of the Act of 1909 three years of service under contract confer upon an employe of a school district a contractual status indefinite in duration which the legislature is powerless to alter or to authorize the board of education to alter. The Supreme Court holds that the Act of 1909 "established a legislative status for teachers, but we fail to see that it established a contractual one that the Legislature may not modify. . . . The status of tenure teachers, while in one sense perhaps contractual, is in essence dependent on a statute, like that of the incumbent of a statutory office, which the Legislature at will may abolish, or whose emoluments it may change."

This court is not bound by the decision of a state court as to the existence and terms of a contract, the obligation of which is asserted to be impaired, but where a statute is claimed to create a contractual right we give weight to the construction of the statute by the courts of the state. Here those courts have concurred in holding that the act of 1909 did not amount to a legislative contract with the teachers of the state and did not become a term of the contracts entered into with employees by boards of education. Unless these views are palpably erroneous we should accept them.

It appears from a stipulation of facts submitted in view of evidence that after a teacher has served in a school district under yearly contracts for three years it has not been customary to enter into further formal contracts with such teacher. From time to time, however, promotions were granted and salary raised for the ensuing year by action of the board. In the case of many of the appellants there have been several such increases in salary.

Although after the expiration of the first three years of service the employe continued in his then position and at his then compensation unless and until promoted or given an increase in salary for a succeeding year, we find nothing in the record to indicate that the board was bound by contract with the teacher for more than the current year. The employe assumed no binding obligation to remain in service beyond that term. Although the act of 1909 prohibited the board, a creature of the state, from reducing the teacher's salary or discharging him without cause, we agree with the courts below that this was but a regulation of the conduct of the board and not a term of a continuing contract of indefinite duration with the individual teacher.

The resolution of June 23, 1933, grouped the existing salaries paid by the board into six classes the lowest of which comprised salaries ranging between $1200 and $1999; and the highest included salaries ranging between $4000 and $5600. The reduction in the lowest class for the coming year was 10 percent; that in the highest class 15 percent. Salaries in the intermediate classes were reduced 11, 12, 13 and 14 percent. It resulted that in some instances a teacher receiving the lowest salary in a given bracket would have his compensation reduced to a figure lower than the reduced compensation of one receiving the highest salary in the next lower bracket. From this circumstance it is argued that the board's action arbitrarily discriminated between the employes and so denied them the equal protection of the laws guaranteed by the Fourteenth Amendment.

We think it was reasonable and proper that the teachers employed by the board should be divided into classes for the application of the percentage reduction. All in a given class were treated alike. Incidental individual inequality resulting in some instances from the operation of the plan does not condemn it as an unreasonable or arbitrary method of dealing with the problem of general salary reductions or deny the equality guaranteed by the Fourteenth Amendment. . . . (127, pp. 484-85)

COMMENT

Here the Court determined that under the relevant statutes of New Jersey the tenure status of the teachers in the state was essentially statutory, and not in the nature of a contractual relationship.

A year later, however, after hearing a comparable case in *Indiana ex rel. Anderson v. Brand*, the Court decided that under the tenure statute existing in that state a teacher held a valid contract which could not be impaired by termination of employment. The *Brand* case follows.

ART. I—LEGISLATIVE DEPT.

Sec. 10—Powers Denied to the States

Cl.   1—Obligation of Contracts

[7] TEACHER TENURE, CONTRACTUAL

INDIANA EX REL. ANDERSON V. BRAND

303 U. S. 95, 58 Sup. Ct. 43 (1938)

The Supreme Court of the United States held that a dismissed teacher had a valid contract which under Article I, section 10 of the federal Constitution the Indiana Legislature could not impair by repealing the tenure law which had applied to the school where the teacher was formerly employed.

A comparison of this case with the one preceding demonstrates the difficulty of determining in abstract fashion or in advance which legislation will afford rights merely statutory and subject to unilateral modification, or which will result in the creation of rights that are contractual. As the Court said here, "a legislative enactment may contain provisions which, when accepted as a basis of action by individuals, become contracts between them and the State and its subdivision within the protection of Article I, section 10" of the federal Constitution.

The background on the case is included within the decision.

Justice Roberts spoke for the Court. He said, in part:

The petitioner sought a writ of mandate to compel the respondent to continue her in employment as a public school teacher. Her complaint alleged that as a duly licensed teacher she entered into a contract in September, 1924, to teach in the township schools and, pursuant to successive contracts, taught continuously to and including the school year 1932-33; that her contract for the school years 1931-32 and 1932-33 contained this clause: "It is further agreed by the contracting parties that all of the provisions of the Teachers' Tenure Law, approved March 8, 1927, shall be in full force and effect in this contract"; and that by force of that act she had a contract, indefinite in duration, which could be cancelled by the respondent only in the manner and for the causes specified in the act. She charged that in July, 1933, the respondent notified her he proposed to cancel her contract for cause; that, after a hearing, he adhered to his decision and the county superintendent affirmed his action; that despite what occurred in July, 1933, the petitioner was permitted to teach during the school year 1933-34, and the respondent was presently threatening to terminate her employment at the end of that year. The complaint alleged the termination of her employment would be a breach of her contract with the school corporation.

The respondent demurred on the grounds that . . . (2) the Teachers' Tenure Law, Acts Ind. 1927, C. 97, had been repealed in respect to teachers in township schools. The demurrer was sustained and the petitioner appealed to the state Supreme Court which affirmed the judgment. The court . . . . held that the repeal did not deprive the petitioner of a vested property right and did not impair her contract within the meaning of the Constitution. In its original opinion the court said: "the relatrix contends . . . that, having become a permanent teacher under the Teachers' Tenure Law before the amendment, she had vested property right in her indefinite contract, which may not be impaired under the Constitution. The question is whether, under the tenure law, there is a grant which cannot lawfully be impaired by a repeal of the statute." . . .

The court below holds that in Indiana teachers' contracts are made but for one year; that the law grants a privilege to one who has taught five years and signed a new contract to continue in employment under given conditions; that the statute is directed merely to the exercise of their powers by the school authorities and the policies therein expressed may be altered at the will of the Legislature; that in enacting laws for the government of public schools, the Legislature exercises a function of sovereignty and the power to control public policy in respect of their management and operation cannot be contracted away by one legislature as to create a permanent public policy unchangeable by succeeding Legislatures. In the alternative the court declares that if the relationship be considered as controlled by the rules of private contract the provision for re-employment from year to year is unenforceable for want of mutuality.

As in most cases brought to this court under the contract clause of the Constitution, the question is as to the nature of the contract and not as to the construction of the law which is supposed to impair it. The principal function of a legislative body is not to make contracts but to make laws which declare the policy of the state and are subject to repeal when a subsequent Legislature shall determine to alter that policy. Nevertheless, it is established that a legislative enactment may contain provisions which, when accepted as the basis of action by individuals, become contracts between them and the State or its subdivisions within the protection of Article 1, Sec. 10. If the people's representatives deem it in the public interest they may adopt a policy of contracting in respect of public business for a term longer than the life of the current session of the Legislature. This the petitioner claims has been done with respect to permanent teachers. The Supreme Court has decided, however, that it is the state's policy not to bind school corporations by contract for more than one year.

In 1927 the State adopted the Teachers' Tenure Law under which the present controversy arises. By this act it was provided that a teacher who has served under contract for five or more consecutive years, and thereafter enters into a contract for further service with the school corporation, shall become a permanent teacher and the contract, upon the expiration of its stated term, shall be deemed to continue in effect for an indefinite period, shall be known as an indefinite contract, and shall remain in force unless succeeded by a new contract or canceled as provided in the act. The corporation may cancel the contract, after notice and hearing, for incompetency, insubordination, neglect of duty, immorality, justifiable decrease in the number of teaching positions, or other good or just cause, but not for political or personal reasons. The teacher may not cancel the contract during the school term nor for a period of 30 days previous to the beginning of any term (unless by mutual agreement) and may cancel only upon 5 days' notice.

By an amendatory act of 1933 township school corporations were omitted from the provisions of the act of 1927. The court below construed this act as repealing the act of 1927 so far as township schools and teachers are concerned and as leaving the respondent free to terminate the petitioner's employment. But we are of the opinion that the petitioner had a valid contract with the respondent, the obligation of which would be impaired by the termination of her employment.

Where the claim is that the state's policy embodied in a statute is to bind its instrumentalities by contract, the cardinal inquiry is as to the terms of the statute supposed to have created such a contract. The State long prior to the adoption of written contracts between teachers and school corporations, specified certain subjects with which such contracts must deal, and required that they be made a matter of public record. These were annual contracts, covering a single school term. The act of 1927 announced a new policy that a teacher who had served for 5 years under successive contracts, upon the execution of another was to become a permanent teacher and the last contract was to be indefinite as to duration and terminable by either party only upon compliance with the conditions set out in the statute. The policy which induced the legislation evidently was that the teacher should have protection against the exercise of the right which would otherwise inhere in the employer, of terminating the employment at the end of any school term without assigned reasons and solely at the employer's pleasure. The state courts in earlier cases so declared.

Until its decision in the present case the Supreme Court of the State had uniformly held that the teacher's right to continued employment by virtue of the indefinite contract created pursuant to the act was contractual.

In School City of Elwood v. State Ex Rel. Griffin et al, 203 Ind. 626, at page 634, 180 N. E. 471, 474, 81 A. L. R. 1027, it was said: "the position of a teacher in the public schools is not a public office, but an employment by contract between the teacher and the school corporation. The relation remains contractual after the teacher has, under the provisions of the Teachers' Tenure Law, become a permanent teacher—but the terms and conditions of the contract are thereafter governed primarily by the statute. . . ."

The respondent urges that every contract is subject to the police power and that in repealing the Teachers' Tenure Act the Legislature validly exercised that reserved power of the State. The sufficient answer is found in the statute. By Section 2 of the act of 1927 power is given to the school corporation to cancel a teacher's indefinite contract for incompetency, insubordination (which is to be deemed to mean willful refusal to obey the school laws of the State or reasonable rules prescribed by the employer), neglect of duty, immorality, justifiable decrease in the number of teaching positions, or other good and just cause. The permissible reasons for cancellation cover every conceivable basis for such action growing out of a deficient performance of the obligations undertaken by the teacher, and diminution of the school requirements. Although the causes specified constitute in themselves just and reasonable grounds for the termination of any ordinary contract of employment, to preclude the assumption that any other valid ground was excluded by the enumeration, the Legislature added that the relation might be terminated for any other good and just cause. Thus in the declaration of the state's policy, ample reservations in aid of the efficient administration of the school system were made. The express prohibitions are that the contract shall not be canceled for political or personal reasons. We do not think the asserted change of policy evidenced by the repeal of the statute is that school boards may be at liberty to cancel a teacher's contract for political reasons. We do not understand the respondent so to contend. The most that can be said for his position is that, by the repeal, township school corporations were again put upon the basis of annual contracts, renewable at the pleasure of the board. It is significant that the act of 1933 left the system of permanent teachers and indefinite contracts untouched as respects school corporations in cities and towns of the State. It is not contended, nor can it be thought, that the Legislature of 1933 determined that it was against public policy for school districts in cities and towns to terminate the employment of teachers of 5 or more years' experience for political or personal reasons and to permit cancellation, for the same reasons, in townships.

Our decisions recognize that every contract is made subject to the implied condition that its fulfillment may be frustrated by a proper exercise of the police power but we have repeatedly said that, in order to have this effect, the exercise of the power must be for an end which is in fact public and the means adopted must be reasonably adapted to that end, and the Supreme Court of Indiana has taken the same view in respect of legislation impairing the obligation of the contract of a State instrumentality. The causes of cancellation provided in the act of 1927 and the retention of the system of indefinite contracts in all municipalities except townships by the act of 1933 are persuasive that the repeal of the earlier act by the later was not an exercise of the police power for the attainment of ends to which its exercise may properly be directed.

As the court below has not passed upon one of the grounds of demurrer which appears to involve no federal question, and may present a defense still open to the respondent, we reverse the judgment and remand the cause for further proceedings not inconsistent with this opinion. . . . (104, pp. 444-50)

Justice Black did not agree. His dissent, much reduced here, included the following:

In my opinion this reversal unconstitutionally limits the right of Indiana to control Indiana's public school system. . . .

I cannot agree that the constitutional prohibitions against impairment of contracts was intended to—or does—transfer in part the determination of the educational policy of Indiana from the legislature of that state to this Court.

Indiana, in harmony with our national tradition, seeks to work out a school system, offering education to all, as "essential to the preservation of free government." That great function of an advancing society has heretofore been exercised by the states. I find no constitutional authority for this Court to appropriate that power. Indiana's highest court has said that the *State did not,* and has strongly indicated that the *Legislature could not,* make contracts with a *few citizens,* that would take away from *all the citizens,* the continuing power to alter the educational policy for the best interests of Indiana school children....

. . . I cannot agree to the majority decision. . . . (104, pp. 450, 453-55)

COMMENT

The majority opinion in this case should not be construed as limiting a contrary decision in the case of *Phelps v. Board of Education* (127) a year earlier. Rather, any seeming difference reflects but an actual difference in the tenure laws of the two states involved.

Not to be overlooked is the Court's deference to the traditions and practice of teacher employment in the two states, a particular point being made of the practice developed through law over the years in Indiana. For, unlike the New Jersey legislation involved in the *Phelps* case, the Indiana Statute considered here had established a contract in the legal sense.

Another difference, but one on which the Court would hardly be expected to speak, may also be noted. In the *Phelps* case the complaining school employees were not threatened with dismissal, but only with a reduction in salary such as came to many others in and out of public employment during those years of economic depression. In the *Brand* case, however, the teacher was being threatened with loss of position in addition to loss of an established tenure status by later legislation. Statutes aside, it would seem that a qualified teacher's right to continue in employment is greater than the right to a fixed position on a salary schedule.

To teachers and legislatures in general the critical point made by the Court in the *Brand* case was that while the laws made by legislatures are ordinarily subject to amendment or repeal they may "contain provisions which, when accepted as the basis of action by individuals, become contracts between them and the state."

ART. I—LEGISLATIVE DEPT.
Sec. 10—Powers Denied to the States
Cl.   1—Obligation of Contracts
AMDT. 14—RIGHTS OF CITIZENS
Sec.   1—Due Process of Law

[8] TEACHER RETIREMENT, STATUTORY

DODGE V. BOARD OF EDUCATION OF CHICAGO
302 U. S. 74, 58 Sup. Ct. 98 (1937)

The Supreme Court of the United States held that an Illinois statute which reduced the payments to retired teachers under previous legislation did not violate the contract clause of the federal Constitution, because the relationship established under the earlier legislation had been intended only as a statutory implementation of policy.

As in the two cases preceding, the question here arose in a time of economic depression and was the response of teachers to similar efforts by a legislature at coping with the problems of a reduced state income. The case involved a "retirement plan" that more accurately might be called "a pension plan," since it was of the noncontributory type with payments made wholly from public funds.

This noncontributory Illinois plan, known as the Miller Law, had been put into effect by legislation and amendments dating from 1926. Then, in 1935, a further amendment lowered the maximum retirement age and reduced the annuities to amounts that in some cases were but one-third of those previously paid. Moreover, the reduced annuities applied not only to teachers subsequently retired, but to those previously retired as well. The teachers contended of this recent amendment that it "impairs the obligation of contracts in contravention of Article I, Section 10, of the Constitution of the United States," and that it deprived them of "a vested right without due process, contrary to the Fourteenth Amendment." (75, p. 98) The Illinois Supreme Court found that a statutory, not a contractual, relationship had been established by the law cited. The teachers' action was dismissed. Thereupon, the teachers took their case to the Supreme Court of the United States on appeal.

Justice Roberts wrote the opinion of the Court. He said, in part:

In determining whether a law tenders a contract to a citizen, it is of first importance to examine the language of the statute. If it provides for the execution of a written contract on behalf of the state, the case for an obligation binding upon the state is clear. Equally clear is the case where a statute confirms a settlement of disputed rights and defines its terms. On the other hand, an act merely fixing salaries of officers creates no contract in their favor, and the compensation named may be altered at the will of the Legislature. This is true also of an act fixing the term of tenure of a public officer or an employee of a state agency. The presumption is that such a law is not intended to create private contractual or vested rights, but merely declares a policy to be pursued until the Legislature shall ordain otherwise. He who asserts the creation of a contract with the state in such a case has the burden of overcoming the presumption. If, upon a construction of the statute, it is found that the payments are gratuities, involving no agreement of the parties, the grant of them creates no vested right.

The Supreme Court of Illinois concluded that neither the language of the Miller Law, nor the circumstances of its adoption, evinced an intent on the part of the Legislature to create a binding contract with the teachers of the state. While we are required to reach an independent judgment as to the existence and nature of the alleged contract, we give great weight to the views of the highest court of the state touching these matters.

The Miller Law is entitled, "An Act to provide for the compulsory and voluntary retirement of teachers, . . . and for the payment of retirement annuities." . . . The relevant words of section 1 are: "In every city in this State . . . the board of education of such city shall retire from active service . . . all teachers (of a given age)." Section 2 provides: "Each person so retired . . . shall be paid the sum of fifteen hundred dollars ($1500.00) annually and for life from the date of such retirement." Section 3 provides that persons

65 years of age or over "shall upon their own request be retired . . . and thereafter be paid annuities for life." Appellants admit that this is not the normal language of a contract, but rely on the circumstance that they, as teachers, especially those who voluntarily retired to do so, rightly understood the state was pledging its faith that it would not recede from the offer held out to them by the statute as an inducement to become teachers and to retire, and that the use of the term "annuities" rather than "pensions" was intended as a further assurance of a vested contractual right. The Supreme Court answered this contention by referring to the fact that for years prior to the adoption of the Miller Law, and by a uniform course of decision, it had held that acts indistinguishable from the Miller Law, establishing similar benefit systems, did not create contracts or vested rights, and that the state was free to alter, amend, and repeal such laws, even though the effect of its action was to deprive the pensioner or annuitant, for the future, of benefits then enjoyed. The cases to which the court refers so decide.

The court further held that the Legislature presumably had the doctrine of these cases in mind when it adopted the act now under review, and that the appellants should have known that no distinction was intended between the rights conferred on them and those adjudicated under like laws with respect to other retired civil servants. We cannot say that this was error.

The appellants urge that the Miller Law, contrary to most of the acts that preceded it, omitted to use the word "pension" and instead used the word "annuity", a choice of terminology based on contract rather than on gift, and implying a consideration received as well as offered. The state Supreme Court (364 Ill. 547, 5 N. E. (2nd) 84, 88) answered the contention by saying: "We are unable to see the distinction. The plan of payment is the same, and use of the term 'annuity' instead of 'pension'—which is but an annuity—does not seem to us to result in the distinction for which counsel for appellants contend."

We are of the same opinion, particularly as an examination of the Illinois statutes indicates that, in acts dealing with the subject, the Legislature has apparently used the terms "pension", "benefits", and "annuities" interchangeably as having the same connotation.

The judgment is affirmed. (75, pp. 100-101)

COMMENT

The foregoing decision reiterates a recognized distinction between a pension system supported wholly by public funds and a retirement plan supported through joint contributions by both the state and the public employee. A commentator on this point and this decision has said:

That pensions are gratuities which may be reduced or abolished is an accepted principle. It does not follow that all annuities based upon joint contributions of employee and employers are contracts which the state may not modify. On this score there is a difference of opinion among the courts, especially in the older cases. The modern view has been that a joint-contributory retirement system creates for its members a vested right which cannot be impaired by the legislature or by the retirement board in its by-laws, at least after a member has retired. . . . (41, p. 204)

The same commentator, writing in 1950, notes that New York alone among the states has enacted a constitutional provision specifying that "all retirement benefits provided in part by public funds create a contractual relation between the members and the state" which the legislature is forbidden to impair. (41, p. 204)

The reasons why participants in retirement plans in other states have not insisted upon language so explicit as to remove all doubt that a contractual relationship is intended can only be conjectured. Possibly one reason is that those who have lobbied for retirement laws or assisted in drafting them were not aware of the distinctions which courts might make from the language.

A meeting of some fifty college-level teachers who were discussing proposed changes in a joint-contributory type retirement plan indicated that the question of statutory versus contractual rights in application to the plan had occurred to few if any of them. Thereafter, while the distinction was being discussed, an attitude expressed by several of the teachers reflects another possible reason why the language of retirement provisions in most states remains less explicit than in New York. It was suggested that the greater practical wisdom lay in reliance upon "adequate" statutory rights; that insistence upon contractual rights might provoke from the legislature and the public an antagonism which might prove damaging to the existing position.

SUMMARY: PART ONE

Answers by the Supreme Court of the United States to questions of state and federal position and function touching on education.

Yes No

(X) ( ) [1] *Dartmouth College Case* (1819). Was a charter granted a private school a contract which the legislature of New Hampshire could not at will revoke?

( ) (X) [2] *Springfield Township v. Quick* (1859). Must a state apportion funds to schools receiving aid from a federal land grant while other schools in the state are below parity with them?

(X) ( ) [3] *International Text-Book Co. v. Pigg* (1910). Is transmission of instruction by correspondence interstate commerce and hence beyond state interference?

(X) ( ) [4] *University of Illinois v. United States* (1933). Must a state, under our dual system of government, pay duty on scientific equipment imported for educational purposes?

(X) ( ) [5] *Allen v. Regents* (1938). Must a state pay the federal excise tax on admissions to athletic contests even though the proceeds are devoted to education?

( ) (X) [6] *Phelps v. Board of Education* (1937). Was New Jersey's action in reducing salaries of teachers on tenure an impairment of contract?

(X) ( ) [7] *Indiana ex rel. Anderson v. Brand* (1938). Was Indiana's action in repealing the tenure law under which a dismissed teacher had held a contract an impairment of contract?

( ) (X) [8] *Dodge v. Board of Education* (1937). Was an Illinois statute which reduced the payments to retired teachers under a pension plan supported wholly by public funds an impairment of contract?

RECAPITULATION

Federal Power held paramount.................   [1] [3] [4] [5]...... 4
State Action upheld ....   [2] [6] [8] 3
Citizen upheld ....   [7] 1

PART TWO

QUESTIONS TOUCHING ON
THE BILL OF RIGHTS

*Which means that a person challenged
some action as denying guarantees of
nonestablishment of religion, of freedom
of religion, and of freedom of speech and
the press.*

5

THE BILL OF RIGHTS

"Bills of Rights are for the most part reactions against evils of the past rather than promises for the future." (44, p. 387) Many of our revolutionary forefathers in the new nation could recall from bitter personal experience the memory of civil rights recently denied them. Moreover, they could review the record of struggles over such rights scattered through centuries of English governmental practice. Yet the framers of the Constitution appear to have given little thought to a bill of rights. Late in the convention it was, however, suggested that a bill of rights "would give great quiet to the people," (19, vol. 2, p. 587) but a motion to appoint a committee to prepare such a bill was defeated on the grounds that it was unnecessary and impracticable. "Who," Pennsylvania's delegate, James Wilson, once wanted to know, "will be bold enough to undertake to enumerate all the rights of the people?" (19, vol. 3, p. 144) It was no doubt pointed out at the Convention that scattered clauses already included in the Constitution safeguarded certain individual liberties.

Subsequently, in the *Federalist*, Alexander Hamilton continued the discussion in a vein approaching sophistry. He pointed out that the Constitution was not a reservation of rights in a compact with a prince but was a sovereign act of "WE, THE PEOPLE," done on purpose to "secure the blessings of liberty to ourselves and our posterity." This, Hamilton maintained, was a "better recognition of popular rights, than volumes of those aphorisms which make the principal figure in several of our State bills of rights, and which would sound much better in a treatise of ethics than in a constitution of government." (21, p. 536)

Nevertheless, at the insistence of certain of the ratifying states, the first Congress under the Constitution submitted twelve amendments to the states. Ten of these were ratified and thus incorporated into the Constitution. (48, p. 39 n) The first eight are commonly called the Bill of Rights. They were based, whether taken in the historical or the rhetorical context, upon the attitude that government was the enemy of freedom. It was against government and government alone that these safeguards were interposed. Only the central government was limited thereby. This is manifest in the First Amendment by the inclusion of the word "Congress." Although the remaining amendments composing the Bill of Rights are rendered less specific by the omission of this word, there is little reason to doubt the historical evidence that their framers intended that they be interposed just as exclusively against usurpation of traditional liberties by the Congress alone. The omission did make it possible to argue that these guarantees were restrictions on states as well as on the central government, but Chief Justice John Marshall was enabled to put an end to the controversy for a time by an opportunity presented in the last decision he handed down. Referring to the Bill of Rights in the case of *Barron v. Baltimore* in 1833 he said: "These amendments contain no expression indicating an intention to apply them to state governments. This court cannot so apply them." (57, p. 250)

Thereafter, for a century, in the case of religion at least, "Congress had little opportunity and less inclination to violate the First Amendment, and what the states did by way of dealing with religious matters was their own business so far as the federal Constitution was concerned." (14, p. 132) Thus there were few Supreme Court decisions dealing with religion or bearing religious connotations until after World War I. The "Mormon cases" in the last quarter of the nineteenth century afford an exception. In one of these, *Reynolds v. United States* (134), the Court held that the religious liberty guaranteed by the First Amendment does not include the right to commit immoral or criminal acts, i.e., polygamy, even though such acts are sanctioned by religious doctrine. Another, earlier exception was the *Girard College* case (154) which is discussed in this chapter.

THE FOURTEENTH AMENDMENT AND THE BILL OF RIGHTS

Following the Civil War a possibility that the guarantees of the Bill of Rights might be extended to the states by the final sentence of

Section One of the Fourteenth Amendment became the subject of bitter controversy. (14, p. 41; and 26, pp. 730-31) The sentence follows:

No state shall make or enforce any law which shall abridge the privileges or immunities of citizens of the United States; nor shall any state deprive any person of life, liberty, or property, without due process of law; nor deny to any person within its jurisdiction the equal protection of the laws.

Many persons understood this as intending that the "privileges and immunities" mentioned were those specified by the first eight amendments, and that the Supreme Court would hold any state interference with them to be in violation of the Fourteenth Amendment. However, many decades were to elapse before the court was persuaded to this view. For, from the *Slaughterhouse* cases in 1873 (142) until the present, the Court has resisted making express equation of *all* the civil liberties in the Bill of Rights with the "privileges and immunities of citizens of the United States." Since the 1930's the number of liberties which have been so equated has been increased by certain decisions. Notable among such decisions are those in "education cases" to be described hereafter.

Likewise, persons who had expected that the clause "nor shall any state deprive any person of life, liberty, or property, without due process of law" would be accepted by the Court as including civil liberties covered in the Bill of Rights were also destined to wait nearly as long. But in this aspect there were more dissenting opinions among the justices than appeared in cases turning upon the "privileges and immunities" clause. In 1923, and again in 1925, in the cases respectively of *Meyer v. Nebraska* (113) and *Pierce v. Society of Sisters* (128) the Court began to bring the Bill of Rights under the extended protection of the "due process" clause. Although the trend is only somewhat more complete in the "due process" aspect than in the "privileges and immunities" aspect, the principle of federal defense against invasions of civil rights in general by the states seems now to have become well established. (48, p. 985) Those of the decisions affecting education included in this chapter and which are dated later than 1922 have contributed to this principle in one or both of the aspects.

RELIGIOUS FREEDOM

Much of the immigration to British Colonial America was composed of Englishmen and continental peoples seeking escape from religious persecution in their homeland. Yet, being almost if not entirely the captives of their age, toleration was a concept largely unknown to them. The stories of Roger Williams and of Anne Hutchinson, expelled from their colonies, and of Quakers and Baptists tied to carts and dragged through colonial towns to be lashed by the populace, is testimony that the majority of the colonists were as insistent upon a special brand of religion as had been their own oppressors. But ultimately, perhaps because of the very diversity of sects and the inescapable necessity of living and working together, the tolerance of religious freedom preached by Williams and practiced in Rhode Island was generally recognized as desirable—so much so that an express safeguard for religious freedom was demanded and secured in the First Amendment.

Under that safeguard the right to hold whatever opinion on religion that one may wish has hardly been challenged. But when opinion turns to practice state authority may prevail. Jefferson, in his "Act Establishing Religious Freedom" in the state of Virginia discusses the distinction. He wrote, in part:

. . . to suffer the civil magistrate to intrude his powers into the field of opinion and to restrain the profession or propagation of principles on supposition of their ill tendency is a dangerous fallacy, which at once destroys all religious liberty. . . . it is time enough for the rightful purposes of civil government for its officers to interfere when principles break out into overt acts against peace and good order. . . . (25, p. 109)

As noted earlier, most of the few Supreme Court decisions on religion in the nineteenth century were in support of the above principle. Such cases could come before the Court only from territories subject to Congress, or from contests wherein a determination of state or federal function was required. Not until the Court interpreted the Fourteenth Amendment's "due process of law" clause as constituting a safeguard against invasions of religious liberty by states were many religious cases likely. The decisions bearing on religion during the last fifteen years have been more numerous and probably more productive of important case law than were all the preceding cases involving religion.

AN ESTABLISHMENT OF RELIGION IN THE SCHOOLS

In certain cases to be discussed ([13] [16]) the Supreme Court deals with questions determining whether governmental action involving only a limited number of citizens had been in violation of the First or Fourteenth Amendments. In the other cases, the Court deals with questions of more direct concern to the citizenry as a whole. These latter contests turn more specifically upon the principle of "separation of church and state." The use of public funds for sectarian advantage is the predominant issue. (Private non-sectarian schools may come within the meaning of the statutes contested and of the case law resulting, but none appear to have involved themselves in the question.) The fact that we have parallel systems of public and parochial schools serving the citizens of a nation wherein education is compulsory has lent complexity to the problem.

Education in early colonial America, even where supported by public funds as in Massachusetts, was in large measure religious. That a system of free, secular, and tax-supported education had developed in the United States around the middle of the nineteenth century was possibly an outcome of Protestantism and its diversity finding accommodation in developing democratic dogma and in our expanding nation. But, as Professor Cushman points out, the Catholic Church, strengthened by floods of immigrants to America, could not, in conscience or in fact, surrender its assertedly rightful function of education to the increasing public schools—schools which to Catholic eyes either shunned any religious training or else afforded it only with a Protestant taint. The resulting growth of parochial schools supported by Catholics left them feeling unjustly burdened by the requirement of contributing also to the support of public schools from which they received no direct benefit. They began to insist that those of their schools which met the accreditation standards and satisfied the compulsory school laws of the state should receive public aid. (14, pp. 144-45)

John Lancaster Spaulding, a Catholic spokesman on matters of faith and education, had the following to say nearly seventy-five years ago:

. . . The state . . . which tolerates different forms of religion is thereby debarred from the right to establish a uniform school system; and yet it is unreasonable to ask the state to do nothing to promote and spread education, since, after religion, education is the chief agent of civilization, and, in the absence of governmental aid and supervision, many parents, and ministers of religion even, will either altogether neglect this most important work or at best perform it in an inefficient and careless manner. In a free state, then, where religious tolerance is a fundamental principle of law, the government, in fostering education, is bound to respect scrupulously the rights of the family and liberty of conscience; and this it cannot do, if the schools are supported by taxation, except by instituting what is known as the denominational system of education. The practical difficulties to be overcome are not insuperable; and since there is question here of a fundamental principle of free government, the obstacles to its practical acceptance and enforcement should but serve to inspire just and enlightened statesmen with a more determined will to remove them. If, however, the state should establish a school system from which religion is excluded, it becomes the imperative duty of Catholics to found schools to which they can, with a safe conscience, send their children. . . . (11, p. 589)

Such logic has not been admitted by the predominantly Protestant nation and, indeed, has seemed only to evoke greater opposition to the Catholic pressure. The actual pressure has been directed both toward a general sharing of public school funds and toward the more limited objective of sharing in such benefits or services as the free textbooks, the free transportation to school, the free lunches, the free medical and dental care, and the special education programs for handicapped children that states have widely provided for the public schools during the last quarter-century. However, since 1947, especially, when the Court's decision in the *Everson* case (77) gave clear re-affirmation to the principle of separation of church and state, yet at the same time sanctioned use of public funds for bus transportation of parochial school children on the ground that the benefit accruing to religion was no more than incidental, the Catholic pressure appears to have been concentrated more upon gaining a share in the services than toward securing a share of the general school funds. Resulting controversy has at its heart the question whether extension of state-provided services to nonpublic schools may violate the clause in the First Amendment which forbids "an establishment of religion."

The other clause of the First Amendment dealing with religion, which forbids Congress from "prohibiting the free exercise thereof," has been that most frequently considered by the various courts. The restraint against establishment of religion has only recently been involved in questions before the Supreme Court. Indeed, not until 1940, in the decision of *Cantwell v. Connecticut* (66), was religion expressly included among the fundamental liberties protected by the "due process" clause of the Fourteenth Amendment from impairment by the states. Two years later this holding received confirmation in *Murdock v. Pennsylvania* (118). It still remained to be determined whether the restraint against an established religion intended only a separation of church and state or a separation of religion and state as well. Then, in 1947, the case of *Everson v. Board of Education* (77), Justice Black, speaking for the Court, asserted relevant constitutional doctrine in broadest terms when he said: "Neither [Congress nor the states] can pass laws which aid one religion, aid all religions, or prefer one religion over another." He continued: "Neither a state nor the Federal Government can, openly or secretly, participate in the affairs of any religious organizations or groups and vice versa." (77, p. 512) The opinion from which the foregoing is quoted sustained, nevertheless, the use of public funds to transport children to parochial schools, for the reasons shown on pages to follow. In the same case, Justice Rutledge, dissenting, observed:

. . . Two great drives are constantly in motion to abridge, in the name of education, the complete division of religion and civil authority which our forefathers made. One is to introduce religious education and observances into the public schools. The other, to obtain public funds for the aid and support of various private religious schools. . . . (77, p. 535)

Movement in the drives to which Justice Rutledge points is measured particularly by cases [11], [12], [17], and [19] following.

The first case to be discussed, however, involved neither of these two drives, nor did it involve the First Amendment at all. Rather, it was a guarantee of religious freedom in Pennsylvania's constitution which the Supreme Court applied to a question which could hardly have reached it had not the state of Pennsylvania been challenged by citizens of France. A notable decision which, in effect, fixed more securely the concept of religious freedom for the whole nation was rendered. In this case, the *Girard College* case (154), an individual's unorthodox attitude towards sectarianism was completely upheld.

6

A NINETEENTH CENTURY ODDITY

(RELIGION, CHARITIES)
Art. III—JUDICIAL DEPT.
Sec. 2—Jurisdiction
Cl. 1—Controversies Between States and Citizens
of a Foreign State; Constitution,
Laws, Treaties

[9] SECTARIAN INSTRUCTION NEED NOT BE INCLUDED IN A
COURSE OF STUDY (THE GIRARD COLLEGE CASE)

VIDAL V. GIRARD'S EXECUTORS

2 How. 127 (U. S. 1844)

The Supreme Court of the United States held that the will of Stephen Girard for the endowment of a college which by its provisions excluded ministers and missionaries from the premises of the college was not so derogatory to the Christian religion as to make such a devise void according to the constitution and laws of Pennsylvania.

The life of Stephen Girard (52) affords an early example of the immigrant to riches story in American fact and folklore. A mogul of commerce and finance, he foreshadowed the tendency of his compeers of a later generation to turn toward philanthrophy, and like Andrew Carnegie, Girard appears to have held doubts concerning sectarian religious expression.

In 1776, as master and part owner of a vessel engaged in trade between the French West Indies and New York, Girard put into Philadelphia with his ship in distress. There he remained and established his mercantile career. His wealth through shipping and banking grew steadily and by the period of the War of 1812 his personal resources were such that he was able to succeed "where the United States Treasury had failed" in absorbing and otherwise disposing of a bond issue to finance the war. (52, pp. 214-16)

In 1831, Girard died with an estate of some six million dollars. Among other of his charitable arrangements was a bequest of real estate and two million dollars for the establishment of a college for "poor, white, male orphans."[7] This praiseworthy object was to proceed, however, only by observance of a restriction which, among other points, was seized upon by disappointed relatives of Girard as a basis for attack in an effort to break the will, which said in part:

XXI. 7 . . . [The scholars] shall be instructed in the various branches of a sound education: comprehending Reading, Writing, Grammar, Arithmetic, Geography, Navigation, Surveying, Practical Mathematics, Astronomy, Natural, Chemical and Experimental Philosophy, the French and Spanish languages, (I do not forbid, but do not recommend the Greek and Latin languages,) and such other learning and science as the capacities of the several scholars may merit or warrant. I would have them taught facts and things, rather than words and signs; and especially I desire that . . . a pure attachment to our republican institutions, and to the sacred rights of conscience, as guaranteed by our happy constitution shall be fostered and formed in the minds of the scholars.

XXI. 9 . . . I enjoin and require that no ecclesiastic, missionary, or minister of any sect whatsoever, shall ever hold or exercise any station or duty whatever in the said College; nor shall any such person ever be admitted for any purpose, or as a visitor, within the premises appropriated to the purposes of the said College. In making this restriction, I do not mean to cast any reflection upon any sect or person whatsoever; but, as there is such a multitude of sects, and such a diversity of opinion amongst them, I desire to keep the tender minds of the orphans . . . free from the excitement which clashing doctrines and sectarian controversy are so apt to produce; my desire is, that all the instructors . . . shall take pains to instill into the minds of the scholars the purest principles of morality, so that on their entrance into active life, they may, from inclination and habit, evince benevolence towards their fellow creatures, and a love of truth, sobriety, and industry, adopting

---

[7]The will is minutely detailed and restrictive as to site, design and specifications for the college building. Passage of time and circumstances has rendered administration of the provisions awkward, and this will has been cited in demonstration of the point that such bequests should be drawn in terms sufficiently flexible that adjustments to the unforeseen future can be made.

In 1949, Girard College enrolled 1300 students. In addition to sixteen million dollars worth of non-income property, it had a revenue-producing endowment of seventy-three million dollars. (25, p. 247)

at the same time such religious tenets as their matured reason may enable them to prefer. . . . (154, p. 137)

The "Mayor, Alderman and Citizens of Philadelphia" were named by Girard to execute the trust established for the school.

Girard's relatives, for the most part rewarded by the will, nevertheless found their legacies small when compared to those left for charitable arrangements. These they determined to have set aside. In this effort heirs Francois Fenelon Vidal and John F. Girard, "citizens of the monarchy of France," were joined by American cousins. (52, pp. 301-02) Their argument was threefold: (1) Philadelphia could not legally accept a bequest of real estate, (2) if the city could accept the bequest it could not legally be held, and moreover (3) "the objects of the charity were altogether indefinite, vague, and uncertain and therefore the trusts were incapable of execution or of being cognizable in law or equity." (52, p. 302)

In 1841 the case was presented before the Circuit Court of the United States, sitting as a Court of Equity for the Eastern District of Pennsylvania. Judgment was in favor of the city, i.e., Girard's executors. The heirs then appealed to the Supreme Court of the United States and secured two powerful attorneys whom the court reporter lists as Jones and Webster—the latter was Daniel, the same who had argued the *Dartmouth College* case a quarter century before.

The points thereafter raised against the will remained essentially those argued before the lower court, but the focus and tone was changed so that the three rather prosaic points now became two resounding questions: (1) Was not Girard's will an invalid charity under common law and under the constitution of the Commonwealth of Pennsylvania, and (2) was not this will intolerably repugnant to a Christian state?

A renowned attorney, Binney, came from retirement to join another, Sergeant, in behalf of the city.

The opposing attorneys argued for days over the laws of charity, developing a mass of citations on the subject that went back solidly to Elizabeth and to Henry VIII before leaping remotely into scriptural history. At last they turned to the question of the will's repugnance in excluding ecclesiastics from the college.

Speaking for the heirs, Jones included the following:

. . . A part of this devise would make it a curse to any civilized land; it is a cruel experiment upon poor orphan boys to shut them up and make them the victims of a philosophical speculation. By the laws of Pennsylvania it is blasphemy to attack the Christian religion, but in this case nothing is to be taught but the doctrines of pure morality, and all the advantages of early impressions upon the youthful mind are entirely abrogated. . . . (154, p. 144)

The attorneys for the trustees turned this argument by showing that Girard had not restricted the religious opinions of the teachers but had, in the lawyer's words, demanded "piety, elevated virtue, and holy lives and character" of them. Was not Mr. Bache[8], selected as president of the college, a "Christian Gentleman"? Mr. Sergeant went on:

. . . The objection assumes that the Bible is not to be taught at all, or that laymen are incapable of teaching it. There is not the least evidence of an intention to prohibit it from being taught. On the contrary, there is an obligation to teach what the Bible alone can teach, viz., a pure system of morality.

. . . Girard has neither prohibited religious instruction nor a professorship. What will the United States do with the Smithsonian legacy [with which Congress cannot connect religion]? . . . Girard is said to have expressed himself in terms derogatory to Christianity. Suppose he had used a different phraseology, and said that none but laymen should be admitted into the college. This would not have been objectionable, and yet precisely the same result has been brought about. . . . (154, p. 169)

Then it was Daniel Webster's turn. He went over the whole ground again, but saved particular rhetoric for an enlargement upon his colleague's charge that "a part of this devise would make it a curse."

A biographer of Girard has described the scene:

. . . In a powerfully emotional argument, Webster denied the power of the city to maintain a college; he refused to admit that such an institution was a charitable use—although he had taken exactly the opposite stand in the famous Dartmouth College case—and he questioned the [state] constitutionality of the whole document. As the climax of a magnificent speech, he asserted that provisions barring ministers from the college grounds showed an attitude "derogatory to the Christian religion, contrary to sound morals and subversive of laws"; hence, he insisted, the will was inimical to public policy and must not stand. . . . (52, p. 303)

But the Supreme Court had the final word. A unanimous opinion written by Justice Story entirely upheld Girard's will.[9] The Court conceded, in connection with the long argument over the history of charities, that "under the Act of 32 and 34 Henry VIII, corporations are excepted from taking a devise," and also that once upon a time "corporations could not take real property in trust," but declared that all this had little to do with Pennsylvania's constitution or tradition.

---

[8]No point was made of the fact that Bache was a great-grandson of Benjamin Franklin.

[9]Girard was even longer—twenty-one or more years after his death—in getting properly and finally buried. Following the arrival of his funeral cortege for Catholic services, "three hundred and ninety-six Masons entered the churchyard." The Bishop "hastily withdrew." The Masons, after waiting awhile deposited the casket in a vault occupied by a general, with the result that "no church ritual was performed." The body was subsequently moved at least twice prior to 1851. (52, pp. 298, 358-59)

Justice Story then turned to the allegedly non-Christian aspect of Girard's will, and said, in part:

. . . All that we can gather from his language is, that he desired to exclude sectarians and sectarianism from the college, leaving the instructors and officers free to teach the purest morality, the love of truth, sobriety and industry by all appropriate means. . . . Is an omission to provide for instruction in Christianity in any scheme for school or college education a fatal defect, which voids it according to the law of Pennsylvania? If the instruction provided for is complete and imperfect, is it equally fatal? . . . Let us take the case of a charitable donation to teach the poor orphans reading, writing, arithmetic, geography, and navigation, and excluding all other studies and instruction; would the donation be void, as a charity in Pennsylvania, as being deemed derogatory to Christianity. Hitherto it has been supposed that a charity for the instruction of the poor might be good and valid in England even if it did not go beyond the establishment of a grammar school. And in America, it has been thought, in the absence of any express legal prohibitions, that the donor might select the studies, as well as the classes of persons, who were to receive his bounty without being compellable to make religious instruction a necessary part of those studies. It has hitherto been thought sufficient, if he does not require anything to be taught inconsistent with Christianity.

Looking to the objection, therefore, in a mere judicial view, which is the only one in which we are at liberty to consider it, we are satisfied that there is nothing in the devise establishing the college, or in the regulations and restrictions contained therein, which are inconsistent with the Christian re-religion, or are opposed to any known policy of the State of Pennsylvania. . . . (154, p. 199)

COMMENT

The free exercise of religion guaranteed by the First Amendment to the federal Constitution was not involved here. That Amendment was at the time a restriction upon Congress alone and not a restriction upon the states. No action of Congress was in question. What was involved in the religious aspect of the case was an article in Pennsylvania's bill of rights—one which the Court observed to be about as comprehensive in the assurance of religious freedom as language would allow. What the Court did do here was to refuse to question a will creating an endowment for a college and providing that no religion be taught there, nor any cleric be allowed on the school grounds.

Beyond insuring the existence of Girard College, the Court's decision possibly had two effects upon education in general, namely: (1) Donors, testators, and school authorities were enabled to gather assurance that sectarian instruction need not be included in a course of study and (2) the publicity attendant upon the case may have had an effect, similar to one in the *Dartmouth College* case (149), of giving assurance to prospective donors and testators that endowments which they might make would remain secure. And, very likely, the decision had the effect of fixing more firmly for the whole nation the concept of religious freedom.

7

CONCESSION OF PUBLIC FUNDS FOR PAROCHIAL SCHOOLS

AMDT. 1—RELIGION, FREE SPEECH, ETC.
An Establishment of Religion

[10] **INDIANS' TRIBAL FUNDS FOR PAROCHIAL SCHOOLS**
QUICK BEAR V. LEUPP
210 U. S. 50, 28 Sup. Ct. 690 (1908)

The Supreme Court of the United States sustained a contract made at the request of Indians that money due them under a treaty be paid by the Commissioner of Indian Affairs for the support of Indian Catholic schools.

The question of permissible monetary aids to religion was first argued before the Court very near the turn of the century. At that time, in the case of *Bradfield v. Roberts* (60), it was held that an agreement whereby a hospital corporation benefited from District of Columbia funds was valid despite the fact that a monastic order and sisterhood constituted the membership of the corporation. That case, the present one, and the two treated on the pages immediately following have developed the significant case law on this question. (48, pp. 763-64) Three of these cases involved schools, and all four resulted in financial concession to religion. The greatest financial concession to religion, however, has been said to lie in practice much older than any of the decisions in these cases—"the practice of exempting religious property from taxation. This traces back to the idea expressed in the Northwest Ordinance that Government has an interest in religion as such." (48, pp. 763-64)

The present case arose from the complaint of Reuben Quick Bear, Ralph Eagle Feathers, and other Indians who were members of the Sioux Tribe living on the Rosebud Agency in South Dakota. They sought to enjoin payment of tribal funds, administered by Charles E. Leupp, Commissioner of Indian Affairs, and by other officers of the United States, for the support of sectarian schools on their reservation.

The Supreme Court of the United States received the case on appeal from both parties to the suit, inasmuch as both had been adversely affected by the judgment of the Court of Appeals of the District of Columbia.

Chief Justice Fuller reviewed the facts of the case in a "statement" preceding the Court's decision. In his words, certain of the assertions of Quick Bear and Eagle Feathers follow:

7. That the Act of June 7, 1897, Section 1 (30 Stat. L. 62, 79, Chap. 3) . . . contains the following: "And it is hereby declared to be the settled policy of the government to hereafter make no appropriation whatever for education in any sectarian school."

8. That in violation of the said provision . . . the Commissioner of Indian Affairs . . . has made . . . a contract with the Bureau of Catholic Indian Missions of Washington, District of Columbia, . . . for the care, education and maintenance . . . of a number of Indian pupils . . . [payment is] to be made from either the . . . Sioux treaty fund, or from the interest of the . . . Sioux trust fund, or from both. (132, p. 691)

The Indians went on to insist that they had never consented to the expenditure for such a purpose of either of the funds mentioned, but on the contrary had protested any use of the funds for sectarian education.

The Commissioner of Indian Affairs admitted all of the above except the violation. He showed that beginning with acts of 1819 and 1820 and continuing through an act of 1870, Congress had regularly authorized similar contracts with sectarian agencies for Indian education, and had made payment therefor from public moneys. Indeed, the practice had continued until 1895 when pressure had caused Congress for the first time to restrict the use of public moneys for sectarian schools to situations in which no other school facilities could be provided. The Commissioner showed, too, that this congressional limitation had not appeared with any Indian appropriation act later than that of 1897, and, moreover, the statement had clearly been intended to apply to appropriations of public moneys, and not to the funds pertaining to the Indians as a matter of right and administered for them by the government.

Chief Justice Fuller delivered an opinion which upheld the view and the action of the Commissioner of Indian Affairs, and which said, in part:

As has been shown, in 1868 the United States made a treaty with the Sioux Indians, under which the Indians made large cessions of land and other rights. In consideration of this the United States agreed that for every thirty children a house should be provided and a teacher competent to teach the elementary branches of our English education should be furnished for twenty years. In 1877, in consideration of further land cessions, the United States agreed to furnish all necessary aid to assist the Indians in the work of civilization, and furnish them schools and instruction in mechanical and agricultural arts, as provided by the treaty of 1868. In 1899, Congress extended the obligation. . . . Thereafter in every annual Indian appropriation act, there was an appropriation to carry out the terms of this treaty, under the heading, "Fulfilling Treaty Stipulation with, and Support of, Indian tribes."

These appropriations rested on different grounds from the gratuitous appropriations of public moneys under the heading, "Support of Schools". The two subjects were separately treated in each act, and naturally they are essentially different in character. One is the gratuitous appropriation of public money in this sense. It is the Indians' money, or, at least, is dealt with by the government as if it belonged to them, as morally it does. It differs from the "trust fund" in this: The trust fund has been set aside for the Indians, and the income expended for their benefit, which expenditure required no annual appropriation. . . . This "trust fund" is held for the Indians, and not distributed *per capita*, being held as property in common. The money is distributed in accordance with the discretion of the Secretary of the Interior, but really belongs to the Indians. The President declared it to be the moral right of the Indians to have this "trust fund" applied to the education of the Indians in schools of their choice[10], and the same view was entertained by the [lower courts]. . . . But the treaty fund has exactly the same characteristics. They are moneys belonging really to the Indians. They are the price of land ceded by the Indians to the government. The only difference is that, in the "treaty fund", the debt to the Indians created and secured by the treaty is paid by annual appropriations of public moneys, but the payment, as we repeat, of a treaty debt in installments. We perceive no justification for applying the proviso or declaration of policy to the payment of treaty obligations, the two things being distinct and different in nature, and having no relation to each other, except that both are technically appropriations.

---

[10]The contract at issue was asserted to be in response to "a petition duly signed and genuinely signed by 212 members of the tribe" who had, on March 26, 1906, requested the contract for 250 Indian children at $108 per capita for the year.

Some reference is made to the Constitution, in respect to this contract with the Bureau of Catholic Indian Missions. It is not contended that it is unconstitutional, and it could not be. Roberts v. Bradfield, 12 App. D. C. 475; Bradfield v. Roberts, 175 U. S. 291, 44 L. ed. 168, 20 Sup. Ct. Rep. 121. But it is contended that the spirit of the Constitution requires that the declaration of policy that the government "shall make no appropriation whatever for education in any sectarian schools" should be treated as applicable, on the ground that the actions of the United States were to always be undenominational, and that, therefore, the government can never act in a sectarian capacity, either in the use of its own funds or in that of the funds of others, in respect of which it is a trustee; hence, that even the Sioux trust fund cannot be applied for education in Catholic schools, even though the owners of the fund so desire it. But we cannot concede the proposition that Indians cannot be allowed to use their own money to educate their own children in the schools of their own choice because the government is necessarily undenominational, as it cannot make any law respecting an establishment of religion or prohibiting the free exercise thereof. The court of appeals well said:

"The 'treaty' and 'trust' moneys are the only moneys which the Indians can lay claim to as a matter of right; the only sums on which they are entitled to rely as theirs for education; and while these moneys are not delivered to them in hand, yet the money must not only be provided, but be expended, for their benefit, and in part for their education; it seems inconceivable that Congress shall have intended to prohibit them from receiving religious education at their own cost if they desire it; such an intent would be one to prohibit the free exercise of religion amongst the Indians, and such would be the effect of the construction for which the complainants contend. . . ." (132, pp. 698-700)

COMMENT

The Court held that this form of monetary aid to religion acting through sectarian schools was permissible, and that the peculiar relationship between the United States and its Indian wards did not really complicate the issue, so far as the funds actually involved were concerned.

Insofar as the Court's reasoning reflected a concept that the obligation to provide education transcended an obligation to maintain the wall between church and state, the "child benefit" theory which the Court developed in the case of *Cochran v. Louisiana* (70), shown next, was heralded here.

Similarly, and perhaps more clearly, the right of parents to "educate their children in schools of their own choice" foretold the Court's decision in *Meyer v. Nebraska* (113) and in *Pierce v. Society of Sisters* (128).

AMDT. 14—RIGHTS OF CITIZENS
Sec.   1—Due Process of Law
(AMDT. 1—RELIGION, FREE SPEECH, ETC.)
(An Establishment of Religion)

[11] FREE TEXTBOOKS FOR PRIVATE SCHOOLS

COCHRAN V. LOUISIANA STATE BOARD OF EDUCATION

281 U. S. 370, 50 Sup. Ct. 335 (1930)

The Supreme Court of the United States sustained a Louisiana statute which provided free textbooks from public funds to children in private schools.

In this case and in the one presented immediately hereafter the Court developed the "child benefit theory." This means, in simplest terms, that it is the view of the Court that the state's obligation to all the school children in the state transcends a too-literal observance of the principle of separation of church and state.

The opinion of the Court in the present case upheld statutes of heavily Catholic Louisiana in granting free textbooks "to the school children of the state." Private schools were not mentioned in the statutes. However, the State Board of Education construed and applied the law to include among "the school children of the state" those children attending nonpublic schools in the state. Thereupon, certain citizens brought suit to restrain the State Board of Education from providing free textbooks in such schools. These citizens argued that public property was being diverted to private purpose in violation of the Fourteenth Amendment.

The Court's opinion asserted that the schools "are not the beneficiaries." Rather, it was declared, "the school children and the state alone are the beneficiaries."

Chief Justice Hughes, in delivering the opinion of the Court, traced the history of the case. He said, in part:

The appellants, as citizens and taxpayers of the State of Louisiana, brought this suit to restrain the state board of education and other state officials from expending any part of the severance tax fund in purchasing school books and in supplying them free of cost to the school children of the state, under Acts No. 100 and No. 143 of 1928, upon the ground that the legislation violated specific provisions of the constitution of the state and also Section 4 of Article IV and the Fourteenth Amendent of the Federal Constitution. The supreme court of the state affirmed the judgment of the trial court, which refused to issue an injunction. 168 La. 1030.

Act No. 100 of 1928 provided that the severance tax fund of the state, after allowing funds and appropriations as required by the state constitution, should be devoted "first, to supplying school books to the school children of the state." The board of education was directed to provide school books for school children free of cost to such children." Act No. 143 of 1928 made appropriations in accordance with the above provisions. The supreme court of the state, following its decision in *Borden v. Louisiana State Board of Education*, 168 La. 1005, held that these acts were not repugnant to either the state or the Federal Constitution. . . .

The contention of the appellant under the Fourteenth Amendment is that taxation for the purchase of school books constituted a taking of public property for a private purpose. . . . The purpose is said to be to aid private, religious, sectarian, and other schools not embraced in the public educational system of the state by furnishing textbooks free to the children attending such private schools. The operation and effect of the legislation in question were described by the supreme court of the state as follows. . . .

"One may scan the acts in vain to ascertain where any money is appropriated for the purchase of school books for the use of any church, private, sectarian, or even public school. The appropriations were made for the specific purpose of purchasing school books for the use of the school children of the state free of cost to them. It was for their benefit and the resulting benefit to the state that the appropriations were made. True, these children attend some school; public or private, the latter, sectarian or nonsectarian, and that the books are to be furnished them for their use, free of cost, whichever they attend. The schools, however, are not the beneficiaries of these appropriations. They obtain nothing from them, nor are they relieved of a single obligation because of them. The school children and the state alone are the beneficiaries. It is also true that the sectarian schools, which some of the children attend, instruct their pupils in religion, and books are used for that purpose, but one may search diligently the acts, though without result, in an effort to find anything to the effect that it is the purpose of the state to furnish religious books for the use of such children. . . . What the statutes contemplate is that the same books that are furnished children attending public schools shall be furnished children attending private schools. This is the only practical way of interpreting and executing the statutes, and this is what the state board of education is doing. Among these books, naturally, none is to be expected, adapted to religious instruction." The court also stated, although the point is not of importance in relation to the federal question, that it was "only the use of the books that is granted to the children or, in other words, the books are lent to them."

Viewing the statute as having the effect thus attributed to it, we cannot doubt that the taxing power of the state is exerted for a public purpose. The legislation does not segregate private schools, or their pupils, as its beneficiaries or attempt to interfere with any matters of exclusively private concern. Its interest is education, broadly; its method, comprehensive. Individual interests are aided only as the common interest is safeguarded. . . . (70, pp. 335-36).

COMMENT

The decision in this case, it will be noted, involved only the Fourteenth and not the First Amendment.

One who inclines toward the child benefit theory may yet find difficulty in the Court's statement that no benefit was conferred upon the private schools by the fact that such schools could avail their children of free textbooks. In any event, this decision would appear so very non-discriminatory that attendance in the private schools, if not the schools themselves, received encouragement.

The Court appears to hint that had the statutes provided religious books to sectarian schools they would then have been held unconstitutional. This does, indeed, seem to be in line with constitutional development, but at the same time one wonders whether provision of religious books might not have been of less benefit than common textbooks to the sectarian schools.

For some time after this opinion was handed down a fair inference could be made that had the statutes in question expressly included parochial schools the court would have held them invalid. However, the decision in the case to follow has rendered such inference questionable.

AMDT. 1—RELIGION, FREE SPEECH, ETC.
An Establishment of Religion
AMDT. 14—RIGHTS OF CITIZENS
Sec.   1—Due Process of Law

[12] **FREE BUS TRANSPORTATION FOR PAROCHIAL SCHOOLS**

EVERSON V. BOARD OF EDUCATION

330 U. S. 1, 67 Sup. Ct. 504 (1947)

The Supreme Court of the United States sustained the right of local school authorities acting under a New Jersey statute to provide free transportation for children attending parochial schools, and declared that the action of the authorities was not in violation of any provision of the federal Constitution.

In this decision the Court enlarged upon the "child benefit theory" which it had begun to develop in the Cochran case just discussed. The majority held that the tax money which paid the fares of children to parochial schools served the purpose of the state in promoting education without regard to religion. Both the First and Fourteenth Amendments were considered.

The Court was sharply divided—not by any difference of opinion as to the unconstitutionality of state aid to religion, but only by a difference of opinion as to whether such aid had occurred. The majority opinion had the effect of granting a monetary concession to religion, but the majority and the dissenting opinions together gave increased definition to the "wall of separation" doctrine.[11] As the *McCollum*

---

[11]In 1802 President Jefferson in writing to certain New England Baptists asserted that it was the purpose of the First Amendment to build "a wall of separation

case (102), to be discussed next, will show, that wall appears to have been strengthened by this added definition.

The present case differs from the *Cochran* case which precedes it here by the fact that the language of the statute in question clearly included parochial schools within its meaning. The relevant part of the statute reads:

Whenever in any district there are children living remote from any school-house, the board of education of the district may make rules and contracts for the transportation of such children to and from school, including the transportation of school children to and from school other than a public school as is operated for profit in whole or in part.

When any school district provides any transportation for public school children to and from school, transportation from any point in such established school route to any other point in such established school route shall be supplied to school children residing in such school district in going to and from school other than a public school, except such school as is operated for profit in whole or in part. . . . (25, pp. 767, 768)

In accordance with this statute a township school board reimbursed parents for the money they spent in sending their children to school on buses of the local transportation system. Some of the reimbursement was made, by express order of the school board, to parents whose children had been sent to Catholic parochial schools. The Catholic schools were so designated in the order of the board. Everson, a taxpayer of the district, then filed suit in a New Jersey court challenging the right of the school board to make any reimbursement to parents of the parochial school students. The state court found against Everson but he pressed the case to the Supreme Court by appeal. Throughout, he insisted that the statute and the action of the district school board under it violated either the state or the federal Constitutions.

Justice Black, speaking for the majority of the sharply divided court, disagreed. He said in part:

The only contention here is that the state statute and the resolution, insofar as they authorized reimbursement to parents of children attending parochial schools, violate the Federal Constitution in these two respects, which to some extent, overlap. *First.* They authorize the State to take by taxation the private property of some and bestow it upon others, to be used for their

---

between Church and State." In a Mormon case, *Reynolds v. United States* (134) in 1878, the Court accepted this as "almost an authoritative declaration of the scope and effect of the Amendment," one which gave Congress freedom "to reach actions which were in violation of social duties or subversive of good order." (48, p. 579) In 1805, in his Second Inaugural Address Jefferson may, however, have given a different opinion of the purpose of the Amendment, when he said: "In matters of religion, I have considered that its free exercise is placed by the Constitution independent of the powers of the general government." (48, p. 760)

own private purposes. This, it is alleged, violated the due process clause of the Fourteenth Amendment. *Second.* The statute and the resolution forced inhabitants to pay taxes to help support and maintian schools which are dedicated to, and which regularly teach, the Catholic Faith. This is alleged to be a use of state power to support church schools contrary to the prohibition of the First Amendment which the Fourteenth Amendment made applicable to the states. . . .

It is much too late to argue that legislation intended to facilitate the opportunity of children to get a secular education serves no public purpose. . . . The same thing is no less true of legislation to reimburse needy parents, or all parents, for payment of the fares of their children so that they can ride in public busses to and from schools rather than run the risk of traffic and other hazards incident to walking or "hitch-hiking." . . . Nor does it follow that a law has a private rather than a public purpose because it provided that tax-raised funds will be paid to reimburse individuals on account of money spent by them in a way which furthers a public program. . . . Subsidies and loans to individuals such as farmers and home owners, and to privately owned transportation systems, as well as many other kinds of businesses, have been commonplace practice in our state and national history. . . .

Second. The New Jersey statute is challenged as a "law respecting the establishment of religion." The First Amendment as made applicable to the states by the Fourteenth . . . commands that a state "shall make no law respecting an establishment of religion, or prohibiting the free exercise thereof." These words of the First Amendment reflected in the minds of early Americans a vivid mental picture of conditions and practices which they fervently wished to stamp out in order to preserve liberty for themselves and for their posterity. Doubtless their goal has not been entirely reached; but so far has the nation moved toward it that the expression "law respecting the establishment of religion," probably does not so vividly remind present-day Americans of the evils, fears, and political problems that caused that expression to be written into our Bill of Rights. Whether this New Jersey law is one respecting the "establishment of religion" requires an understanding of the meaning of that language, particularly with respect to the imposition of taxes. Once again, therefore, it is not inappropriate briefly to review the background and environment of the period in which that constitutional language was fashioned and adopted.

A large proportion of the early settlers of this country came here from Europe to escape the bondage of laws which compelled them to support and attend government-favored churches. The centuries immediately before and contemporaneous with the colonization of America had been filled with turmoil, civil strife, and persecutions, generated in large part by established sects determined to maintain their absolute political and religious supremacy. With the power of government supporting them, at various times and places, Catholics had persecuted Protestants, Protestants had persecuted Catholics, Protestant sects had persecuted other Protestant sects, Catholics of one shade of belief had persecuted Catholics of another shade of belief, and all of these had from time to time persecuted Jews. In efforts to force loyalty to whatever religious group happened to be on top and in league with the government of a particular time and place, men and women had been fined, cast in jail, cruelly tortured, and killed. Among the offenses for which these punishments had been inflicted were such things as speaking disrespectfully of the views of ministers of government-established churches, non-attendance at those churches, expressions of non-belief in their doctrines, and failure to pay taxes and tithes to support them.

These practices of the old world were transplanted to and began to thrive in the soil of the new America. The very charters granted by the English Crown to the individuals and companies designated to make the laws which would control the destinies of the colonials authorized these individuals and companies to erect religious establishments which all, whether believers or non-believers, would be required to support and attend. An exercise of this authority was accompanied by a repetition of many of the old world practices and persecutions. Catholics found themselves hounded and proscribed because of their faith; Quakers who followed their conscience went to jail; Baptists were peculiarly obnoxious to certain dominant Protestant sects; men and women of varied faiths who happened to be in a minority in a particular locality were persecuted because they steadfastly persisted in worshipping God only as their own consciences dictated. And all of these dissenters were compelled to pay tithes and taxes to support government-sponsored churches whose ministers preached inflammatory sermons designed to strengthen and consolidate the established faith by generating a burning hatred against dissenters.

These practices became so commonplace as to shock the freedom loving colonials into a feeling of abhorrence. The imposition of taxes to pay ministers' salaries and to build and maintain churches and church property aroused their indignation. It was these feelings which found expression in the First Amendment. No one locality and no one group throughout the Colonies can rightly be given entire credit for having aroused the sentiment that culminated in adoption of the Bill of Rights' provisions embracing religious liberty. But Virginia, where the established church had achieved a dominant influence in political affairs and where many excesses attracted wide public attention, provided a great stimulus and able leadership for the movement. The people there, as elsewhere, reached the conviction that individual religious liberty could be achieved best under a government which was stripped of all power to tax, to support, or otherwise to assist any or all religions, or to interfere with the beliefs of any religious individual or group.

The movement toward this end reached its dramatic climax in Virginia in 1785-86 when the Virginia legislative body was about to renew Virginia's tax levy for the support of the established church. Thomas Jefferson and James Madison led the fight against this tax. Madison wrote his great Memorial and Remonstrance against the law. In it, he eloquently argued that a true religion did not need the support of law; that no person, either believer or non-believer, should be taxed to support a religious institution of any kind; that the best interest of a society required that the minds of men always be wholly free; and that cruel persecutions were the inevitable result of government-established religions. Madison's Remonstrance received strong support throughout Virginia, and the Assembly postponed consideration of the proposed tax measure until its next session. When the proposal came up for consideration at that session, it not only died in committee, but the Assembly enacted the famous "Virginia Bill for Religious Liberty" originally written by Thomas Jefferson. The preamble to that Bill stated among other things that

"Almighty God had created the mind free; that all attempts to influence it by temporal punishments, or burthens, or by civil incapacitations, tend only to beget habits of hypocrisy and meanness, and are a departure from the plan of the Holy author of our religion who being Lord both of body and mind, yet chose not to propagate it by coercions on either . . .; that to compel a man to furnish contributions of money for the propagation of opinions which he disbelieves, is sinful and tyrannical; that even the forcing him to support this or that teacher of his own religious persuasion, is depriving him of the comfortable liberty of giving his contributions to the particular pastor, whose morals he would make his pattern . . ."

And the statute itself enacted:

"That no man shall be compelled to frequent or support any religious worship, place, or ministry whatsoever, nor shall be enforced, restrained, molested, or burthened, in his body or goods, nor shall otherwise suffer on account of his religious opinions or belief . . ."

This Court has previously recognized that the provisions of the First Amendment, in the drafting and adoption of which Madison and Jefferson played such leading roles, had the same objective and were intended to provide the same protection against governmental intrusion on religious liberty as the Virginia statute . . . Prior to the adoption of the Fourteenth Amendment, the First Amendment did not apply as a restraint against the states. Most of them did soon provide similar constitutional protection for religious liberty. But some states persisted for about half a century in imposing restraints upon the free exercise of religion and in discriminating against particular religious groups. In recent years, so far as the provision against the establishment of a religion is concerned, the question has most frequently arisen in connection with proposed state aid to church schools and efforts to carry on religious teachings in the public schools in accordance with the tenets of a particular sect. Some churches have either sought or accepted state financial support for their schools. Here again the efforts to obtain state aid or acceptance of it have not been limited to any one particular faith. The state courts, in the main, have remained faithful to the language of their own constitutional provisions designed to protect religious freedom and to separate religions and governments. Their decisions, however, show the difficulty in drawing the line between tax legislation which provides funds for the welfare of the general public and that which is designed to support institutions which teach religion. . . .

The "establishment of religion" clause of the First Amendment means at least this: Neither a state nor the federal government can set up a church. Neither can pass laws which aid one religion, aid all religions, or prefer one religion over another. Neither can force nor influence a person to go to or to remain away from church against his will or force him to profess a belief or disbelief in any religion. No person can be punished for entertaining or professing religious beliefs or disbeliefs, for church attendance or non-attendance. No tax in any amount, large or small, can be levied to support any religious activities or institutions, whatever they may be called, or whatever form they may adopt to teach or practice religion. Neither a state nor the federal government can, openly or secretly, participate in the affairs of any religious organizations or groups and *vice versa*. In the words of Jefferson, the clause against establishment of religion by law was intended to erect "a wall of separation between Church and State." . . .

Measured by those standards, we cannot say that the First Amendment prohibits New Jersey from spending tax-raised funds to pay the bus fares of parochial school pupils as a part of a general program under which it pays the fares of pupils attending public and other schools. It is undoubtedly true that children are helped to get to church schools. There is even a possibility that some of the children might not be sent to the church schools if the parents were compelled to pay their children's bus fares out of their own pockets when transportation to a public school would have been paid for by the state. The same possibility exists where the state requires a local transit company to provide reduced fares to school children including those attending parochial schools, or where a municipally owned transportation system undertakes to carry all school children free of charge. Moreover, state-paid policemen, detailed to protect children going to and from church schools from the very real hazards of traffic, would serve much the same purpose and accomplish much the same result as state provisions intended to guarantee free transportation of a kind which the state deems to be best for the school children's welfare. And parents might refuse to expose their children to the serious danger of traffic accidents going to and from parochial schools, the approaches to which were not protected by policemen. Similarly, parents might be reluctant to permit their children to attend schools which the state had cut off from such general government services as ordinary police and fire protection, connections for sewage disposal, public highways and sidewalks. Of course, cutting off church schools from these services, so separate and so indisputably marked off from the religious function, would make it far more difficult for the schools to operate. But such is obviously not the purpose of the First Amendment. That Amendment requires the state to be a neutral in its relations with groups of religious believers and non-believers; it does not require the state to be their adversary. State power is no more to be used so as to handicap religions that it is to favor them.

This Court has said that parents may, in the discharge of their duty under state compulsory education laws, send their children to a religious rather than a public school if the school meets the secular educational requirements which the state has power to impose. See Pierce v. Society of Sisters, 268 U. S. 510. It appears that these parochial schools meet New Jersey's requirements. The state contributes no money to the schools. It does not support them. Its legislation, as applied, does no more than provide a general program to help parents get their children, regardless of their religion, safely and expeditiously to and from accredited schools.

The First Amendment has erected a wall between church and state. That wall must be kept high and impregnable. We could not approve the slightest breach. New Jersey has not breached it here.

Affirmed. (77, pp. 506-13)

Justice Jackson, joined by Justice Frankfurter agreed with taxpayer Everson's viewpoint in a dissenting opinion. Justice Jackson said, in part:

The Court sustains this legislation by assuming two deviations from the facts of this particular case; first, it assumes a state of facts the record does not support, and secondly, it refuses to consider facts which are inescapable on the record. . . .

The Township of Ewing is not furnishing transportation to the children in any form; it is not operating school busses itself or contracting for their operation; and it is not performing any public service of any kind with this taxpayer's money. All school children are left to ride as ordinary paying passengers on the regular busses operated by the public transportation system. What the township does, and what the taxpayer complains of, is at stated intervals to reimburse parents for the fares paid, provided the children attend either public schools or Catholic Church schools. This expenditure of tax funds has no possible effect on the child's safety or expedition in transit. As passengers on the public busses they travel as fast and no faster, and are as safe and no safer, since their parents are reimbursed as before.

In addition to thus assuming a type of service that does not exist, the Court also insists that we must close our eyes to a discrimination which does exist. The resolution which authorizes disbursement of this taxpayer's money limits reimbursement to those who attend public schools and Catholic schools. That is the way the act is applied to this taxpayer.

The New Jersey act in question makes the character of the school, not the needs of the children, determine the eligibility of parents to reimbursement. . . .

It seems to me that the basic fallacy in the Court's reasoning, which accounts for its failure to apply the principles it avows, is in ignoring the essentially religious test by which beneficiaries of this expenditure are selected. A policeman protects a Catholic, of course—but not because he is a Catholic; it is because he is a man and member of our society. The fireman protects the church school—but not because it is a church school; it is because it is property, part of the assets of our society. Neither the fireman nor the policeman has to ask before he renders aid, "Is this man or building identified with the Catholic Church?" But before these school authorities draw a check to reimburse for a student's fare they must ask just that question, and if the school is a Catholic one they may render aid because it is such, while if it is of any other faith or is run for profit, the help must be withheld. . . .

But we cannot have it both ways. Religious teaching cannot be a private affair when the state seeks to impose regulations which infringe on it indirectly, and a public affair when it comes to taxing citizens of one faith to aid another, or those of no faith to aid at all. If these principles seem harsh in prohibiting aid to Catholic education, it must not be forgotten that it is the same Constitution that alone assures Catholics the right to maintain these schools at all when predominant local sentiment would forbid them. Pierce v. Society of Sisters, (268 U. S. 510). Nor should I think that those who have done so well without this aid would want to see this separation between Church and State broken down. If the state may aid these religious schools, it may therefore regulate them. Many groups have sought aid from tax funds only to find that it carried political controls with it. Indeed this Court has declared that "It is hardly lack of due process for the government to regulate that which it subsidizes."

But in any event, the great purposes of the Constitution do not depend on the approval or convenience of those they restrain. I cannot read the history of the struggle to separate political from ecclesiastical affairs, well summarized in the opinion of Mr. Justice Rutledge in which I generally concur, without a conviction that the Court today is unconsciously giving the clock's hands a backward turn. (77, pp. 5131-7)

Justice Rutledge wrote a separate dissenting opinion with Justice Burton joining in agreement that the majority should have upheld taxpayer Everson. Justice Rutledge, beginning with quotations, said, in part:

"Congress shall make no law respecting an establishment of religion, or prohibiting the free exercise thereof. . . ."

"Well aware that Almighty God hath created the mind free; . . . that to compel a man to furnish contributions of money for the propagation of opinions which he disbelieves, is sinful and tyrannical:

"We the General Assembly [of Virginia, 1786], *do enact* [in a Bill for Establishing Religious Freedom], that no man shall be compelled to frequent or support any religious worship, place, or ministry whatsoever, nor shall be enforced, restrained, molested, or burthened in his body or goods, nor shall otherwise suffer on account of his religious opinions or belief. . . ."

I cannot believe that the great author of those words, or the men who made them law, could have joined in this decision. Neither so high nor so impregnable today as yesterday is the wall raised between church and state by Virginia's great statute of religious freedom and the First Amendment, now made applicable to all the states by the Fourteenth. New Jersey's statute sustained is the first, if indeed it is not the second breach to be made by this Court's action. That a third, and a fourth, and still others will be attempted, we may be sure. For just as Cochran v. Board of Education, 281 U. S. 370, has opened the way by oblique ruling for this decision, so will the two make wider the breach for a third. Thus with time the most solid freedom steadily gives way before continuing corrosive decision.

This case forces us to determine squarely for the first time what was "an establishment of religion" in the First Amendment's conception; and by that measure to decide whether New Jersey's action violates its command. . . .

I

Not simply an established church, but any law respecting an establishment of religion is forbidden. The Amendment was broadly but not loosely phrased. It is the compact and exact summation of its author's views formed during his long struggle for religious freedom. In Madison's own words characterizing Jefferson's Bill for Establishing Religious Freedom, the guaranty he put in our national charter, like the bill he piloted through the Virginia Assembly, was a "Model of technical precision, and perspicuous brevity." Madison could not have confused "church" and "religion", or "an established church" and "an establishment of religion."

The Amendment's purpose was not to strike merely at the official establishment of a single sect, creed or religion, outlawing only a formal relation such as had prevailed in England and some of the colonies. Necessarily it was to uproot all such relationships. But the object was broader than separating church and state in this narrow sense. It was to create a complete and permanent separation of the spheres of religious activity and civil authority by comprehensively forbidding every form of public aid or support for religion. In proof the Amendment's wording and history unite with this Court's consistent utterances whenever attention has been fixed directly upon the question.

No one would claim today that the Amendment is constricted, in "prohibiting the free exercise" of religion, to securing the free exercise of some formal or creedal observance, of one sect or of many. It secures all forms of religious expression, creedal, sectarian or nonsectarian wherever and however taking place, except conduct which trenches upon the like freedoms of others or clearly and presently endangers the community's good order and security. For the protective purposes of this phase of the basic freedom street preaching, oral or by distribution of literature, has been given "the same high estate under the First Amendment as . . . worship in the churches and preaching from the pulpits." And on this basis parents have been held entitled to send their children to private, religious schools. Pierce v. Society of Sisters, 268 U. S. 510. Accordingly, daily religious education commingled with secular is "religion" within the guaranty's comprehensive scope. So are religious training and teaching in whatever form. The word connotes the broadest content, determined not by the form or formality of the teaching or where it occurs, but by its essential nature regardless of those details.

"Religion" has the same broad significance in the twin prohibition concerning "an establishment." The Amendment was not duplicitous. "Religion" and "establishment" were not used in any formal or technical sense. The prohibition broadly forbids state support, financial or other, of religion in any guise, form or degree. It outlaws all use of public funds for religious purposes.

II

No provision of the Constitution is more closely tied to or given content by its generating history than the religious clause of the First Amendment. It is at once the refined product and the terse summation of that history. The history includes not only Madison's authorship and the proceedings before the First Congress, but also the long and intensive struggle for religious freedom in America, more especially in Virginia, of which the Amendment was the direct culmination. In the documents of the times, particularly of Madison, who was leader in the Virginia struggle before he became the Amendment's sponsor, but also in the writings of Jefferson and others and in the issues which engendered them is to be found irrefutable confirmation of the Amendment's sweeping content. . . .

All the great instruments of the Virginia struggle for religious liberty thus became warp and woof of our constitutional tradition, not simply by the course of history, but by the common unifying force of Madison's life, thought and sponsorship. He epitomized the whole of that tradition in the Amendment's compact, but nonetheless comprehensive, phrasing.

As the Remonstrance discloses throughout, Madison opposed every form and degree of official relation between religion and civil authority. For him religion was a wholly private matter beyond the scope of civil power either to restrain or to support. Denial or abridgment of religious freedom was a violation of rights both of conscience and of natural equality. State aid was no less obnoxious or destructive to freedom and to religion itself than other forms of state interference. "Establishment" and "free exercise" were correlative and coextensive ideas, representing only different facets of the single great and fundamental freedom. The Remonstrance, following the Virginia statute's example, referred to the history of religious conflicts and the effects of all sorts of establishments, current and historical, to suppress religion's free exercise. With Jefferson, Madison believed that to tolerate any fragment of establishment would be by so much to perpetuate restraint upon that freedom. Hence he sought to tear out the institutions not partially but root and branch, and to bar its return forever.

In no phase was he more unrelentingly absolute than in opposing state support or aid by taxation. Not even "three pence" contribution was thus to be exacted from any citizen for such a purpose. Remonstrance, Par. 3. Tithes had been the life blood of establishment before and after other compulsions disappeared. Madison and his co-workers made no exceptions or abridgments to the complete separation they created. Their objection was not to small tithes. It was to any tithes whatsoever. "If it were lawful to impose a small tax for religion the admission would pave the way for oppressive levies." Not the amount but "the principle of assessment was wrong." And the principle was as much to prevent "the interference of law in religion" as to restrain religious intervention in political matters. In this field the authors of our freedom would not tolerate "the first experiment on our liberties" or "wait till usurped power had strengthened itself by exercise, and entangled the question in precedents." Remonstrance, Par. 3. Nor should we.

In view of this history no further proof is needed that the Amendment forbids any appropriation, large or small, from public funds to aid or support any and all religious exercises. . . .

III

Does New Jersey's action furnish support for religion by use of the taxing power? Certainly it does, if the test remains undiluted as Jefferson and Madison made it, that money taken by taxation from one is not to be used or given to support another's religious training or belief, or indeed one's own. Today as then the furnishing of "contributions of money for the propagation of opinions which he disbelieves" is the forbidden exaction; and the prohibition is absolute whatever measures bring that consequence and whatever amount may be sought or given to that end.

The funds used here were raised by taxation. The Court does not dispute, nor could it, that their use does in fact give aid and encouragement to religious instruction. It only concludes that this aid is not "support" in law. But Madison and Jefferson were concerned with aid and support in fact, not as a legal conclusion "entangled in precedents". Remonstrance, Par. 3. Here parents pay money to send their children to parochial schools and funds raised by taxation are used to reimburse them. This not only helps the children to get to school and the parents to send them. It aids them in a substantial way to get the very thing which they are sent to the particular school to secure, namely, religious training and teaching.

Believers of all faiths, and others who do not express their feelings toward ultimate issues of existence in any creedal form, pay the New Jersey tax. When the money so raised is used to pay for transportation to religious schools, the Catholic taxpayer to the extent of his proportionate share pays for the transportation of Lutheran, Jewish and otherwise religiously affiliated children to receive their non-Catholic religious instruction. Their parents likewise pay proportionately for the transportation of Catholic children to receive Catholic instruction. Each thus contributes to "the propagation of opinions which he disbelieves" in so far as their religions differ, as do others who accept no creed without regard to those differences. Each thus pays taxes also to support the teaching of his own religion, an exaction equally forbidden since it denies "the comfortable liberty" of giving one's contribution to the particular agency of instruction he approves.

New Jersey's action therefore exactly fits the type of exaction and the kind of evil at which Madison and Jefferson struck. Under the test they framed it cannot be said that the cost of transportation is no part of the cost of education or of religious instruction given. That it is a substantial and a necessary element is shown most plainly by the continuing and increasing demand for the state to assume it. Nor is there pretense that it relates only to the secular instruction given in religious schools or that any attempt is or could be made toward allocating proportional shares as between the secular and the religious instruction. It is precisely because the instruction is religious and relates to a particular faith, whether one or another, that parents send their children to religious schools under the Pierce doctrine. And the very purpose of the state's contribution is to defray the cost of conveying the pupil to the place where he will receive not simply secular, but also and primarily religious, teaching and guidance. . . .

Finally, transportation, where it is needed, is as essential to education as any other element. Its cost is as much a part of the total expense, except at times in amount, as the cost of textbooks, of school lunches, of athletic equipment, of writing and other materials; indeed of all other items composing the total burden. Now as always the core of the educational process is the teacher-pupil relationship. Without this the richest equipment and facilities would go for naught. . . . But the proverbial Mark Hopkins conception no longer suffices for the country's requirements. Without buildings, without equipment, without library, textbooks and other materials, and without transportation to bring teacher and pupil together in such an effective teaching environment, there can be not even the skeleton of what our times require. Hardly can it be maintained that transportation is the least essential of these items, or that it does not in fact aid, encourage, sustain and support, just as they do, the very process which is its purpose to accomplish. No less essential is it, or the payment of its cost, than the very teaching in the classroom or payment of the teacher's sustenance. Many types of equipment, now considered essential, better could be done without. . . .

IV

But we are told that the New Jersey statute is valid in its present application because the appropriation is for a public, not a private purpose, namely, the promotion of education, and the majority accept this idea in the conclusion that all we have here is "public welfare legislation". If that is true and the Amendment's force can be thus destroyed, what has been said becomes all the more pertinent. For then there could be no possible objection to more extensive support of religious education by New Jersey.

If the fact alone be determinative that religious schools are engaged in education, thus promoting the general and individual welfare, together with the legislature's decision that the payment of public moneys for their aid makes their work a public function, then I can see no possible basis, except one of dubious legislative policy, for the state's refusal to make full appropriation for support of private, religious schools, just as is done for public instruction. There could not be, on that basis, valid constitutional objection.

We have here then one substantial issue, not two. To say that New Jersey's appropriation and her use of the power of taxation for raising the funds appropriated are not for public purposes but are for private ends, is to say that they are for the support of religion and religious teaching. Conversely, to say that they are for public purposes is to say that they are not for religious ones.

This is precisely for the reason that education which includes religious training and teaching, and its support, have been made matters of private right and function, not public, by the very terms of the First Amendment. That is the effect not only in its guaranty of religion's free exercise, but also in the prohibition of establishments. It was on this basis of the private character of the function of religious education that this Court held parents entitled to send their children to private, religious schools. Pierce v. Society of Sisters, *supra*. Now it declares in effect that the appropriation of public funds to defray part of the cost of attending those schools is for a public purpose. If so, I do not understand why the state cannot go farther or why this case approaches the verge of its power. . . .

Our constitutional policy is exactly the opposite. It does not deny the value or the necessity for religious training, teaching or observance. Rather it secures their free exercise. But to that end it does deny that the state can undertake or sustain them in any form or degree. For this reason the sphere of religious activity, as distinguished from the secular intellectual liberties, has been given the twofold protection and, as the state cannot forbid neither can it perform or aid in performing the religious function. The dual prohibition makes that function altogether private. It cannot be made a public one by legislative act. This was the very heart of Madison's Remonstrance, as it is of the Amendment itself.

It is not because religious teaching does not promote the public or the individual's welfare, but because neither is furthered when the state promotes religious education, that the Constitution forbids it to do so. Both legislatures and courts are bound by that distinction. In failure to observe it lies the fallacy of the "public function" "logical legislation" argument, a fallacy facilitated by easy transference of the argument's basing from due process unrelated to any religious aspect to the First Amendment. . . .

The reasons underlying the Amendment's policy have not vanished with time or diminished in force. Now as when it was adopted the price of religious freedom is double. It is that the church and religion shall live both within and upon that freedom. There cannot be freedom of religion, safeguarded by the state, and intervention by the church or its agencies in the state's domain or dependency on its largesse. Madison's Remonstrance, Pars. 6, 8. The great condition of religious liberty is that it be maintained free from sustenance, as also from other interference, by the state. For when it comes to rest upon that secular foundation it vanishes with the resting. Id., Pars. 7, 8. Public money devoted to payment of religious costs, educational or other, brings the quest for more. It brings too the struggle of sect against sect for the larger share or for any. Here one by numbers alone will benefit most, there another. That is precisely the history of societies which have had an established religion and dissident groups. It is the very thing Jefferson and Madison experienced and sought to guard against, whether in its blunt or in its more screened forms. The end of such strife cannot be other than to destroy the cherished liberty. The dominating group will achieve the dominant benefit; or all will embroil the state in their dissensions. . . .

This is not therefore just a little case over bus fares. In paraphrase of Madison, distant as it may be in its present form from a complete establishment of religion, it differs from it only in degree; and is the first step in that direction. . . .

The realm of religious training and belief remains, as the Amendment made it, the kingdom of the individual man and his God. It should be kept inviolately private, not "entangled . . . in precedents" or confounded with what legislatures legitimately may take over into the public domain.

V

No one conscious of religious values can be unsympathetic toward the burden which our constitutional separation puts on parents who desire religious instruction mixed with secular for their children. They pay taxes for others' children's education, at the same time the added cost of instruction for their own. Nor can one happily see benefits denied to children which others receive, because in conscience they or their parents for them desire a different kind of training others do not demand.

But if those feelings should prevail, there would be an end to our historic constitutional policy and command. No more unjust or discriminatory fact is it to deny attendants at religious schools the cost of their transportation than it is to deny them tuitions, sustenance for their teachers, or any other educational expense which others receive at public cost. Hardship in fact there is which none can blink. But, for assuring to those who undergo it the greater, the most comprehensive freedom, it is one written by design and firm intent into our basic law. . . .

That policy necessarily entails hardship upon persons who forego the right to educational advantages the state can supply in order to secure others it is precluded from giving. Indeed this may hamper the parent and the child forced by conscience to that choice. But it does not make the state unneutral to withhold what the Constitution forbids it to give. On the contrary it is only by observing the prohibition rigidly that the state can maintain its neutrality and avoid partisanship in the dissensions inevitable when sect opposes sect over demands for public moneys to further religious education, teaching or training in any form or degree, directly or indirectly. Like St. Paul's freedom, religious liberty with a great price must be bought. And for those who exercise it most fully, by insisting upon religious education for their children mixed with secular, by the terms of our Constitution the price is greater than for others.

The problem then cannot be cast in terms of legal discrimination or its absence. This would be true, even though the state in giving aid should treat all religious instruction alike. Thus, if the present statute and its application were shown to apply equally to all religious schools of whatever faith, yet in the light of our tradition it could not stand. For then the adherent of one creed still would pay for the support of another, the childless taxpayer with others more fortunate. Then too there would seem to be no bar to making appropriations for transportation and other expenses of children attending public or other secular schools, after hours in separate places and classes for their exclusively religious instruction. The person who embraces no creed also would be forced to pay for teaching what he does not believe. Again, it was the furnishing of "contributions of money for the propagation of opinions which he disbelieves" that the fathers outlawed. That consequence and effect are not removed by multiplying to all-inclusiveness the sects for which support is exacted. The Constitution requires, not comprehensive identification of state with religion, but complete separation. . . .

Two great drives are constantly in motion to abridge, in the name of education, the complete division of religion and civil authority which our forefathers made. One is to introduce religious education and observance into the public schools. The other, to obtain public funds for the aid and support of various private religious schools . . . In my opinion both avenues were closed by the Constitution. Neither should be opened by this Court. The matter is not one of quantity, to be measured by the amount of money expended. Now as in Madison's day it is one of principle, to keep separate the separate spheres as the First Amendment drew them; to prevent the first experiment upon our liberties; and to keep the question from becoming entangled in corrosive precedents. We should not be less strict to keep strong and untarnished the one side of the shield of religious freedom than we have been of the other.

The judgment should be reversed. (77, pp. 517-35)

COMMENT

Earlier, mention was made of the fact that the separate opinions of the Justices in this case add to a broad interpretation of the "establishment of religion" clause. Nevertheless, the majority opinion held that the facts for review in the case were not in violation of any provision of the federal Constitution. Both of the dissenting opinions insist that the majority, after enunciating strong principles, then proceeded to contravene them in application to the question.

Schoolmen inclined to accept the Court's reasoning on the Louisiana textbook law in the *Cochran* case would probably find the Court's reasoning on this New Jersey transportation law similarly warranted, except, that as Justice Jackson points out, the township school board extended the authorization for reimbursement of fares for children attending only the Catholic parochial schools.

Professor Cushman noted of the decision in this case that it:

. . . leaves several questions unanswered. How far may the state validly go, under the "child benefit theory", in granting benefits to parochial school children? If it may provide free textbooks and bus transportation, may it also provide free lunches, free gymnasiums and swimming pools, free school clinics, and so on? Also, if a community is not forbidden to give free bus service to all school children including parochial school children, may Catholic parents demand such service as a constitutional right from communities which now extend it only to public school children? . . . (14, p. 145)

The questions just raised are, of course, evoked by the decision of the Court on the specific facts under review. The broad interpretation which the Court gave the "establishment of religion" clause in erecting the background against which to review the facts of the case was disturbing to a variety of commentators. Their viewpoint is summarized as follows, and again the words are Professor Cushman's. He notes that the Court did not question that government aid to religion "would be bad," and then goes on:

> Religious leaders, both Catholic and Protestant, together with some lay critics, have challenged the basic rule which the Court has announced. They urged that the Founding fathers did not intend by the First Amendment to forbid all government aid to religion, but only such aid as favors one religion over another. . . . (14, p. 146)

Out of all the foregoing attitudes toward the *Everson* decision we find a curious bifurcation of the thought provoked. For, although as Justice Rutledge in his dissenting opinion warned, "neither so high nor impregnable today as yesterday is the wall raised between church and state," we may justifiably continue the metaphor and say that the wall appears, notwithstanding, to run farther. (This may be demonstrated by the next case discussed.) Harry N. Rosenfeld, writing in the *Nation's Schools* and considering whether the decision in the *Everson* case may have limited, rather than extended, "the constitutional possibilities of public aid for sectarian schools," notes the difficulty of applying such principle. He says:

> . . . [The decision] may mean that payments made to parents or school children are valid while payments made directly to sectarian schools may be unconstitutional . . .
> . . . [And it] may mean that the crucial issue is not the character of the recipient but rather the nature of the aid . . . A third possible interpretation, although hardly a rationale, runs along different lines. The school board operated no high school. Therefore . . . it had to make some arrangement to meet its obligation to . . . its children. This interpretation would limit the decision to the very narrow point of the unavailability of public facilities within the school district. . . . (42, p. 43)

The present case, it should be clearly understood, did not sanction the use of public funds for the establishment of religion. It merely sanctioned, by the majority view, the use of public funds for a public purpose which brought no more than incidental benefit to religion.

The Court did not have under review the question of the New Jersey statute's apparent discrimination against children who attended other parochial schools or private schools operated for profit, although both majority and minority noted that this point was of sufficient import for resolving the case quite aside from the religious issue.

Some persons would surely agree with Justice Rutledge and his belief that the manifest discrimination against children attending other than Catholic non-profit schools constituted the real issue— was, in fact, the issue before the Court.

Whereas this and the preceding two cases have dealt primarily with questions of the use of public funds for the benefit of sectarian schools, three later cases ([17], [18], and [19]) are related more specifically to the express application of the "establishment of religion" clause to questions arising from school practices involving religious instruction.

Meanwhile the matters of military training (cases [13] and [14]) and of the flag salute (cases [15] and [16]) are considered in connection with schools.

8

RELIGIOUS CONVICTION
VERSUS NATIONALISM

AMDT. 1—RELIGION, FREE SPEECH, ETC.
An Establishment of Religion.

[13] COMPULSORY MILITARY TRAINING IN A STATE UNIVERSITY
PEARSON V. COALE
290 U. S. 597, 54 Sup. Ct. 131 (1933)

The Supreme Court of the United States dismissed an appeal "for want of a substantial Federal question" and thereby sustained the right of the State of Maryland to compel male students in its state university to take military training.

This case and the one following arose within the peculiar context of attitudes developed by Americans from the conflict produced by mingled idealism and disillusionment following World War I. The period was one in which the Kellogg-Briand Peace Pact of 1928, "the most thoroughgoing commitment to peace which great powers had ever made," could be ratified by the Senate on the same January day in 1929 that it turned to "consideration of a bill authorizing construction of fifteen cruisers." (28, vol. 2, p. 500) Munition makers, the "Merchants of Death," acquired a place among the over-simplifications in the explanation of war, and attempts were made to reinterpret even the American Civil War as a plot of industrialists.

The present case arose when Ennis Coale, a member of the Epworth League of the Methodist Episcopal Church registered in the University of Maryland in the fall of 1932. The university was a "land grant college" benefiting under the terms of the Morrill Act of 1862 and was consequently obligated to provide instruction in military tactics— the Reserve Officers Training Corps program. During the summer preceding his enrollment Ennis Coale had read a resolution by the general council of his church urging that Methodists be exempt from Reserve Officers Training Corps programs and that the United States cease financial support of military instruction in all civil schools. Also, at his request he had received from a "Committee on Militarism and Education" a pamphlet and advice on how he might avoid military training in college.

Accordingly, Ennis Coale refused to participate in the Reserve Officers Training Corps program at the University of Maryland and was suspended until such time as he was willing to comply with the regulations of the university.

His father sought a writ of mandamus [12] in the superior court of Baltimore to compel the university to admit the son. This court granted the writ, but upon the case being taken by the university authorities to the court of appeals of Maryland, the highest state court, the order for the writ was reversed.

This state court found reason to doubt Ennis Coale's sincerity, and it cited a written statement he had submitted in connection with his refusal to take military training at the time he registered.

The decision against Ennis Coale (123, pp. 54-60) was appealed to the Supreme Court of the United States. That Court, in a per curiam[13] decision dismissed the appeal "for want of a substantial Federal question." (124, p. 131) The right of the University of Maryland to compel its qualified male students to take the Reserve Officers Training Corps program was thereby sustained.

COMMENT

The facts and presentation of this case provided nothing which the Supreme Court would recognize as reason for questioning Maryland's requirement for compulsory military training as a condition for attendance at its university. In the following year, however, a similar California case with the question somewhat more skillfully developed was decided by the Court. That case follows.

---

[12]An order to compel a public agency or its officers to perform an act.

[13]A per curiam decision is one by the whole court and not prepared by any one Justice.

AMDT. 1—RELIGION, FREE SPEECH, ETC.
An Establishment of Religion
AMDT. 14—RIGHTS OF CITIZENS
Sec.   1—Due Process of Law

[14] COMPULSORY MILITARY TRAINING IN A STATE UNIVERSITY—2

HAMILTON V. REGENTS OF THE UNIVERSITY OF CALIFORNIA

293 U. S. 245, 55 Sup. Ct. 197 (1934)

The Supreme Court of the United States held that although the religious beliefs of a student were protected by due process of law, he was not being compelled to attend the University and could claim no constitutional right to do so without complying with the requirement that all physically able male students take military training.

Among the freshmen who registered for the fall term, 1933, at the University of California were two young men who conformed to all requirements except the compulsory course in military science and tactics. This course, they later asserted, was "an integral part of the military establishment of the United States," and not connected in any way with the militia or military establishment of California. (97, p. 199)

As the Supreme Court of the United States was to observe, their sincerity was beyond question. Both were sons of ordained ministers in the Methodist Episcopal Church, both were themselves members of that church and its Epworth League, and both adhered to certain resolutions in which local and national conferences of their church had urged that the United States "cease to support financially all military training in civil educational institutions," or else exempt Methodist students on the grounds of conscientious objection. The two students therefore petitioned the university for exemption but their petition was denied. Their next recourse was another petition in which the bishop of the church for California joined them in addressing the regents. This petition was likewise denied. In addition, the regents suspended the two students until they should be willing to comply with the regulations requiring military training at the University of California. These regulations rested upon the statute by which the state had accepted the terms of the Morrill Act of 1862 providing for federal endowment of "land grant colleges" which would offer certain specified subjects, including military tactics. (97, pp. 199-200)

The two students, through their fathers, thereupon sought from the California supreme court a mandate to compel the university to admit them without imposing the requirement for military training. The state court refused to issue the writ and the case was taken to the Supreme Court of the United States on appeal. The two students asserted that the state statute was repugnant to the Constitution and laws of the United States. More specifically they asserted that, contrary to the Fourteenth Amendment, their privileges and immunities as citizens of the United States were being abridged and their liberty and property were being denied them without due process of law. They reiterated their religious convictions and conscientious objection to military training and, finally, challenged the California statute as being also repugnant to the Kellogg-Briand Peace Pact, ratified by the Senate in 1929.[14] (97, pp. 197-202)

The Supreme Court held that the Reserve Officers Training Corps program at the University of California was hardly an integral part of the military establishment of the United States. (97, p. 203) And as for the Kellogg-Briand Peace Pact—this, said the Court, "requires little consideration," and it went on:

... In that instrument the United States and the other high contracting parties declare that they condemn recourse to war for the solution of international controversies. . . . Clearly there is no conflict between the regent's order and the provisions of this treaty. . . . (97, p. 205)

The Court devoted most attention to the claims of the students under the Fourteenth Amendment. Justice Butler, with Justice Cardozo rendering a separate concurring opinion, delivered the unanimous opinion of the court. Justice Butler said, in part:

The clauses of the Fourteenth Amendment invoked by appellants declare: "No State shall make or enforce any law which shall abridge the privileges or immunities of citizens of the United States; nor shall any State deprive any person of life, liberty, or property, without due process of law." Appellants' contentions are that the enforcement of the order prescribing instruction in military science and tactics abridges some privilege or immunity covered by the first clause and deprives of liberty safeguarded by the second. The "privileges and immunities" protected are only those that belong to citizens of the United States as distinguished from citizens of the states— those that arise from the Constitution and laws of the United States as contrasted with those that spring from other sources. . . Appellants assert— unquestionably in good faith—that all war, preparation for war, and the training required by the University are repugnant to the tenets and discipline of their church, to their religion, and to their consciences. The "privilege" of attending the University as a student comes not from federal sources but is given by the state. It is not within the asserted protection. The only "immunity" claimed by these students is freedom from obligation to comply

---

[14] The attempt here was to show that the California statute conflicted with a treaty which, by virtue of its ratification, was included within the "supreme law of the land." As the decision in this case demonstrates, the proponents of the "Bricker Amendment" were afforded no ammunition.

with the rule prescribing military training. But that "immunity" cannot be regarded as not within, or as distingushable from, the "liberty" of which they claim to have been deprived by the enforcement of the regents' order. If the regents' order is not repugnant to the due process clauses, then it does not violate the privileges and immunities clause. Therefore we need only decide whether by state action the "liberty" of these students has been infringed.

There need be no attempt to enumerate or comprehensively to define what is included in the "liberty" protected by the due process clause. Undoubtedly it does include the right to entertain the beliefs, to adhere to the principles, and to teach the doctrines on which these students base their objections to the order prescribing military training. . . . The fact that they are able to pay their way in this University but not in any other institution in California is without significance upon any constitutional or other question here involved. California has not drafted or called them to attend the University. They are seeking education offered by the state and at the same time insisting that they be excluded from the prescribed course solely upon grounds of their religious beliefs and conscientious objections to war, preparation for war, and military education. Taken on the basis of the facts alleged in the petition, appellants' contentions amount to no more than an assertion that the due process clause of the Fourteenth Amendment as a safeguard of "liberty" confers the right to be students in the State University free from obligations to take military training as one of the conditions of attendance.

Viewed in the light of our decisions, that proposition must at once be put aside as untenable.

Government, federal and state, each in its own sphere owes a duty to the people within its jurisdiction to preserve itself in adequate strength to maintain peace and order and to assure the just enforcement of law. And every citizen owes the reciprocal duty, according to his capacity, to support and defend government against all enemies. . . .

United States v. Schwimmer, 279 U. S. 644, 49 S. Ct. 448, 73 L. Ed. 889, involved a petition for naturalization by one opposed to bearing arms in defense of country. Holding the applicant not entitled to citizenship we said (page 650 of 279 U. S. 49 S. Ct. 448, 450): "That it is the duty of citizens by force of arms to defend our government against all enemies whenever necessity arises is a fundamental principle of the Constitution . . . Whatever tends to lessen the willingness of citizens to discharge their duty to bear arms in the country's defense detracts from the strength and safety of the government."

In United States v. Macintosh[15], 283 U. S. 605 S. Ct. 570, 571, 75 L. Ed. 1302, a later naturalization case, the applicant was unwilling, because of conscientious objections, to take unqualifiedly the statutory oath of allegiance which contains this statement: "That he will support and defend the Constitution and laws of the United States against all enemies, foreign and domestic, and bear true faith and allegiance to the same." 8 U. S. C. Section 381 (8 USCA Section 831). His petition stated that he was willing, if necessary, to take up arms in defense of this country, "but I should want to be free to judge of the necessity". In amplification he said: "I do not undertake to support 'my country, right or wrong' in any dispute which may arise

---

[15]This case and the *Schwimmer* case cited in the preceding paragraph have been overruled by the decision in *Girouard v. United States*, 1946. (91)

and I am not willing to promise beforehand, and without knowing the cause for which my country may go to war, either that I will or that I will not 'take up arms in defense of this country', however 'necessary' the war may seem to be to the Government of the day." The opinion of this court quotes from petitioner's brief a statement to the effect that it is a "fixed principle of our Constitution, zealously guarded by our laws, that a citizen cannot be forced and need not bear arms in a war if he has conscientious religious scruples against doing so." And referring to that part of the argument in behalf of the applicant, this court said (page 623 of 283 U. S., 51 S. Ct. 570, 575): "This, if it means what it seems to say, is an astonishing statement. Of course, there is no such principle of the Constitution, fixed or otherwise. The conscientious objector is relieved from the obligation to bear arms in obedience to no constitutional provision, express or implied; but because, and only because, it has accorded with the policy of Congress thus to relieve him . . . The privilege of the native born conscientious objector to avoid bearing arms comes, not from the Constitution, but from the acts of Congress. That body may grant or withhold the exemption as in its wisdom it sees fit; and, if it be withheld, the native-born conscientious objector cannot successfully assert the privilege. No other conclusion is compatible with the well-nigh limitless extent of the war powers as above illustrated, which include, by necessary implication, the power, in the last extremity, to compel the armed service of any citizen in the land, without regard to his objections or his views in respect of the justice or morality of the particular war or of war in general. In Jacobson v. Massachusetts, 196 U. S. 11, 29, 25 S. Ct. 358, 362, 49 L. Ed. 643, 3 Ann. Cas. 765, this court [upholding a state compulsory vaccination law], speaking of the liberties guaranteed to the individual by the Fourteenth Amendment, said: "And yet he may be compelled, by force if need be, against his will and without regard to his personal wishes or his pecuniary interests, or even his religious or political convictions, to take his place in the ranks of the army of his country, and risk the chance of being shot down in its defense."

And see Pearson v. Coale, 165 Md. 224, 167 A. 54, a case, similar to that now before us, decided against the contention of a student in the University of Maryland who on conscientious grounds objected to military training there required. His appeal to this Court was dismissed for the want of a substantial federal question. Coale v. Pearson, 290 U. S. 597, 54 S. Ct. 131, 78 L. Ed. 525.

Plainly there is no ground for the contention that the regents' order, requiring able-bodied male students under the age of twenty-four as a condition of their enrollment to take the prescribed instruction in military science and tactics, transgresses any constitutional right asserted by these appellants. . . . (97, pp. 203-05)

COMMENT

The gist of the Court's decision here was that the California statute did not require military service, nor, in the words of a commentator, did it "peremptorily command submission to Military training." It did make the obligation to take such training "a condition of attendance at the university." (48, p. 768) The imposition of this obligation was shown to be a state power not in conflict with the federal Constitution.

A subsequent decision involving a related issue may be of interest to those persons, including teachers, who occupy a semipublic position. In the 1945 case of *In re Summers* (103) the Court reviewed a state supreme court's finding that a license could be withheld from an attorney "on the premise that a conscientious belief in non-violence to the extent that the believer would not use force to prevent wrong, no matter how aggravated, made it impossible for him to swear in good faith" to support the state constitution. The Supreme Court held that the requirement of such an oath and its interpretation "to require a willingness to perform military service, did not abridge religious freedom." Four dissenting justices insisted, in the words of Justice Black, that they could not agree that a state could "lawfully bar from a semipublic position a well-qualified man of good character solely because he entertains a religious belief which might prompt him at some time in the future to violate a law which has not yet been and may never be enacted." (48, p. 768)

In re Summers did not, of course, either confirm or limit the decision in *Hamilton v. Regents*.

AMDT. 1—RELIGION, FREE SPEECH, ETC.

An Establishment of Religion

[15] COMPULSORY FLAG SALUTING—1

MINERSVILLE SCHOOL DISTRICT V. GOBITIS

310 U. S. 586, 60 Sup. Ct. 1011 (1940)

The Supreme Court of the United States sustained a Pennsylvania school board rule that students should salute the flag as a condition for school attendance. This decision was reversed in *West Virginia State Board of Education v. Barnette* in 1943.

In this case and the one to follow two of the most powerful forces in contemporary society—nationalism and religion—were arrayed in conflict before the Court. Wartime nationalism faced religious conviction in one of its most dissentious and aggressively active forms. Thus, militant Christianity, strengthened by the democratic dogma that the state may not encroach unduly upon individual rights, confronted that same state standing secure but uncomfortable in the right and obligation to support itself by all reasonable means. It was an ancient problem, one that has found no express answer in law or theory, but only quasi-solutions in working balance.

Jehovah's Witnesses, once known as "Russellites," are a sect in which every member holds himself to be a minister of the gospel. Each minister or "Witness" further holds that his justification lies in spreading an interpretation of the Bible and a special doctrine emphasizing calculations of Christ's coming and the battle of Armageddon. All institutionalized churches, say the Witnesses, are spawned by the devil. These teachings are most zealously disseminated through many resources but especially through personal contacts, sale or giving away religious literature, and by house to house preachments. (43, p. 1056) The zeal and fanaticism of the Witnesses has brought considerable attention from the courts. Between 1938 and 1950 they appeared before the Supreme Court of the United States in "more than twenty major cases involving religious liberty issues. In a majority of these they were successful. These decisions have done much to clarify our constitutional law relating to freedom of religion." (14, p. 132)

Ceremony in religion is contrary to the tenets of the Witnesses. Likewise, although they declare "respect" for the flag they refuse to salute it, contending that to do so is contrary to their literal interpretation of Exodus, Chapter 20, verses 4 and 5, wherein is found an injunction against bowing down before any "graven image."

Therefore, when the school board of Minersville, Pennsylvania, school district ruled that all its children should salute the flag each day on pain of expulsion, the children of Witness Walter Gobitis refused, and were expelled. The father brought suit to enjoin the school board from enforcing the flag-salute ceremony as a condition of school attendance. Both the District Court and the Circuit Court found in Gobitis' favor. The Supreme Court, having made counter disposition of several similar cases in per curiam decisions[16], now granted certiorari in order "to give the matter full reconsideration." (43, p. 1059) The Court spoke of the *Gobitis* case as presenting "phases of the profoundest problem confronting a democracy."

Justice Frankfurter delivered the opinion. He said, in part:

A grave responsibility confronts this Court whenever in course of litigation it must reconcile the conflicting claims of liberty and authority. But when the liberty invoked is liberty of conscience, and the authority is authority to safeguard the nation's fellowship, judicial conscience is put to its severest test. Of such a nature is the present controversy.

Lillian Gobitis, aged twelve, and her brother William, aged ten, were ex-

---

[16]These opinions refusing to review flag salute requirements were in the following cases: *Leoles v. Landers* (1937) (109); *Herring v. State Board of Education* (1938) (100); *Gabrielli v. Knickerbocker* (1939) (84); and *Johnson v. Deerfield* (1939) (107). They are indicative of the Court's general attitude that it should not decide a constitutional issue unless the necessity for so doing is strong.

pelled from the public schools of Minersville, Pennsylvania, for refusing to salute the national flag as part of a daily school exercise. The local Board of Education required both teachers and pupils to participate in this ceremony. The ceremony is a familiar one. The right hand is placed on the breast and the following pledge recited in unison: "I pledge allegiance to my flag, and to the Republic for which it stands; one nation indivisible, with liberty and justice for all." While the words are spoken, teacher and pupils extend their right hands in salute to the flag. The Gobitis family are affiliated with "Jehovah's Witnesses", for whom the Bible as the word of God is the supreme authority. The children had been brought up conscientiously to believe that such a gesture of respect for the flag was forbidden by command of Scripture.

The Gobitis children were of an age for which Pennsylvania makes school attendance compulsory. Thus they were denied a free education and their parents had to put them into private schools. To be relieved of the financial burden thereby entailed, their father, on behalf of the children and in his own behalf, brought this suit. He sought to enjoin the authorities from continuing to exact participation in the flag-salute ceremony as a condition of his children's attendance at the Minersville school. After trial of the issues, Judge Maris gave relief in the District Court on the basis of a thoughtful opinion; his decree was affirmed by the Circuit Court of Appeals. Since this decision ran counter to several per curiam dispositions of this Court, we granted certiorari to give the matter full reconsideration. By their able submissions, the Committee on the Bill of Rights of the American Bar Association and the American Civil Liberties Union, as friends of the Court, have helped us to our conclusion.

We must decide whether the requirement of participation in such a ceremony, exacted from a child who refuses upon sincere religious grounds, infringes without due process of law the liberty guaranteed by the Fourteenth Amendment.

Centuries of strife over the erection of particular dogmas as exclusive or all-comprehending faiths led to the inclusion of a guarantee for religious freedom in the Bill of Rights. The First Amendment, and the Fourteenth through its absorption of the First, sought to guard against repetition of those bitter religious struggles by prohibiting the establishment of a state religion and by securing to every sect the free exercise of its faith. So pervasive is the acceptance of this previous right that its scope is brought into question, as here, only when the conscience of individuals collides with the felt necessities of society.

Certainly the affirmative pursuit of one's convictions about the ultimate mystery of the universe and man's relation to it is placed beyond the reach of law. Government may not interfere with organized or individual expression of belief or disbelief, propagation of belief—or even of disbelief in the supernatural—is protected, whether in church or chapel, mosque or synagogue, tabernacle or meetinghouse. Likewise the Constitution assures generous immunity to the individual from imposition of penalties for offending, in the course of his own religious activities, the religious views of others, be they a minority or those who are dominant in government.

But the manifold character of man's relations may bring his conception of religious duty into conflict with the secular interests of his fellowmen. When does the constitutional guarantee compel exemption from doing what society thinks necessary for the promotion of some great common end, or from a penalty for conduct which appears dangerous to the general good? To state the problem is to recall the truth that no single principle can answer all of life's complexities. The right to freedom of religious belief, however dissident and however obnoxious to the cherished beliefs of others—even of a majority—is itself the denial of an absolute. But to affirm that the freedom to follow conscience has itself no limits in the life of a society would deny that very plurality of principles which, as a matter of history, underlies protection of religious toleration. Compare Mr. Justice Holmes in Hudson County Water Co. v. McCarter, 209 U. S. 349, 355. Our present task then, as so often the case with courts, is to reconcile two rights in order to prevent either from destroying the other. But, because in safeguarding conscience we are dealing with interests so subtle and so dear, every possible leeway should be given to the claims of religious faith.

In the judicial enforcement of religious freedom we are concerned with a historic concept. See Mr. Justice Cardozo in Hamilton v. Regents, 293 U. S. 245, at page 265. The religious liberty which the Constitution protects has never excluded legislation of general scope not directed against doctrinal loyalties of particular sects. Judicial nullification of legislation cannot be justified by attributing to the framers of the Bill of Rights views for which there is no historic warrant. Conscientious scruples have not, in the course of the long struggle for religious toleration, relieved the individual from obedience to a general law not aimed at the promotion or restriction of religious beliefs. The mere possession of religious convictions which contradict the relevant concerns of a political society does not relieve the citizen from the discharge of political responsibilities. The necessity for this adjustment has again and again been recognized. In a number of situations the exertion of political authority has been sustained, while basic considerations of religious freedom have been left inviolate. Reynolds v. United States, 90 U. S. 145; Davis v. Beason, 133 U. S. 333; Selective Draft Law Cases, 245 U. S. 366; Hamilton v. Regents, 293 U. S. 245. In all these cases the general laws in question, upheld in their application to those who refused obedience from religious conviction, were manifestations of specific powers of government deemed by the legislature essential to secure and maintain that orderly, tranquil, and free society without which religious toleration itself is unattainable. Nor does the freedom of speech assured by Due Process move in a more absolute circle of immunity than that enjoyed by religious freedom. Even if it were assumed that freedom of speech goes beyond the historic concept of full opportunity to utter and to disseminate views, however heretical or offensive to dominant opinion, and includes freedom from conveying what may be deemed an implied but rejected affirmation, the question remains whether school children, like the Gobitis children, must be excused from conduct required of all the other children in the promotion of national cohesion. We are dealing with an interest inferior to none in the hierarchy of legal values. National unity is the basis of national security. To deny the legislature the right to select appropriate means for its attainment presents a totally different order of problem from that of the propriety of subordinating the possible ugliness of littered streets to the free expression of opinion through distribution of handbills. Compare Schneider v. State of New Jersey, 308 U. S. 147.

Situations like the present are phases of the profoundest problem confronting a democracy—the problem which Lincoln cast in memorable dilemma: "Must a government of necessity be too strong for the liberties of its people, or too weak to maintain its own existence?" No mere textual reading or logical talisman can solve the dilemma. And when the issue demands judicial determination, it is not the personal notion of judges of what wise adjustment requires which must prevail.

Unlike the instances we have cited, the case before us is not concerned with an exertion of legislative power for the promotion of some specific need or interest of secular society—the protection of the family, the promotion of health, the common defense, the raising of public revenue to defray the cost of government. But all these specific activities of government presuppose the existence of an organized political society. Such a sentiment is fostered by all those agencies of the mind and spirit which may serve to gather up the traditions of a people, transmit them from generation to generation, and thereby create that continuity of a treasured common life which constitutes a civilization. "We live by symbols". The flag is the symbol of our national unity, transcending all internal differences, however large, within the framework of the Constitution. This Court has had occasion to say that ". . . the flag is the symbol of the nation's power,—the emblem of freedom in its truest, best sense . . . it signifies government resting on the consent of the governed; liberty regulated by law; the protection of the weak against the strong; security against the exercise of arbitrary power; and absolute safety for free institutions against foreign aggression." Halter v. Nebraska, 205 U. S. 34.

The case before us must be viewed as though the legislature of Pennsylvania had itself formally directed the flag-salute for the children of Minersville; had made no exemption for children whose parents were possessed of conscientious scruples like those of the Gobitis family, and had indicated its belief in the desirable ends to be secured by having its public school children share a common experience at those periods of development when their minds are supposedly receptive to its assimilation, by an exercise appropriate in time and place and setting, and one designed to evoke in them appreciation of the nation's hopes and dreams, its sufferings and sacrifices. The precise issue, then, for us to decide is whether the legislatures of the various states and the authorities in a thousand counties and school districts of this country are barred from determining the appropriateness of various means to evoke that unifying sentiment without which there can ultimately be no liberties, civil or religious. To stigmatize legislative judgment in providing for this universal gesture of respect for the symbol of our national life in the setting of the common school as a lawless inroad on that freedom of conscience which the Constitution protects, would amount to no less than the pronouncement of pedagogical and psychological dogma in a field where courts possess no marked and certainly no controlling competence. The influences which help toward a common feeling for the common country are manifold. Some may seem harsh and others no doubt are foolish. Surely, however, the end is legitimate. And the effective means for its attainment are still so uncertain and so unauthenticated by science as to preclude us from putting the widely prevalent belief in flag-saluting beyond the pale of legislative power. It mocks reason and denies our whole history to find in the allowance of a requirement to salute our flag on fitting occasions the seeds of sanction for obeisance to a leader.

The wisdom of training children in patriotic impulses by those compulsions which necessarily pervade so much of the educational process is not for our independent judgment. Even were we convinced of the folly of such a measure, such belief would be no proof of its unconstitutionality. For ourselves, we might be tempted to say that the deepest patriotism is best engendered by giving unfettered scope to the most crochety beliefs. Perhaps it is best, even from the standpoint of those interests which ordinances like the one under review seek to promote, to give to the least popular sect leave from conformities like those here in issue. But the court-room is not the arena for debating issues of educational policy. It is not our province to choose among competing considerations in the subtle process of securing effective loyalty to the traditional ideals of democracy, while respecting at the same time individual idiosyncrasies among a people so diversified in racial origins and religious allegiances. So to hold would in effect make us the school board for the country. That authority has not been given to this Court, nor should we assume it.

We are dealing here with the formative period in the development of citizenship. Great diversity of psychological and ethical opinion exists among us concerning the best way to train children for their place in society. Because of these differences and because of reluctance to permit a single, iron-cast system of education to be imposed upon a nation compounded of so many strains, we have held that, even though public education is one of our most cherished democratic institutions, the Bill of Rights bars a state from compelling all children to attend the public schools. Pierce v. Society of the Sisters of the Holy Name of Jesus and Mary, 268 U. S. 510. But it is a very different thing for this Court to exercise censorship over the conviction of legislatures that a particular program or exercise will best promote in the minds of children who attend the common schools an attachment to the institutions of their country.

What the school authorities are really asserting is the right to awaken in the child's mind considerations as to the significance of the flag contrary to those implanted by the parent. In such an attempt the state is normally at a disadvantage in competing with the parent's authority, so long—and this is the vital aspect of religious toleration—as parents are unmolested in their right to counteract by their own persuasiveness the wisdom and rightness of those loyalties which the state's educational system is seeking to promote. Except where the transgression of constitutional liberty is too plain for argument, personal freedom is best maintained—so long as the remedial channels of the democratic process remain open and unobstructed—when it is ingrained in a people's habits and not enforced against popular policy by the coercion of adjudicated law. That the flag-salute is an allowable portion of a school program for those who do not invoke conscientious scruples is surely not debatable. But for us to insist that, though the ceremony may be required, exceptional immunity must be given to dissidents, is to maintain that there is no basis for a legislative judgment that such an exemption might introduce elements of difficulty into the school discipline, might cast doubts in the minds of the other children which would themselves weaken the effect of the exercise.

The preciousness of the family relation, the authority and independence which give dignity to parenthood, indeed the enjoyment of all freedom, presuppose the kind of ordered society which is summarized by our flag. A society which is dedicated to the preservation of these ultimate values of civilization may in self-protection utilize the educational process for inculcating those almost unconscious feelings which bind men together in a comprehending loyalty, whatever may be their lesser differences and difficulties. That is to say, the process may be utilized so long as men's right to believe as they please, to win others to their way of belief, and their right to assemble in their chosen places of worship for the devotional ceremonies of their faith, are all fully respected.

Judicial review, itself a limitation on popular government, is a fundamental part of our constitutional scheme. But to the legislature no less than to courts is committed the guardianship of deeply-cherished liberties. Where all the effective means of inducing political changes are left free from interference, education in the abandonment of foolish legislation is itself a training in liberty. To fight out the wise use of legislative authority in the forum of public opinion and before legislative assemblies rather than to transfer such a contest to the judicial arena, serves to vindicate the self-confidence of a free people.

Reversed. (114, pp. 1011-16)

COMMENT

The Supreme Court, in reversing the lower courts and thereby upholding the Minersville school board, based its decision on the theory that the state had the right to require the flag salute as a means for achieving national feeling and unity. Accordingly, even though the school board's regulation was a command to perform an act rather than a prohibition of action, where such command and performance contributed to national unity, individual freedoms could in a degree be subordinated thereto. The Court did not expressly decide whether the flag salute constituted a religious ceremony, and consequently the question of whether the compulsory nature of the school board's regulation was in conflict with the First Amendment was likewise not specifically determined.

Justice Frankfurter's opinion observed that the Courts are not proper settings for debates on educational policy. Yet the key point in the question would seem to have been whether the particular educational policy of requiring the flag salute constituted an undue interference with individual rights. Moreover, when the Court said, in effect, that the schools could be used to instill patriotism through requirement of specific performance to that end an educational policy was clearly fostered. One comment made by the Court in its consideration of patriotism may stand as a challenge to educators. Since the "best" method of fitting students to the cultural demand for patriotism has not been discovered, school boards and legislatures, said the Court, should be permitted to work out their own best method. That the legislative search (by a school board) for the "best" method may have been at the heart of the difficulty in this unhappy case seems to have been noted, but yet without full recognition by the Court.

In any event, as Victor Rotnem and F. G. Folsom, two members of the Department of Justice, have shown, the Court's opinion that the flag salute was a means toward inculcating patriotism became all too frequently a public opinion that the flag salute was also the measure of patriotic sentiment. The two years following the decision "reflect an uninterrupted record of violence and persecution of the Witnesses," say Rotnem and Folsom. They go on:

Attempts have been made to persecute school children who had been expelled under the "salute or be expelled" regulations on the ground that such children were incorrigible delinquents. The parents have been persecuted for failure to make their children attend school. . . .

. . . Mississippi has enacted a statute, allegedly prompted by the stand of the Jehovah's Witnesses against the flag salute, making it a crime to distribute matter calculated to encourage disloyalty to the United States. Numerous Witnesses have been indicted under this act because they distributed literature explaining the sect's opposition to the flag salute. The flag has been used in a manner bordering on immorality by mobs which have baited Jehovah's Witnesses throughout the country. . . .

This ugly picture . . . is an eloquent argument in support of the minority contention of Mr. Justice Stone [in the Gobitis Case]. The placing of symbolic exercises on a higher plane than freedom of conscience has made this symbol an instrument of oppression of a religious minority. The flag has been violated by its misuse to deny the very freedoms it is intended to represent— the freedoms which themselves best engender a healthy "cohesive" respect for national institutions. . . .

How much more effective an instrument of patriotic education it would be if the flag salute itself were made a practical daily exercise of a fundamental liberty, a liberty which is one of the four great freedoms which this nation upholds. . . . (43, pp. 1062-63)

These and similar events and considerations were shortly to cause misgivings among certain Justices who had voted with the majority. As the following case shows, such misgivings were instrumental in bringing about a reversal.

AMDT. 1—RELIGION, FREE SPEECH, ETC.
An Establishment of Religion

[16] COMPULSORY FLAG SALUTING—2

WEST VIRGINIA STATE BOARD OF
EDUCATION V. BARNETTE
319 U. S. 624, 63 Sup. Ct. 1178 (1943)

The Supreme Court of the United States held that a state board rule requiring all students to salute the flag and recite the pledge of allegiance thereto as a condition of school attendance violated the First Amendment of the Federal Constitution which guaranteed the exercise of freedom of religion. This decision reversed that in *Minersville School District v. Gobitis* three years earlier.

By its 1940 decision in the case of *Minersville School District v. Gobitis* just discussed, the Supreme Court had declared that a local school board ruling requiring school children to salute the flag as a condition of attendance did not unconstitutionally restrict freedom of religion. For, said the Court, freedom of religion is not absolute; therefore it cannot be compromised by the requirements of national unity in producing national security. Three years later the Court decided that to compel students to salute the flag and pledge allegiance to it was a violation which "invades the sphere of intellect and spirit which it is the purpose of the First Amendment of our Constitution to reserve from all official control."

Not only had the earlier decision been sharply criticized by commentators such as those quoted on the pages just preceding, but certain Justices who had voted with Justice Frankfurter in the eight-to-one majority of the *Gobitis* case apparently began to regret that they had not joined Justice Stone in dissenting. For, within two years, these Justices found an opportunity to state their misgivings in the 1942 decision in *Jones v. Opelika* (108). This case involved a Jehovah's Witness who had been convicted of violating an Opelika, Alabama, anti-peddling ordinance by taking as a contribution a sum equivalent to the price of a piece of religious literature. The Supreme Court upheld the ordinance,[17] but Justices Black, Douglas, and Murphy joined in a dissenting opinion which adverted to the *Gobitis* case, and said in part:

> The opinion of the Court sanctions a device which in our opinion suppresses or tends to suppress the free exercise of a religion practiced by a minority group. This is but another step in the direction which Minersville School District v. Gobitis . . . took against the same religious minority and is a logical extension of the principles upon which that decision rested. Since we joined in the opinion in the Gobitis case, we think this is an appropriate occasion to state that we now believe it was also wrongly decided. Certainly our democratic form of government functioning under the historic Bill of Rights has a high responsibility to accommodate itself to the religious views of minorities, however unpopular those views may be. The First Amendment does not put the right freely to exercise religion in a subordinate position. We fear, however, that the opinions in this and the Gobitis case do exactly that. . . . (108, pp. 1251-52)

When the three members of the Court making this statement were added to Justice Stone, the lone dissenter at the time the *Gobitis*

---

[17]Later, in the 1943 case of *Murdock v. Pennsylvania* (118) this decision, like the "flag salute" decision, was also reversed.

decision was handed down, only one more was lacking for a majority. Then, when President Roosevelt appointed Justice Rutledge to replace Justice Byrnes early in 1943 that majority, it developed, was more than secure. Justice Jackson joined them for the reversal soon to be made.

The new flag-salute case involved some differences. One was of no great import in that a state board of education rather than a local school board had made the ruling now challenged. Of more importance was the fact that under this ruling action could be taken against parents of children "unlawfully absent" in consequence of their dismissal for refusing to salute the flag. Meanwhile, that is, in the interval between the two cases, Congress had dealt definitively with the matter of respect due the flag by an act of 1942. Section seven of the act recites the familiar words of the pledge and prescribes the usual salute, but it also says: "However, civilians will always show full respect to the flag when the pledge is given by merely standing at attention, men removing the headdress."

When, however, the West Virginia State Board of Education, no doubt encouraged by the decision in the *Gobitis* case, had made the ruling described above, members of the Jehovah's Witnesses sued in the United States District Court to restrain enforcement of the ruling. This court decided in their favor. Thereupon the State Board appealed to the Supreme Court.

Justice Jackson, in delivering the opinion of the Court said, in part:

This case calls upon us to reconsider a precedent decision, as the Court throughout its history often has been required to do. Before turning to the Gobitis case, however, it is desirable to notice certain characteristics by which this controversy is distinguished.

The freedom asserted by these respondents does not bring them into collision with rights asserted by any other individual. It is such conflicts which most frequently require intervention of the State to determine where the rights of one end and those of another begin. But the refusal of these persons to participate in the ceremony does not interfere with or deny rights of others to do so. Nor is there any question in this case that their behavior is peaceable and orderly. The sole conflict is between authority and rights of the individual. The State asserts power to condition access to public education on making a prescribed sign and profession and at the same time to coerce attendance by punishing both parent and child. The latter stand on a right of self-determination in matters that touch individual opinion and personal attitude.

As the present Chief Justice said in dissent in the Gobitis case, the State may "require teaching by instruction and study of all in our history and in the structure and organization of our government, including the guaranties of civil liberty which tend to inspire patriotism and love of country." 310 U. S. at page 604. Here, however, we are dealing with a compulsion of students to declare a belief. They are not merely made acquainted with the flag salute so that they may be informed as to what it is or even what it means. The issue here is whether this slow and easily neglected route to aroused loyalties constitutionally may be short-cut by substituting a compulsory salute and slogan. This issue is not prejudiced by the Court's previous holding that where a State, without compelling attendance extends college facilities to pupils who voluntarily enroll, it may prescribe military training as part of the course without offense to the Constitution. It was held that those who take advantage of its opportunities may not on ground of conscience refuse compliance with such conditions. In the present case attendance is not optional. That case is also to be distinguished from the present one because, independently of college privileges or requirements, the State has power to raise militia and impose the duties of service therein upon its citizens.

There is no doubt that, in connection with the pledges, the flag salute is a form of utterance. Symbolism is a primitive but effective way of communicating ideas. The use of an emblem or flag to symbolize some system, idea, institution, or personality, is a short cut from mind to mind. Causes and nations, political parties, lodges and ecclesiastical groups seek to knit the loyalty of their following to a flag or banner, a color or design. The state announces rank, function, and authority through crowns and maces, uniforms and black robes; the church speaks through the Cross, the Crucifix, the altar and shrine, and clerical raiment. Symbols of State often convey political ideas just as religious symbols come to convey theological ones. Associated with many of these symbols are appropriate gestures of acceptance of respect: a salute, a bowed or bared head, a bended knee. A person gets from a symbol the meaning he puts into it, and what is one man's comfort and inspiration is another's jest and scorn. . . .

It is also to be noted that the compulsory flag salute and pledge requires affirmation of a belief and an attitude of mind. It is not clear whether the regulation contemplates that pupils forego any contrary convictions of their own and become unwilling converts to the prescribed ceremony or whether it will be acceptable if they simulate assent by words without belief and by a gesture barren of meaning. It is now a commonplace that censorship or suppression of expression of opinion is tolerated by our Constitution only when the expression presents a clear and present danger of action of a kind the State is empowered to prevent and punish. It would seem that involuntary affirmation could be commanded only on even more immediate and urgent grounds than silence. But here the power of compulsion is invoked without any allegation than remaining passive during a flag salute ritual creates a clear and present danger that would justify an effort even to muffle expression. To sustain the compulsory flag salute we are required to say that a Bill of Rights which guards the individual's right to speak his own mind, left it open to public authorities to compel him to utter what is not in his mind.

Whether the First Amendment to the Constitution will permit officials to order observance of ritual of this nature does not depend upon whether as a voluntary exercise we would think it to be good, bad or merely innocuous. Any credo of nationalism is likely to include what some disapprove or to omit what others think essential, and to give off different overtones as it takes on different accents or interpretations. If official power exists to coerce acceptance of any patriotic creed, what it shall contain cannot be decided by courts, but must be largely discretionary with the ordaining authority, whose power to prescribe would no doubt include power to amend. Hence validity of the asserted power to force an American citizen publicly to profess any statement of belief or to engage in any ceremony of assent to one presents questions of power that must be considered independently of any idea we may have as to the utility of the ceremony in question.

Nor does the issue as we see it turn on one's possession of particular religious views or the sincerity with which they are held. While religion supplies respondents' motive for enduring the discomforts of making the issue in this case, many citizens who do not share these religious views hold such a compulsory rite to infringe constitutional liberty of the individual. It is not necessary to inquire whether non-conformist beliefs will exempt from the duty to salute unless we first find power to make the salute a legal duty.

The Gobitis decision, however, assumed, as did the argument in that case and in this, that power exists in the State to impose the flag salute discipline upon school children in general. The Court only examined and rejected a claim based on religious beliefs of immunity from an unquestioned general rule. The question which underlies the flag salute controversy is whether such a ceremony so touching matters of opinion and political attitude may be imposed upon the individual by official authority under powers committed to any political organization under our Constitution. We examine rather than assume existence of this power and, against this broader definition of issues in this case, re-examine specific grounds assigned for the Gobitis decision.

1. It was said that the flag-salute controversy confronted the Court with "the problem which Lincoln cast in memorable dilemma: 'Must a government of necessity be too strong for the liberties of its people, or too weak to maintain its own existence?' " and that the answer must be in favor of strength . . .

. . . Such over-simplification, so handy in political debate, often lacks the precision necessary to postulates of judicial reasoning. If validly applied to this problem, the utterance cited would resolve every issue of power in favor of those in authority and would require us to override every liberty thought to weaken or delay execution of their policies.

Government of limited power need not be anemic government. Assurance that rights are secure tends to diminish fear and jealousy of strong government, and by making us feel safe to live under it makes for its better support. Without promise of a limiting Bill of Rights it is doubtful if our Constitution could have mustered enough strength to enable its ratification. To enforce those rights today is not to choose weak government over strong government. It is only to adhere as a means of strength to individual freedom of mind in preference to officially disciplined uniformity for which history indicates a disappointing and disastrous end.

The subject now before us exemplifies this principle. Free public education, if faithful to the ideal of secular instruction and political neutrality, will not be partisan or enemy of any class, creed, party, or faction. If it is to impose any ideological discipline, however, each part of denomination must seek to control, or failing that, to weaken the influence of the educational system. Observance of the limitations of the Constitution will not weaken government in the field appropriate for its exercise.

2. It was also considered in the Gobitis case that functions of educational officers in states, counties and school districts were such that to interfere with their authority "would in effect make us the school board for the country."

The Fourteenth Amendment, as now applied to the States, protects the citizen against the State itself and all of its creatures—Boards of Education not excepted. These have, of course, important, delicate, and highly discretionary functions, but none that they may not perform within the limits of the Bill of Rights. That they are educating the young for citizenship is reason for scrupulous protection of Constitutional freedoms of the individual, if we are not to strangle the free mind at its source and teach youth to discount important principles of our government as mere platitudes.

Such Boards are numerous and their territorial jurisdiction often small. But small and local authority may feel less sense of responsibility to the Constitution, and agencies of publicity may be less vigilant in calling it to account. The action of Congress in making flag observance voluntary and respecting the conscience of the objector in a matter so vital as raising the Army contrasts sharply with these local regulations in matters relatively trivial to the welfare of the nation. There are village tyrants as well as village Hampdens, but none who acts under color or law is beyond reach of the Constitution.

3. The Gobitis opinion reasoned that this is a field "where courts possess no marked and certainly no controlling competence", that it is committed to the legislatures as well as the courts to guard cherished liberties and that it is constitutionally appropriate to "fight out the wise use of legislative authority in the forum of public opinion and before legislative assemblies rather than to transfer such a contest to the judicial arena", since all the "effective means of inducing political changes are left free".

The very purpose of a Bill of Rights was to withdraw certain subjects from the vicissitudes of political controversy, to place them beyond the reach of majorities and officials and to establish them as legal principles to be applied by the courts. One's right to life, liberty, and property, to free speech, a free press, freedom of worship and assembly, and other fundamental rights may not be submitted to vote; they depend on the outcome of no elections.

In weighing arguments of the parties it is important to distinguish between the due process clause of the Fourteenth Amendment as an instrument for transmitting the principles of the First Amendment and those cases in which it is applied for its own sake. The test of legislation which collides with the Fourteenth Amendment, because it also collides with the principles of the First, is much more definite than the test when only the Fourteenth is involved. Much of the vagueness of the due process clause disappears when the specific prohibitions of the First becomes its standard. The right of a State to regulate, for example, a public utility may well include, so far as the due process test is concerned, power to impose all of the restrictions which a legislature may have a "rational basis" for adopting. But freedoms of speech and of press, of assembly, and of worship may not be infringed on such slender grounds. They are susceptible of restriction only to prevent grave and immediate danger to interests which the state may lawfully protect. It is important to note that while it is the Fourteenth Amendment which bears directly upon the State it is the more specific limiting principles of the First Amendment that finally govern this case.

Nor does our duty to apply the Bill of Rights to assertions of official authority depend upon our possession of marked competence in the field where the invasion of rights occurs. True, the task of translating the majestic generalities of the Bill of Rights, conceived as part of the pattern of liberal government in the eighteenth century, into concrete restraints on officials dealing with the problems of the twentieth century, is one to disturb self-confidence. These principles grew in soil which also produced a philosophy that the individual was the center of society, that his liberty was attainable through mere absence of governmental restraints, and that government should be entrusted with few controls and only the mildest supervision over men's affairs. We must transplant these rights to a soil in which the laissez-faire concept or principle of non-interference has withered at least as to economic affairs, and social advancements are increasingly sought through closer integration of society and through expanded and strengthened government control. These changed conditions often deprive precedents of reliability and cast us more than we would choose upon our own judgment. But we act in these matters not by authority of our competence but by force of our commissions. We cannot, because of modest estimates of our competence in such specialties as public education, withhold the judgment that history authenticates as the function of this Court when liberty is infringed.

4. Lastly, and this is the very heart of the Gobitis opinion, it reasons that "National unity is the basis of national security", that the authorities have "the right to select appropriate means for its attainment", and hence reaches the conclusion that such compulsory measures toward "national unity" are constitutional. Upon the verity of this assumption depends our answer in this case.

National unity as an end which officials may foster by persuasion and example is not in question. The problem is whether under our Constitution compulsion as here employed is a permissible means for its achievement.

Struggles to coerce uniformity of sentiment in support of some end thought essential to their time and country have been waged by many good as well as by evil men. Nationalism is a relatively recent phenomenon but at other times and places the ends have been racial or territorial security, support of a dynasty or regime, and particular plans for saving souls. As first and moderate methods to attain unity have failed, those bent on its accomplishment must resort to an ever-increasing severity. As governmental pressure toward unity becomes greater, so strife becomes more bitter as to whose unity it shall be. Probably no deeper division of our people could proceed from any provocation than from finding it necessary to choose what doctrine and whose program public educational officials shall compel youth to unite in embracing. Ultimate futility of such attempts to compel coherence is the lesson of every such effort from the Roman drive to stamp out Christianity as a disturber of its pagan unity, the Inquisition, as a means to religious and dynastic unity, the Siberian exiles as a means to Russian unity, down to the fast failing efforts of our present totalitarian enemies. Those who begin coercive elimination of dissent soon find themselves exterminating dissenters. Compulsory unification of opinion achieves only the unanimity of the graveyard.

It seems trite but necessary to say that the First Amendment to our Constitution was designed to avoid these ends by avoiding these beginnings. There is no mysticism in the American concept of the State or of the nature or origin of its authority. We set up government by consent of the governed, and the Bill of Rights denies those in power any legal opportunity to coerce that consent. Authority here is to be controlled by public opinion, not public opinion by authority.

The case is made difficult not because the principles of its decision are obscure but because the flag involved is our own. Nevertheless, we apply the limitations of the Constitution with no fear that freedom to be intellectually and spiritually diverse or even contrary will disintegrate the social organization. To believe that patriotism will not flourish if patriotic ceremonies are voluntary and spontaneous instead of a compulsory routine is to make an unflattering estimate of the appeal of our institutions to free minds. We can have intellectual individualism and the rich cultural diversities that we owe to exceptional minds only at the price of occasional eccentricity and abnormal attitudes. When they are so harmless to others or to the State as those we deal with here, the price is not too great. But freedom to differ is not limited to things that do not matter much. That would be a mere shadow of freedom. The test of its substance is the right to differ as to things that touch the heart of the existing order.

If there is any fixed star in our constitutional constellation, it is that no official, high or petty, can prescribe what shall be orthodox in politics, nationalism, religion, or other matters of opinion or force citizens to confess by work or act their faith therein. If there are any circumstances which permit an exception, they do not now occur to us.

We think the action of the local authorities in compelling the flag salute and pledge transcends constitutional limitations on their power and invades the sphere of intellect and spirit which it is the purpose of the First Amendment to our Constitution to reserve from all official control.

The decision of this Court in Minersville School District v. Gobitis and the holdings of those few per curiam decisions which preceded and foreshadowed it are overruled, and the judgment enjoining enforcement of the West Virginia Regulation is affirmed. (158, pp. 1179-87)

Justice Frankfurter, with Justices Roberts and Reed, dissented. Justice Frankfurter said, in part:

. . . As a member of this Court I an not justified in writing my private notions of policy into the Constitution, no matter how deeply I may cherish them or how mischievous I may deem their disregard. The duty of a judge who must decide which of two claims before the Court shall prevail, that of a state to enact and enforce laws within its general competence or that of an individual to refuse obedience because of the demands of his conscience, is not that of the ordinary person. It can never be emphasized too much that one's own opinion about the wisdom or evil of a law should be excluded altogether when one is doing one's duty on the bench. The only opinion of our own even looking in that direction that is material is our opinion whether legislators could in reason have enacted such a law. In the light of all the circumstances, including the history of this question in this Court, it would require more daring than I possess to deny that reasonable legislators could have taken the action which is before us for review. Most unwillingly, therefore, I must differ from my brethren with regard to legislation like this. I cannot bring my mind to believe that the "liberty" secured by the Due Process Clause gives this Court authority to deny to the State of West Virginia the attainment of that which we all recognize as a legitimate legislative end, namely, the promotion of good citizenship, by employment of the means here chosen. . . . (158, pp. 1189-90)

COMMENT

This decision appears to have provoked much less unfavorable comment in the press than did that in the earlier flag-salute case. Therefore, it would seem to be in closer adjustment with the attitudes of the more articulate section of the public toward our First Amendment and our schools. For this section of the public appears to agree with the Court that it is not within the province of legislatures and educational authorities to determine for individuals what is and what is not a religious ceremony. Only the individual in the exercise of free conscience can determine what is contrary to his religious principles and what is not. Therefore to compel the flag salute and pledge of allegiance contrary to conscience "invades the sphere of intellect and spirit which it is the purpose of the First Amendment to our Constitution to reserve from all official control." Likewise there is an apparent agreement that patriotism can hardly be legislated, and finally again, that the admitted authority of legislatures and educational authorities in governing schools does not extend to religious conviction, particularly when such conviction is demonstrated merely by noncompliance with an act that is only symbolic.

However, the foregoing paragraph is not to be taken as an argument that the conflicting religious and social issues involved in the two cases are or can be clear and simple in a nation of diverse sects and separated church and state. It may be noted that of the sixteen Justices who participated in the two cases, four abandoned the eight-to-one majority in the first case to reverse themselves in the second. Three of these four, while voting with the majority in the second case, joined in presenting a different set of reasons for doing so. And the three dissenters in the second case steadfastly asserted the right of the state to exercise power that the majority had denied.

It should be observed that nothing in this decision restrains schools from including patriotic exercises in their programs or from requiring all pupils, except those with true conscientious objections, to participate in such exercises.

9

ASSISTANCE BY
PUBLIC SCHOOLS
TO RELIGIOUS GROUPS

AMDT. 1—RELIGION, FREE SPEECH, ETC.
An Establishment of Religion

AMDT. 14—RIGHTS OF CITIZENS
Sec.   1—Due Process of Law

[17] **RELEASED TIME FOR ON-PREMISE RELIGIOUS INSTRUCTION**

ILLINOIS EX REL. MC COLLUM V.
BOARD OF EDUCATION
333 U. S. 203, 68 Sup. Ct. 461 (1948)

The Supreme Court of the United States held that religious instruction in the public school buildings during public school time as practiced in the schools of Champaign, Illinois, was invalid, in that under the First (and Fourteenth) Amendment to the federal Constitution it amounted to an establishment of religion.

This case assumes particular significance by the fact that it appears to be the first in which either federal or state action was declared by the Court to result in "an establishment of religion." The decision was, however, stated in such general terms, and was at the same time so carefully confined to the facts of the case, that its application to variants of the practice in Champaign remained doubtful. Indeed, within four years, in the case of *Zorach v. Clauson* (163), the Court itself upheld a variant practice of religious instruction connected with public schools in New York. The *Zorach* case is discussed as the next but one, and the two should be considered in combination. In both cases the decision turns upon a "released time" arrangement for religious instruction of public school children. Such arrangements have become common since the period of World War I. Most of them have been devised because "the use of public-school funds is expressly unconstitutional in many states, and impliedly unconstitutional in most other states." (41, p. 381) Two general types of "released time" programs exist. The most common plan, and the one questioned in the *Zorach* case later, involves religious instruction, off the public school premises although during the public school time, by sects acceptable to individuals. Less common was the plan declared unconstitutional here in the *McCollum* case. Under this plan both the public school buildings and the public school time were utilized for religious instruction.

The defense ordinarily made for either type arrangement insists that the religious instruction achieved thereby is not in the public school curriculum but is merely an "adjunct" to it. This in turn rests upon the idea expressed in the Ordinance of 1787 that society and government are interested in religion. And, as it is sometimes phrased in deference to the nation's multiplicity of sects, "All religion is good, even though some of it is better." Likewise, as Justice Reed pointed out in his dissenting opinion here, the states and the federal government have recognized Christian and other religious ceremonial in many ways—from providing chaplains for the armed services and in prisons, to opening legislative sessions and a school day with prayer or a verse from the Bible. The constitutionality "of such religious exercises was challenged in many states with conflicting results," but until the *McCollum* case, "the question never came before the Supreme Court." (14, p. 145) The facts in the *McCollum* case were at least seven years in the making before the Court reviewed them.

In 1940 the Champaign, Illinois, school board agreed that religious education should be given in the local schools to those children in grades four through nine whose parents signed "request cards." Such children were instructed approximately forty-five minutes a week by agents of the Council on Religious Education, an organization of Catholic, Jewish, and some Protestant faiths. The Council paid the religious teachers but the public school authorities supervised them. The classes were conducted during regular school hours and in the school building. Attendance was compulsory for the designated children and roll was taken and reported as for regular classes. Those children whose parents had not requested them excused for the religious instruction were required to leave the regular classrooms and go to another part of the building to make way for the religious classes.

Vashti McCollum, mother of a son in attendance and a resident and taxpayer in the district, petitioned for a writ of mandamus to compel the school board to stop permitting religious classes in the schools during regular school hours. As an avowed atheist Vashti McCollum had not, of course, signed a "request card" for the son who, she felt, was by the fact of the "released time" program and the details of its operation rendered conspicuous and left exposed to ridicule as the unbeliever which he nevertheless had every right to be. This "newsworthy" aspect of the case tended to obscure the overriding issue from many observers.

The Illinois circuit court dismissed Vashti McCollum's petition, and this dismissal was affirmed by the state's supreme court. Thereupon, Mrs. McCollum's case was taken by appeal to the Supreme Court of the United States, which reversed the state court by holding with Vashti McCollum that the Champaign "released time" plan violated the "establishment of religion" clause of the First Amendment and conflicted with the "due process of law" clause of the Fourteenth. This decision, by an eight-to-one majority, was written by the same Justice who had given the Court's decision in the *Everson* case (77) a year earlier. In addition, two concurring opinions were rendered. Thus, with the lone dissent, four opinions are recorded for the nine Justices in the *McCollum* case.

Justice Black, in handing down the Court's decision, said in part:

This case relates to the power of a state to utilize its tax-supported public school system in aid of religious instruction insofar as that power may be restricted by the First and Fourteenth Amendments to the Federal Constitution.

The appellant, Vashti McCollum, began this action for mandamus against the Champaign Board of Education in the Circuit Court of Champaign County, Illinois. Her asserted interest was that of a resident and taxpayer of Champaign and of a parent whose child was then enrolled in the Champaign public schools. Illinois has a compulsory education law which, with exceptions, requires parents to send their children, aged seven to sixteen, to its tax-supported public schools where the children are to remain in attendance during the hours when the schools are regularly in session. Parents who violate this law commit a misdemeanor punishable by fine unless the children attend private or parochial schools which meet educational standards fixed by the State. District boards of education are given general supervisory powers over the use of the public school buildings within the school districts. Ill. Rev. Stat. ch. 122, sections 123, 301 (1943).

Appellant's petition for mandamus alleged that religious teachers, employed by private religious groups, were permitted to come weekly into the school buildings during the regular hours set apart for secular teaching, and then and there for a period of thirty minutes substitute their religious teaching for the secular education provided under the compulsory education law. The petitioner charged that this joint public-school religious group program violated the First and Fourteenth Amendments to the United States Constitution. The prayer of her petition was that the Board of Education be ordered to "adopt and enforce rules and regulations prohibiting all instruction in and teaching of religious education in all public schools in Champaign School District Number 71 . . . and in all public school houses and buildings in said district when occupied by public schools . . ."

The foregoing facts, without reference to others that appear in the record, show the use of tax-supported property for religious instruction and the close cooperation between the school authorities and the religious council in promoting religious education. The operation of the State's compulsory education system thus assists and is integrated with the program of religious instruction carried on by separate religious sects. Pupils compelled by law to go to school for secular education are released in part from their legal duty upon the condition that they attend the religious classes. This is beyond all question a utilization of the tax-established and tax-supported public school system to aid religious groups to spread their faith. And it falls squarely under the ban of the First Amendment (made applicable to the States by the Fourteenth) as we interpreted it in *Everson v. Board of Education*, 330 U. S. 1. There we said: "Neither a state nor the Federal Government can set up a church. Neither can pass laws which aid one religion, aid all religions, or prefer one religion over another. Neither can force or influence a person to go to or to remain away from church against his will or force him to profess a belief or disbelief in any religion. No person can be punished for entertaining or professing religious beliefs or disbeliefs, for church attendance or non-attendance. No tax in any amount, large or small, can be levied to support any religious activities or institutions, whatever they may be called, or whatever form they may adopt to teach or practice religion. Neither a state nor the Federal Government can, openly or secretly, participate in the affairs of any religious organization or groups and *vice versa*. In the words of Jefferson, the clause against establishment of religion by law was intended to erect "a wall of separation between church and state." *Id*. at 15-16. The majority in the *Everson* case, and the minority as shown by quotations from the dissenting views in our notes 6 and 7, agreed that the First Amendment's language, properly interpreted, had erected a wall of separation between Church and State. They disagreed as to the facts shown by the record and as to the proper application of the First Amendment's language to those facts.

Recognizing that the Illinois program is barred by the First and Fourteenth Amendments if we adhere to the views expressed both by the majority and the minority in the *Everson* case, counsel for the respondents challenge those views as dicta and urge that we reconsider and repudiate them. They argue that historically the First Amendment was intended to forbid only government preference of one religion over another, not an impartial governmental assistance of all religions. In addition they ask that we distinguish or overrule our holding in the *Everson* case that the Fourteenth Amendment made the "establishment of religion" clause of the First Amendment applicable as a prohibition against the States. After giving full consideration to the arguments presented we are unable to accept either of these contentions.

To hold that a state cannot consistently with the First and Fourteenth Amendments utilize its public school system to aid any or all religious faiths or sects in the dissemination of their doctrines and ideals does not, as counsel urge, manifest a governmental hostility to religion or religious teachings. A manifestation of such hostility would be at war with our national tradition as embodied in the First Amendment's guaranty of the free exercise of religion. For the First Amendment rests upon the promise that both religion and the government can best work to achieve their lofty aims if each is left free from the other within its respective sphere. Or, as we said in the *Everson* case, the First Amendment has erected a wall between Church and State which must be kept high and impregnable.

Here not only are the State's tax-supported public school buildings used for the dissemination of religious doctrines. The State also affords sectarian groups an invaluable aid in that it helps to provide pupils for the religious classes through use of the State's compulsory public school machinery. This is not separation of Church and State.

The cause is reversed and remanded to the State Supreme Court for proceeding not inconsistent with this opinion. (102, pp. 462-66)

The four dissenters in the Everson case joined here in a concurring opinion. With Justice Burton, Justice Jackson, and Justice Rutledge agreeing, Justice Frankfurter said, in part:[18]

. . . Of course, "released time" as a generalized conception, undefined by differentiating particularities, is not an issue for constitutional adjudication. Local programs differ from each other in many and crucial respects. Some "released time" classes are under separate denominational auspices, others are conducted jointly by several denominations, often embracing all the religious affiliations of a community. Some classes in religion teach a limited sectarianism; others emphasize democracy, unity and spiritual values not anchored in a particular creed. Insofar as these are manifestations merely of the free exercise of religion, they are quite outside the scope of judicial concern, except insofar as the Court may be called upon to protect the right of religious freedom. It is only when challenge is made to the share that the public schools have in the execution of a particular "released time" program that close judicial scrutiny is demanded of the exact relation between the religious instruction and the public educational system in the specific situation before the Court. . . .

. . . Religious education [as found in Champaign schools and] so conducted on school time and property is patently woven into the working scheme of the school. The Champaign arrangement thus presents powerful elements of inherent pressure by the school system in the interest of religious sects.

---

[18]In addition to the portions quoted, Justice Frankfurter includes a "documented account of the elimination of sectarianism from American school system which is re-interpreted as a fight for the secularization of public supported education." Horace Mann, who appears as "Justice Frankfurter's principal figure in the fight against sectarianism," may have been misunderstood by the Justice. (48, pp. 760, 761n)

The fact that this power has not been used to discriminate is beside the point. Separation is a requirement to abstain from fusing functions of government and of religious sects, not merely to treat them all equally. . . .

We do not consider, as indeed we could not, school programs not before us which, though colloquially characterized as "released time", present situations differing in aspects that may well be constitutionally crucial. Different forms which "released time" has taken during more than 30 years of growth include programs which, like that before us, could not withstand the test of the Constitution; others may be found unexceptionable. . . . (102, pp. 466-75)

In a separate concurring opinion Justice Jackson alludes to Mrs. McCollum's atheism and finds her contention to be in demand of more than the end of a "released time" program. Also he points out that the Court's decision will establish little to guide the state court to which the case is returned. He said, in part:

. . . The relief demanded in this case is the extraordinary writ of mandamus to tell the local board of education what it must do. The prayer for relief is that a writ issue against the board of education "ordering it to immediately adopt and enforce rules and regulations prohibiting all instruction in and teaching of religious education in all public schools . . . and in all public-school houses and buildings in said district when occupied by public schools." The plaintiff, as she has every right to be, is an avowed atheist. What she has asked of the courts is that they not only end the "released-time" plan but also ban every form of teaching which suggests or recognizes that there is a God. She would ban all teaching of the Scriptures. She especially mentions as an example of invasion of her rights "having pupils learn and recite such statements as, "The Lord is my Shepherd, I shall not want." And she objects to teaching that the King James' version of the Bible "is called the Christian's Guide Book, the Holy Writ and the Word of God", and many other similar matters. This Court is directing the Illinois courts generally to sustain plaintiff's complaint without exception of any of these grounds of complaint, without discriminating between them and without laying down any standards to define the limits of the effect of our decision.

To me, the sweep and detail of these complaints is a danger signal which warns of the kind of local controversy we will be required to arbitrate if we do not place appropriate limitations on our decision and exact strict compliance with jurisdictional requirements. . . . Nothing but educational confusion and discrediting of the public-school system can result from subjecting it to constant law suits.

While we may and should end such formal and explicit instruction as the Champaign plan and can at all times prohibit teaching of creed and catechism and ceremonial, and can forbid forthright proselyting in the schools, I think it remains to be demonstrated whether it is possible, even if desirable, to comply with such demands as plaintiff's completely to isolate and cast out of secular education all that some people may reasonably regard as religious instruction. . . .

The task of separating the secular from the religious in education is one of magnitude, intricacy, and delicacy. To lay down a sweeping constitutional doctrine as demanded by complainant and apparently approved by the Court, applicable alike to all school boards of the nation, "to immediately adopt and enforce rules and regulations prohibiting all instruction in and teaching of religious education in all public schools" is to decree a uniform, rigid, and, if we are consistent, an unchanging standard for countless school boards representing and serving highly localized groups which not only differ from each other but which themselves, from time to time, change attitudes. It seems to me that to do so is to allow zeal for our own ideas of what is good in public instruction to induce us to accept the role of a super board of education for every school district in the nation. . . .   (102, pp. 476-78)

Justice Reed, in dissent, maintained that the Court failed to establish any exact grounds upon which to find the Champaign "released time" plan invalid. He said, in part:

. . . As I am convinced that this interpretation of the First Amendment is erroneous, I feel impelled to express the reasons for my disagreement. By directing attention to the many instances of close association of church and state in American society and by recalling that many of these relations are so much a part of our tradition and culture that they are accepted without more, this dissent may help in an appraisal of the meaning of the clause of the First Amendment concerning the establishment of religion and of the reasons which lead to the approval or disapproval of the judgment below. . . .

It seems clear to me that the "aid" referred to by the Court in the Everson case could not have been those incidental advantages that religious bodies, with other groups similarly situated, obtain as a by-product of organized society. This explains the well-known fact that all churches receive "aid" from government in the form of freedom from taxation. The Everson decision itself justified the transportation of children to church schools by New Jersey for safety reasons. It accords with *Cochran v. Louisiana State Board of Education*, 281 U. S. 370, where this Court upheld a free textbook statute of Louisiana against a charge that it aided private schools on the ground that the books were for the education of the children, not to aid religious schools. Likewise the National School Lunch Act aids all school children attending tax-exempt schools. In *Bradfield v. Roberts*, 175 U. S. 291, this Court held proper the payment of money by the Federal Government to build an addition to a hospital, chartered by individuals who were members of a Roman Catholic sisterhood, and operated under the auspices of the Roman Catholic Church. This was done over the objection that it aided the establishment of religion. While obviously in these instances the respective churches, in a certain sense, were aided, this Court has never held that such "aid" was in violation of the First or Fourteenth Amendment. . . .

. . . Whatever may be the wisdom of the arrangement as to the use of the school buildings made with the Champaign Council of Religious Education, it is clear to me that past practice shows such cooperation between the schools and a nonecclesiastical body is not forbidden by the First Amendment. . . . The prohibition of enactments respecting the establishment of religion do not bar every friendly gesture between church and state. It is not an absolute prohibition against every conceivable situation where the two may work together any more than the other provisions of the First Amendment—free speech, free press—are absolutes. . . .

This Court cannot be too cautious in upsetting practices embedded in our society by many years of experience. A state is entitled to have great leeway in its legislation when dealing with the important social problems of its population. A definite violation of legislative limits must be established. The Constitution should not be stretched to forbid national customs in the way courts act to reach arrangements to avoid federal taxation. Devotion to the great principle of religious liberty should not lead us into a rigid interpretation of the Constitutional guarantee that conflicts with accepted habits of our people. This is an instance where, for me, the history of past practices is determinative of the meaning of a constitutional clause, not a decorous introduction to the study of its text. . . . (102, pp. 478, 483-84, 486-87)

COMMENT

Not many Supreme Court decisions have inspired so much reflection and so much re-examination of the policies of public schools relating to either sectarian or nonsectarian religious instruction, yet appear to have resulted in such little action. For the specifics of the decision were so limited within a field of practice so complex that neither educators nor constitutional lawyers could derive much certainty therefrom.

There was, of course, the fact that "released time" programs according to the Champaign plan were invalid for the two-fold reason that, (1) public, tax-supported school buildings had been used for teaching religious doctrines and (2) the school system's compulsory machinery had assisted the religious Council's sectarian groups in spreading their faith. This, to repeat the Court's words, stood "squarely under the ban of the First Amendment (made applicable to the states by the Fourteenth) as we interpreted it in *Everson v. Board of Education.*" By this present holding the Court again spelled out the principle enunciated in the *Everson* case when it had said: "Neither [Congress nor the states] can pass laws which aid one religion, aid all religions, or prefer one religion over another." Thus the Court had twice held that the Constitution required not only (1) separation of church and state but of religion and state as well,[19] and likewise that (2) the First Amendment's "establishment of religion" clause must be applied equally to Congress and the states.

But for all this, the question remained whether another type of "released time" program might not be acceptable. Champaign's school board believed it would and merely modified its own program to conform with the other general type wherein religious instruction was given off the public school premises. (41, p. 298)

---

[19]This view does not seem supported by the text of the proposed First Amendment as James Madison introduced it into Congress, nor does it appear to square with Joseph Story's explanation of the "establishment of religion" clause in his *Commentaries on the Constitution.* (48, pp. 758-59)

Also, in consequence of the Court's decision, some school administrators gave sincere thought, and some others merely expedient thought, to "character education" in situations where a prevailing "released time" program appeared indefensible. Some, too, no doubt used the Court's decision as leverage with which to rid themselves of responsibility for any form of such programs. To most educators it was obvious that the Court had not excluded from the schools the study of ethics or of the value or nature of religion.

The reading of the Bible in the schools, with or without comment, was regarded by some as possibly in conflict with the Court's decision. This question of Bible reading was later taken to the Court, but jurisdiction was rejected as shown in the case next following.

Concurrently, a case testing the constitutionality of the "off-premise" type of "released time" program was also being pressed in New York. This case follows as the next but one.

AMDT. 1—RELIGION, FREE SPEECH, ETC.

An Establishment of Religion

[18] **BIBLE READING IN THE PUBLIC SCHOOLS**

DOREMUS V. BOARD OF EDUCATION

342 U. S. 429, 72 Sup. Ct. 394 (1952)

AND

GIDEONS INTERNATIONAL V. TUDOR

348 U. S. 816, 75 Sup. Ct. 25 (1954)

The Supreme Court of the United States refused on jurisdictional grounds to question the validity of a New Jersey statute which required certain Bible reading in the public schools and, thereby, sustained the right of the state to maintain the practice.

In neither the *McCollum* case (102) just discussed nor in the *Zorach* case (163), to follow, was the question of Bible reading in the public schools an issue before the Supreme Court. As shown below the case here failed of adjudication, and the matter has not again passed into the Court's view.

The *Doremus* case was initiated by a parent and taxpayer who contested, on the ground that it conflicted with the First Amendment, a New Jersey statute requiring that each public school day open with the reading of five verses from the Old Testament. The statute at the same time prohibited religious exercises other than Bible reading and repeating the Lord's Prayer in schools receiving funds appropriated for public schools. The state courts expressed uncertainty of the existence of an adjudicable issue, but did declare that the Bible reading was not in conflict with the First Amendment of the Constitution. The case was taken to the Supreme Court of the United States on an appeal which the Court rejected six-to-three. The majority held that (1) the Appellants' interest as taxpayers was in this instance not sufficient to constitute a case acceptable to the Court, and that (2) since the question of the rights of the child involved in the case had become moot through her graduation from high school, no controversy on that issue remained.

Of the latter point the Court remarked that "no decision we could render now would protect any rights she may once have had, and this Court does not sit to decide arguments after events have put them to rest." Moreover, noted the Court, the child had been under no compulsion to "accept" or respond in any way to "any dogma or creed or even to listen when the Scriptures were read." (76, p. 396)

The dissenting Justices maintained that, because the state court had heard and decided the case, the Supreme Court should accept it upon the same merits.

COMMENT

The majority on the Court in this case would probably not subscribe to an educational theory which holds that some teaching is bound to "brush off on" the student, whatever his motivation.

Had this case been accepted as a justiciable controversy, certain questions on the bounds of sectarian instruction as against merely "religious" or "ethical" instruction in the public schools might have been answered. The Court itself had afforded an opportunity for such questions by declaring in the *Everson* case that the First Amendment separated state and religion as well as state and church. The decision in the *McCollum* case had not resolved the questions—nor does the decision in the *Zorach* case which follows.

The question of Bible distribution through public schools was, however, raised very recently in New Jersey Courts. The Rutherford, New Jersey, Board of Education had accepted an offer by Gideon International to give copies of the New Testament which included the Old Testament's Psalms and Proverbs, to public school children upon written request of their parents. A Jewish parent, initially joined by a Catholic, sought an injunction against the project. This injunction, granted in lower court, was sustained by the New Jersey supreme court in December, 1953. It was the opinion of the supreme court that: "Distribution of the King James version in the public schools of this state would . . . cast aside all progress made in the United

States and throughout New Jersey in the field of religious toleration and freedom." Moreover, in refusing to grant the injunction the state supreme court said: "We would be renewing the ancient struggles among the various religious faiths to the detriment of all. This we must decline to do." (4, p. 29) The Supreme Court of the United States was asked to review this matter also, but in *Tudor v. Board of Education* (150 and 89) certiorari was denied in 1954 and this case likewise was left in the hands of New Jersey's courts.

AMDT. 1—RELIGION, FREE SPEECH, ETC.
An Establishment of Religion

[19] **RELEASED TIME FOR OFF-PREMISE RELIGIOUS INSTRUCTION**

ZORACH V. CLAUSON

343 U. S. 306, 72 Sup. Ct. 679 (1952)

The Supreme Court of the United States upheld a New York statute and the action of the school board of the City of New York in providing a "released time" program for religious instruction during public school hours but away from public school buildings as not being in conflict with the First Amendment to the Federal Constitution.

Within a few weeks following its rejection of appeal in the *Doremus* case on Bible reading in the schools the Court returned to a religious issue similar to one previously considered. Now, it was to uphold a type of "released time" program more common than the Champaign plan which had been declared unconstitutional in the *McCollum* case four years earlier.

The majority opinion here in the *Zorach* case includes a digest of arguments by certain citizens in New York who sought to show that the plan prevailing there, as well as that dealt with in Illinois, was unconstitutional. The Court recorded the following:

. . . [Tessim Zorach and Esta Gluck] who are tax-payers and residents of New York City and whose children attend its public schools, challenge the present law, contending it is in essence not different from the one involved in the *McCollum* case. Their argument, stated elaborately in various ways, reduces itself to this: the weight and influence of the school is put behind a program for religious instruction; public school teachers police it, keeping tab on students who are released; the classroom activities come to a halt while the students who are released for religious instruction are on leave; the school is a crutch on which the churches are leaning for support in their religious training; without the cooperation of the schools this "released time" program, like the one in the *McCollum* case, would be futile and ineffective. . . . (163, pp. 680-82)

This argument had, of course, been presented earlier to the New York Court of Appeals. On July 11, 1951, that court had sustained the "released time" plan in question and had distinguished it from the one invalidated by the *McCollum* case by declaring:

. . . In the New York City program there is neither supervision nor approval of religious teachers and no solicitation of pupils or distribution of cards. The religious instruction must be outside the school building and grounds. There must be no announcement of any kind in the public schools relative to the program and no comment by any principal or teacher on the attendance or non-attendance of any pupil upon religious instruction. All that the school does besides excusing the pupil is to keep a record—which is not available for any other purpose—in order to see that the excuses are not taken advantage of and the school deceived, which is, of course, the same procedure the school would take in respect of absence for any other reason. . . . (48, p. 762)

The decision by the New York Court was taken to the Supreme Court of the United States on appeal and the state court was sustained, six-to-three. Justice Douglas said for the Court, in part:

. . . Our problem reduces itself to whether New York by this system has either prohibited the "free exercise" of religion or has made a law "respecting an establishment of religion" within the meaning of the First Amendment.

It takes obtuse reasoning to inject any issue of the "free exercise" of religion into the present case. No one is forced to go to the religious classroom and no religious exercise or instruction is brought to the classrooms of the public schools. A student need not take religious education. He is left to his own desires as to the manner or time of his religious devotions, if any.

There is a suggestion that the system involves the use of coercion to get public school students into religious classrooms. There is no evidence in the record before us that supports that conclusion. The present record indeed tells us that the school authorities are neutral in this regard and do no more than release students whose parents so request. If in fact coercion were used, if it were established that any one or more teachers were using their office to persuade or force students to take the religious instruction, a wholly different case would be presented. Hence we put aside that claim of coercion both as respects the "free exercise" of religion and "an establishment of religion" within the meaning of the First Amendment.

Moreover, apart from that claim of coercion, we do not see how New York by this type of "released time" program has made a law respecting an establishment of religion within the meaning of the First Amendment. There is much talk of the separation of Church and State in the history of the Bill of Rights and in the decisions clustering around the First Amendment. . . . There cannot be the slightest doubt that the First Amendment reflects the philosophy that Church and State should be separated. And so far as interference with the "free exercise" of religion and an "establishment" of religion are concerned, the separation must be complete and unequivocal. The First Amendment within the scope of its coverage permits no exception; the prohibition is absolute. The First Amendment, however, does not say that in every and all respects there shall be a separation of Church and State. Rather, it studiously defines the main, the specific ways, in which there shall be no concert or union or dependency one on the other. That is the common sense of the matter. Otherwise the state and religion would be aliens to each other—

hostile, suspicious, and even unfriendly. Churches could not be required to pay even property taxes. Municipalities would not be permitted to render police or fire protection to religious groups. Policemen who helped parishioners into their places of worship would violate the Constitution. Prayers in our legislative halls; the appeals to the Almighty in the messages of the Chief Executive; the proclamation making Thanksgiving Day a holiday; "so help me God" in our courtroom oaths—these and all other references to the Almighty that run through our laws, our public rituals, our ceremonies would be flouting the First Amendment. A fastidious atheist or agnostic could even object to the supplication with which the Court opens each session: "God save the United States and this Honorable Court."

We would have to press the concept of separation of Church and State to these extremes to condemn the present law on constitutional grounds. The nullification of this law would have wide and profound effects. A Catholic student applies to his teacher for permission to leave the school during hours on a Holy Day of Obligation to attend a mass. A Jewish student asks his teacher for permission to be excused for Yom Kippur. A Protestant wants the afternoon off for a family baptismal ceremony. In each case the teacher, in order to make sure the student is not a truant, goes further and requires a report from the priest, the rabbi, or the minister. The teacher in other words cooperates in a religious program to the extent of making it possible for her students to participate in it. Whether she does it occasionally for a few students, regularly for one, or pursuant to a systematized program designed to further the religious needs of all the students does not alter the character of the act.

We are a religious people whose institutions presuppose a Supreme Being. We guarantee the freedom to worship as one chooses. We make room for as wide a variety of beliefs and creeds as the spiritual needs of man deem necessary. We sponsor an attitude on the part of government that shows no partiality to any one group and that lets each flourish according to the zeal of its adherents and the appeal of its dogma. When the state encourages religious instruction or cooperates with religious authorities by adjusting the schedule of public events to sectarian needs, it follows the best of our traditions. For it then respects the religious nature of our people and accommodates the public service to their spiritual needs. To hold that it may not would be to find in the Constitution a requirement that the government show a callous indifference to religious groups. That would be preferring those who believe in no religion over those who do believe. Government may not finance religious groups nor undertake religious instruction nor blend secular and sectarian education or use secular institutions to force one or some religion on any person. But we find no constitutional requirement which makes it necessary for government to be hostile to religion and to throw its weight against efforts to widen the effective scope of religious influence. The government must be neutral when it comes to competition between sects. It may not thrust any sect on any person. It may not make a religious observance compulsory. It may not coerce anyone to attend church, to observe a religious holiday, or to take religious instruction. But it can close its doors or suspend its operations as to those who want to repair to their religious santcuary for worship or instruction. No more than that is undertaken here.

This program may be unwise and improvident from an educational or a community viewpoint. That appeal is made to us on a theory, previously advanced, that each case must be decided on the basis of "our own pre-possessions". . . . Our individual preferences, however, are not the constitutional standard. The constitutional standard is the separation of Church and State. The problem, like many problems in constitutional law, is one of degree. . . .

In the *McCollum* case the classrooms were used for religious instruction and the force of public school was used to promote that instruction. Here, as we have said, the public schools do no more than accommodate their schedules to a program of outside religious instruction. We follow the *McCollum* case. But we cannot expand it to cover the present released time program unless separation of Church and State means that public institutions can make no adjustments of their schedules to accommodate the religious needs of the people. We cannot read into the Bill of Rights such a philosophy of hostility to religion.

Affirmed. (163, pp. 682-85)

Justice Black, Justice Frankfurter, and Justice Jackson each delivered a separate dissenting opinion. Justice Black asserted that he could "see no significant difference between the invalid Illinois system and that of New York," and added that "except for the use of the school building in Illinois there is no difference between the systems which I consider even worthy of mention." He said further that in the *McCollum* case the Court had found it unconstitutional for the schools to "manipulate the compelled classroom hours of its compulsory school machinery so as to channel children into sectarian classes." Yet, by its present decision, "that is exactly what the Court holds New York can do." He went on to hint that the Court's faith in the enduring value of the wall between Church and State, expressed as recently as the *Everson* and *McCollum* decisions, already needed reaffirmation, then continued: (Justice Black, dissenting)

. . . Difficulty of decision in the hypothetical situations mentioned by the Court, but not now before us, should not confuse the issues in this case. Here the sole question is whether New York can use its compulsory education laws to help religious sects get attendants presumably too unenthusiastic to go unless moved to do so by the pressure of this state machinery. That this is the plan, purpose, design, and consequence of the New York program cannot be denied. The state thus makes religious sects beneficiaries of its power to compel children to attend secular schools. Any use of such coercive power by the state to help or hinder some religious sects or to prefer all religious sects over nonbelievers or vice versa is just what I think the First Amendment forbids. In considering whether a state has entered this forbidden field the question is not whether it has entered too far but whether it has entered at all. New York is manipulating its compulsory education laws to help religious sects get pupils. This is not separation but combination of Church and State.

The Court's validation of the New York system rests in part on its statement that Americans are "a religious people whose institutions presuppose a Supreme Being." This was at least as true when the First Amendment was adopted; and it was just as true when eight justices of this Court invalidated the released time system in *McCollum* on the premise that a state can no more "aid all religions" than it can aid one. It was precisely because Eighteenth Century Americans were a religious people divided into many fighting sects that we were given the constitutional mandate to keep church and state completely separate. Colonial history had already shown that, here as elsewhere, zealous sectarians entrusted with governmental power to further their causes, would sometimes torture, maim, and kill those they branded "heretics", "atheists", or "agnostics". The First Amendment was therefore to insure that no one powerful sect or combination of sects could use political or governmental power to punish dissenters whom they could not convert to their faith. Now, as then, it is only by wholly isolating the state from the religious sphere and compelling it to be completely neutral, that the freedom of each and every denomination and of all nonbelievers can be maintained. It is this neutrality the Court abandons today when it treats New York's coercive system as a program which *merely* "encourages religious instruction or cooperates with religious authorities". The abandonment is all the more dangerous to liberty because of the Court's legal exaltation of the orthodox and its derogation of unbelievers.

Under out system of religious freedom, people have gone to their religious sanctuaries not because they feared the law but because they loved their God. The choice of all has been as free as the choice of those who answered the call to worship moved only by the music of the old Sunday morning church bells. The spiritual mind of man has thus been free to believe, disbelieve, or doubt, without repression, great or small, by the heavy hand of government. Statutes authorizing such repression have been stricken. Before today, our judicial opinions have refrained from drawing invidious distinctions between those who believe in no religion and those who do believe. The First Amendment has lost much if the religious follower and the atheist are no longer to be judicially regarded as entitled to equal justice under law.

State help to religion injects political and party prejudices into a holy field. It too often substitutes force for prayer, hate for love, and persecution for persuasion. Government should not be allowed, under cover of the soft euphemism of "co-operation," to steal into the sacred area of religious choice. (163, pp. 686-87)

Justice Frankfurter writes almost disdainfully of the Court's opinion. He is in particular agreement with Justice Jackson whose dissent follows his, and also with Justice Black. He says, in part:

The Court tells us that in the maintenance of its public schools, "[The State government] can close its doors or suspend its operations" so that its citizens may be free for religious devotions or instruction. If that were the issue, it would not rise to the dignity of a constitutional controversy. Of course a State may provide that the classes in its schools shall be dismissed, for any reason, or no reason, on fixed days, or for special occasions. The essence of this case is that the school system did not "close its doors" and did not "suspend its operations". There is all the difference in the world between letting the children out of school and letting some of them out of school into religious classes. If every one is free to make what use he will of time wholly unconnected from schooling required by law—those who wish sectarian instruction devoting it to that purpose, those who have ethical instruction at home, to that, those who study music, to that—then of course there is no conflict with the Fourteenth Amendment.

The pith of the case is that formalized religious instruction is substituted for other school activity which those who do not participate in the released-time program are compelled to attend. The school system is very much in operation during this kind of released time. If its doors are closed, they are closed upon those students who do not attend the religious instruction in order to keep them within the school. That is the very thing which raises the constitutional issue. It is not met by disregarding it. Failure to discuss this issue does not take it out of the case. . . .

The result in the *McCollum* case, 333 U. S. 203, was based on principles that received unanimous acceptance by this Court, barring only a single vote. I agree with Mr. Justice Black that those principles are disregarded in reaching the result in this case. Happily they are not disavowed by the Court. From this I draw the hope that in future variations of the problem which are bound to come here, these principles may again be honored in the observance.

The deeply divisive controversy aroused by the attempts to secure public school pupils for sectarian instruction would promptly end if the advocates of such instruction were content to have the school "close its doors or suspend operations"—that is, dismiss classes in their entirety, without discrimination—instead of seeking to use the public schools as the instrument for security of attendance at denominational classes. The unwillingness of the promoters of this movement to dispense with such use of the public schools betrays a surprising want of confidence in the inherent power of the various faiths to draw children to outside sectarian classes—an attitude that hardly reflects the faith of the greatest religious spirits. (163, pp. 687-88)

If Justice Frankfurter's dissent approached the disdainful, that of Justice Jackson got even closer to the sarcastic. His brief dissent is quoted in its entirety:

This released time program is founded upon a use of the State's power of coercion, which, for me, determines its unconstitutionality. Stripped to its essentials, the plan has two stages, first, that the State compel each student to yield a large part of his time for public secular education and, second, that some of it be "released" to him on condition that he devote it to sectarian religious purposes.

No one suggests that the Constitution would permit the State directly to require this "released time" to be spent "under the control of a duly constituted religious body". This program accomplishes that forbidden result by indirection. If public education were taking so much of the pupils' time as to injure the public or the student's welfare by encroaching upon their religious opportunity, simply shortening everyone's school day would facilitate voluntary and optional attendance at Church classes. But that suggestion is rejected upon the ground that if they are made free many students will not go to the Church. Hence, they must be deprived of freedom for this period, with Church attendance put to them as one of the two permissible ways of using it.

The greater effectiveness of this system over voluntary attendance after school hours is due to the truant officer who, if the youngster fails to go to the Church school, dogs him back to the public schoolroom. Here schooling is more or less suspended during the "released time" so the nonreligious attendants will not forge ahead of the churchgoing absentees. But it serves as a temporary jail for a pupil who will not go to Church. It takes more subtlety of mind than I possess to deny that this is governmental constraint in support of religion. It is as unconstitutional, in my view, when exerted by indirection as when exercised forthrightly.

As one whose children, as a matter of free choice, have been sent to privately supported Church schools, I may challenge the Court's suggestion that opposition to this plan can only be anti-religious, atheistic, or agnostic. My evangelistic brethren confuse an objection to compulsion with an objection to religion. It is possible to hold a faith with enough confidence to believe that what should be rendered to God does not need to be decided and collected by Caesar.

The day that this country ceases to be free for irreligion it will cease to be free for religion—except for the sect that can win political power. The same epithetical jurisprudence used by the Court today to beat down those who oppose pressuring children into some religion can devise as good epithets tomorrow against those who object to pressuring them into a favored religion. And, after all, if we concede to the State power and wisdom to single out "duly constituted religious" bodies as exclusive alternates for compulsory secular instruction, it would be logical to also uphold the power and wisdom to choose the true faith among those "duly constituted". We start down a rough road when we begin to mix compulsory public education with compulsory godliness.

A number of Justices just short of a majority of the majority that promulgates today's passionate dialectics joined in answering them in *Illinois ex rel. McCollum v. Board of Education*, 333 U. S. 203. The distinction attempted between that case and this is trivial, almost to the point of cynicism, magnifying its nonessential details and disparaging compulsion which was the underlying reason for invalidity. A reading of the Court's opinion in that case along with its opinion in this case will show such difference of overtones and undertones as to make clear that the *McCollum* case has passed like a storm in a teacup. The wall which the Court was professing to erect between Church and State has become even more warped and twisted than I expected. Today's judgment will be more interesting to students of psychology and of the judicial processes than to students of constitutional law. (163, p. 689)

COMMENT

One cannot but be reminded by this case of Justice Jackson's remark concerning the disparity between the principles enunciated and the decision handed down in the *Everson* case (77) five years earlier. He had at that time compared the majority on the Court with Byron's Julia who "Whispering 'I will ne'er consent':—consented."

This case did remove from the minds of authorities responsible for public school "released time" programs much of the uncertainty raised by the Court's decision in the *McCollum* case (102). (See comment following the case.) School authorities were assured that they need only accord their law and program to the New York plan.

The gist of the Court's expressed attitude toward public school participation with sectarian religious instruction is, in simplest terms, that (1) where done in public schools and with particular administrative cooperation it amounts to an unconstitutional establishment of religion, but that (2) where done outside the school and with only the necessary minimum of administrative cooperation it does not amount to an establishment of religion.

As has been noted in connection with the *Doremus* case (76) the Court has never passed upon the question of Bible reading or of "just religion" in the public schools. But the fact that the *Doremus* case and the *Tudor* case (150 and 89) have lately appeared in the New Jersey courts[20] lends respectability to the speculation that it may do so. With the two major versions of the Bible—the Protestant King James and the Catholic Douay—presenting some substantial differences, a contentious partisan of one or the other of the two great branches of Western Christendom may discover substantial aggrievement through his children. Regardless of the version, an agnostic or a Mormon or a Jew could likewise be aggrieved.

The bitterness centering around the question of religion in the schools may be exemplified by the reflection it appears to have cast through the opinions in this case.

---

[20]See comment on *Doremus* case, preceding this case.

10

LOYALTY TESTS, LOYALTY OATHS, AND FREEDOM OF EXPRESSION

AMDT. 1—RELIGION, FREE SPEECH, ETC.
Freedom of Speech and of Peaceable
Assembly (Loyalty Tests)
AMDT. 14—RIGHTS OF CITIZENS
Sec.   1—Due Process of Law

[20] TEACHERS' FREEDOM OF SPEECH AND
ANTI-SUBVERSIVE LEGISLATION

ADLER V. BOARD OF EDUCATION
342 U. S. 485, 72 Sup. Ct. 380 (1952)

The Supreme Court of the United States sustained as in violation of no rule, constitutional or otherwise, New York's Civil Service Law and "Feinberg Law" which make ineligible for employment in the public schools of the state any member of an organization advocating overthrow of the government by unlawful means.

Perhaps no guarantee in the Bill of Rights is taken more as a matter of course than is freedom of speech. Yet this safeguard was not in the proposed draft submitted by Madison to the first Congress, possibly because it had not yet been firmly posited as a fundamental freedom. No state constitution included the guarantee in 1789 when the proposal for a Bill of Rights in the federal Constitution was submitted to the House. (50, pp. 84-85) But the House committee did add free-

134

dom of speech to Madison's proposed freedom of the press, and since then Americans have come to claim more of it than they may actually possess.

The Senate in that first Congress made another significant change in Madison's draft. He had proposed that the Bill of Rights restrict the states as well as Congress, but the Senate, upon the objection that the federal government was already thought by many to be interfering with the states too much, limited the application of the Bill of Rights to Congress alone.

However, in 1833, while John Marshall was still Chief Justice, the Supreme Court was faced by a contender who asserted that in the Bill of Rights the Fifth Amendment, "declares principles which regulate the legislation of the states, for the protection of the people in each and all the states." To this the Court replied: "These amendments contain no expression indicating an intention to apply them to the state governments. This court cannot so apply them." (57, p. 250)

There, so far as the Court was concerned, the matter rested for nearly a century. But, meanwhile, following proclamation of the Fourteenth Amendment in 1868, persistent attempts were made to persuade the Court to identify the personal rights in the Bill of Rights with the liberty which states may not take away without due process of law. The Court remained adamant. Then, in 1925, in *Gitlow v. New York* (92), speaking quite casually and almost as if reiterating doctrine long established, the Court while upholding a conviction for criminal anarchy, remarked: "For present purposes we may and do assume that freedom of speech and of the press—which are protected by the First Amendment from abridgement by Congress—are among the fundamental personal rights and 'liberties' protected by the due process clause of the Fourteenth Amendment from impairment by the states." (92, p. 630) This dictum became accepted doctrine in 1927 when in *Fiske v. Kansas* (81) the Court invalidated an antisubversive statute on the ground that it abridged freedom of speech contrary to the "due process" clause of the Fourteenth Amendment.[21]

Again, in 1931, the Court spoke to the same effect against a California law which prohibited display of a red flag. A Miss Yetta Stromberg, leader in a youth camp, offended the statute by leading her group

---

[21]In continuing the process, freedom of religion, *Cantwell v. Connecticut* (1940) (66); freedom of the press, *Near v. Minnesota* (1931) (120); freedom of assembly, *DeJonge v. Oregon* (1937) (74); and the right of assistance of counsel, *Powell v. Alabama* (1932) (130); have likewise been brought under the protection of the Fourteenth Amendment. *Palko v. Connecticut* (1937) (122), contains an excellent discussion of the relationship of the "due process" clause of the Fourteenth Amendment to the guarantees in the first eight amendments.

in a salute to the flag of the Union of Soviet Socialist Republics, while reciting a pledge of her own composition: "To the Workers' Flag, and to the cause for which it stands; one aim throughout our lives, freedom for the working class." Her California conviction was reversed, not unanimously, and the Court asserted categorically: "The conception of liberty under the due process clause of the Fourteenth Amendment embraces free speech." (145)

The *Stromberg* case is, of course, reminiscent of the two flag-salute cases discussed earlier as religious issues in the schools, but the decision in it, and in the *Gitlow* and *Fiske* cases just mentioned, would seem worth remembering while the *Adler* (53) and *Wieman* (160) cases involving teachers' loyalty are considered hereafter.

But before those two cases are discussed, a certain theme with regard to freedom of speech may deserve mention. It harks back to 1925 and the *Gitlow* case which, as has been noted, involved violation of a New York statute directed at criminal anarchy. The question was one where, in the words of the Court, "the legislative body has previously determined the danger of substantive evil arising from utterances of a specified character," i.e., advocating the overthrow of organized government by force or violence. (92, pp. 631-32)

Justice Holmes, joined by Justice Brandeis, there wrote a dissent notable for its fatalism concerning freedom of speech. He said:

. . . If what I think is the correct test is applied, it is manifest that there was no present danger of an attempt to overthrow the government by force on the part of the admittedly small minority who shared the defendant's views. It is said that this Manifesto was more than a theory, that it was an incitement. Every idea is an incitement. It offers itself for belief, and, if believed, it is acted upon unless some other belief outweighs it, or some failure of energy stifles the movement at its birth. The only difference between the expression of an opinion and an incitement in the narrower sense is the speaker's enthusiasm for the result. Eloquence may set fire to reason. But whatever may be thought of the redundant discourse before us, it has no chance of starting a present conflagration. If, in the long run, the beliefs expressed in proletarian dictatorship are destined to be accepted by the dominant forces of the community, the only meaning of free speech is that they should be given their chance and have their way. . . . (92, p. 632)

Possibly, in writing these words the Justice hardly envisaged the incendiarism which some states came to feel was practiced so artfully upon the immature in classrooms and which caused those states to react with provisions for teachers' loyalty tests, particularly just following each of the two World Wars.

At the same time Congress also required loyalty tests as, for example, in the Taft-Hartley Act of 1947.

The recent state legislation has resulted in three significant cases before the Supreme Court. In the first of these, *Garner v. Los Angeles Board of Public Works* (87), the Court sustained the constitutionality of a municipal ordinance requiring a loyalty oath of employees and barring from employment those who advise, teach, or advocate the violent overthrow of the government, or those who are or become members of any group or organization doing so. This decision was cited by the Court in both of the "education cases" to follow.

The case of *Adler v. Board of Education* arose from a challenge of New York legislation designed to keep subversive influences out of schools. The so-called Feinberg law on which the Court ruled dates from 1949, but it rests in turn upon certain older laws.

In 1917, the state legislature provided for the removal of superintendents, teachers and employees in any school district "for the utterance of any treasonable or seditious word or words or the doing of any treasonable or seditious act or acts while holding such positions." Twelve years later, in 1929, the state supplemented the foregoing with a provision for disqualifying from public employment those who advise, advocate, or teach the overthrow of the government of the United States or any of its subdivisions by violent means, or who belong to organizations doing so. This law provided that those affected could demand hearings. (53, pp. 383-84)

Apparently not satisfied with the operation of this legislation, the state supplemented it with the Feinberg law in 1949. The rather long preamble shows clearly the thought of the legislature. It reads:

> The legislature hereby finds and declares that there is a common report that members of subversive groups, and particularly of affiliated organizations, have infiltrated into public employment in the public schools of the state. . . . The consequence of any such infiltration into the public schools is that subversive propaganda can be disseminated among children of tender years by those who teach them and to whom the children look for guidance, authority and leadership.
>
> The legislature finds that members of such groups frequently use their office or position to advocate and teach subversive doctrines. The legislature finds that members of such groups are frequently bound by an oath, agreement, pledge or understanding to follow, advocate and teach a prescribed party line or group dogma or doctrine without regard to truth or free inquiry. The legislature finds that such dissemination of propaganda may be and frequently is sufficiently subtle to escape detection in the classroom. . . .
>
> . . . The legislature deplores the failure heretofore to prevent such infiltration, which threatens dangerously to become a commonplace in our schools. To this end, the board of regents, which is charged primarily with the responsibility of supervising the public school systems in the state, should be admonished and directed to take affirmative action to meet this grave menace and to report thereon regularly to the state legislature. (53, pp. 383-84)

The text of the Feinberg law is in three parts. The first part charges the board of regents to enforce the law through necessary rules and regulations.

The second part requires that the board make a list of organizations which, after inquiry, notice and hearing, are held to be subversive. The board is authorized to use any similar list established under federal law, and the board is required to make membership in any organization included in either the state or federal lists prima facie evidence for barring or dismissing an individual from employment.

The third part requires of the board of regents an annual report to the legislature on the measures taken under the law. (53, pp. 383-84)

Certainly this was legislation which would find challengers among teachers. One Irving Adler, with others, brought an action in the Kings County supreme court to have the law declared invalid. That court granted the injunction sought. On appeal by the board of regents the state supreme court, appellate division, reversed the lower court, and this decision was subsequently affirmed by the New York court of appeals. Thereupon Adler appealed to the Supreme Court of the United States. He contended that the Feinberg law and the board's rules under it abridged certain rights protected by the First Amendment.

In reply, Justice Minton, speaking for the majority in a Court divided six-to-three, said in part:

It is first argued that the Feinberg Law and the rules promulgated thereunder constitute an abridgment of the freedom of speech and assembly of persons employed or seeking employment in the public schools of the State of New York.

It is clear that such persons have the right under our law to assemble, speak, think and believe as they will. . . . It is equally clear that they have no right to work for the state in the school system on their own terms. . . . They may work for the school system upon the reasonable terms laid down by the proper authorities of New York. If they do not choose to work on such terms, they are at liberty to retain their beliefs and associations and go elsewhere. Has the State thus deprived them of any right to free speech or assembly? We think not. Such persons are or may be denied, under the statutes in question, the privilege of working for the school system of the State of New York because, first, of their advocacy of the overthrow of the government by force or violence, or, secondly, by unexplained membership in an organization found by the school authorities, after notice and hearing, to teach and advocate the overthrow of the government by force or violence, and known by such persons to have such purpose.

The constitutionality of the first proposition is not questioned here. . . .

As to the second, it is rather subtly suggested that we should not follow our recent decision in Garner v. Board of Public Works of Los Angeles, 341 U. S. 716, 71 S. Ct. 909, 95 L. Ed. 1317. We there said: "We think that a municipal employer is not disabled because it is an agency of the state from inquiring of its employees as to matters that may prove relevant to their fitness and suitability for the public service. Past conduct may well relate to present fitness; past loyalty may have a reasonable relationship to present and future trust. Both are commonly inquired into in determining fitness for both high and low positions in private industry and are not less relevant in public employment." 341 U. S. at page 720, 71 S. Ct. at page 912.

We adhere to that case. A teacher works in a sensitive area in a schoolroom. There he shapes the attitude of young minds towards the society in which they live. In this, the state has a vital concern. It must preserve the integrity of the schools. That the school authorities have the right and the duty to screen the officials, teachers, and employees as to their fitness to maintain the integrity of the school as a part of ordered society, cannot be doubted. One's associates, past and present, as well as one's conduct, may properly be considered in determining fitness and loyalty. From time immemorial, one's reputation has been determined in part by the company he keeps. In the employment of officials and teachers of the school system, the state may very properly inquire into the company they keep, and we know of no rule, constitutional or otherwise, that prevents the state, when determining the fitness and loyalty of such persons, from considering the organizations and persons with whom they associate.

If, under the procedure set up in the New York law, a person is found to be unfit and is disqualified from employment in the public school system because of membership in a listed organization, he is not thereby denied the right of free speech and assembly. His freedom of choice between membership in the organization and employment in the school system might be limited, but not his freedom of speech or assembly, except in the remote sense that limitation is inherent in every choice. Certainly such limitation is not one the state may not make in the exercise of its police power to protect the schools from pollution and thereby to defend its own existence.

It is next argued by appellants that the provision in Section 3022 directing the Board of Regents to provide in rules and regulations that membership in any organization listed by the Board after notice and hearing, with provisions for review in accordance with the statute, shall constitute prima facie evidence of disqualification, denies due process, because the fact found bears no relation to the fact presumed. In other words, from the fact found that the organization was one that advocated the overthrow of government by unlawful means and that the person employed or to be employed was a member of the organization and knew of its purpose, to presume that such member is disqualified for employment is so unreasonable as to be a denial of due process of law. We do not agree.

"The law of evidence is full of presumptions either of fact or law. The former are, of course, disputable, and the strength of any inference of one fact from proof of another depends upon the generality of the experience upon which it is founded. . . .

"Legislation providing that proof of one fact shall constitute *prima facie* evidence of the main fact in issue is but to enact a rule of evidence, and quite within the general power of government. Statutes, national and state, dealing with such methods of proof in both civil and criminal cases, abounds, and the decisions upholding them are numerous." . . .

Membership in a listed organization found to be within the statute and known by the member to be within the statute is a legislative finding that the member by his membership supports the thing the organization stands for, namely, the overthrow of government by unlawful means. We cannot say that such a finding is contrary to fact or that "generality of experience" points to a different conclusion. Disqualification follows therefore as a reasonable presumption from such membership and support. Nor is there here a problem of procedural due process. The presumption is not conclusive but arises only in a hearing where the person against whom it may arise has full opportunity to rebut it. . . .

Without raising in the complaint or in the proceedings in the lower courts the question of the constitutionality of Section 2031 of the Education Law of New York, appellants urge here for the first time that this section is unconstitutionally vague. The question is not before us. We will not pass upon the constitutionality of a state statute before the state courts have had an opportunity to do so. . . .

It is also suggested that the use of the word "subversive" is vague and indefinite. But the word is first used in Section 1 of the Feinberg Law, which is the preamble of the Act, and not in a definitive part thereof. When used in subdivision 2 of Section 3022, the word has a very definite meaning, namely, an organization that teaches and advocates the overthrow of government by force or violence.

We find no constitutional infirmity in Section 12-a of the Civil Service Law of New York or in the Feinberg Law which implemented it, and the judgment is affirmed. (53, pp. 384-87)

Justice Frankfurter wrote a dissent based on jurisdictional grounds. He said, in part:

We are asked to pass on a scheme to counteract what are currently called "subversive" influences in the public school system of New York. The scheme is formulated partly in statutes and partly in administrative regulations, but all of it is still an unfinished blueprint. We are asked to adjudicate claims against its constitutionality before the scheme has been put into operation, before the limits that it imposes upon free inquiry and association, the scope of scrutiny that it sanctions, and the procedural safeguards that will be found to be implied for its enforcement have been authoritatively defined. I think we should adhere to the teaching of this Court's history to avoid constitutional adjudications on merely abstract or speculative issues and to base them on the concreteness afforded by an actual, present, defined controversy, appropriate for judicial judgment, between adversaries immediately affected by it. In accordance with the settled limits upon our jurisdiction. I would dismiss this appeal. . . . (53, p. 387)

Justice Black also dissented, saying in part:

While I fully agree with the dissent of Mr. Justice DOUGLAS [which follows], the importance of his holding prompts me to add these thoughts.

This is another of those rapidly multiplying legislative enactments which make it dangerous—this time for school teachers—to think or say anything except what a transient majority happen to approve at the moment. Basically these laws rest on the belief that government should supervise and limit the flow of ideas into the minds of men. The tendency of such governmental policy is to mould people into a common intellectual pattern. Quite a different governmental policy rests on the belief that government should leave the mind and spirit of man absolutely free. Such a governmental policy encourages varied intellectual outlooks in the belief that the best views will prevail. This policy of freedom is in my judgment embodied in the First Amendment and made applicable to the states by the Fourteenth. Because of this policy public officials cannot be constitutionally vested with powers to select the ideas people can think about, censor the public views they can express, or choose the persons or groups people can associate with. Public officials with such powers are not public servants; they are public masters.

I dissent from the Court's judgment sustaining this law which effectively penalizes school teachers for their thoughts and their associates. (53, pp. 387-92)

Like Justice Black, Justice Douglas attacked the merits of the majority decision. He said:

I have not been able to accept the recent doctrine that a citizen who enters the public service can be forced to sacrifice his civil rights. I cannot for example find in our constitutional scheme the power of a state to place its employees in the category of second-class citizens by denying them freedom of thought and expression. The Constitution guarantees freedom of thought and expression to everyone in our society. All are entitled to it; and none needs it more than the teacher.

The public school is in most respects the cradle of our democracy. The increasing role of the public school is seized upon by proponents of the type of legislation represented by New York's Feinberg law as proof of the importance and need for keeping the school free of "subversive influences". But that is to misconceive the effect of this type of legislation. Indeed the impact of this kind of censorship on the public school system illustrates the high purpose of the First Amendment in freeing speech and thought from censorship.

The present law proceeds on a principle repugnant to our society—guilt by association. A teacher is disqualified because of her membership in an organization found to be "subversive". The finding as to the "subversive" character of the organization is made in a proceeding to which the teacher is not a party and in which it is not clear that she may even be heard. To be sure, she may have a hearing when charges of disloyalty are leveled against her. But in that hearing the finding as to the "subversive" character of the organization apparently may not be reopened in order to allow her to show the truth of the matter. The irrebuttable charge that the organization is "subversive" therefore hangs as an ominous cloud over her own hearing. The mere fact of membership in the organization raises a *prima facie* case of her own guilt. She may, it is said, show her innocence. But innocence in this case turns on knowledge; and when the witch hunt is on, one who must rely on ignorance leans on a feeble reed.

The very threat of such a procedure is certain to raise havoc with academic freedom. Youthful indiscretions, mistaken causes, misguided enthusiasms—all long forgotten—become the ghosts of a harrowing present. Any organization committed to a liberal cause, any group organized to revolt against an hysterical trend, any committee launched to sponsor an unpopular program becomes suspect. These are the organizations into which Communists often infiltrate. Their presence infects the whole, even though the project was not conceived in sin. A teacher caught in that mesh is almost certain to stand condemned. Fearing condemnation, she will tend to shrink from any association that stirs controversy. In that manner freedom of expression will be stifled.

But that is only part of it. Once a teacher's connections with a listed organization is shown, her views become subject to scrutiny to determine whether her membership in the organization is innocent or, if she was formerly a member, whether she has *bona fide* abandoned her membership.

The law inevitably turns the school system into a spying project. Regular loyalty reports on the teachers must be made out. The principals become detectives; the students, the parents, the community become informers. Ears are cocked for tell-tale signs of disloyalty. The prejudices of the community come into play in searching out the disloyal. This is not the usual type of supervision which checks a teacher's competency; it is a system which searches for hidden meanings in a teacher's utterances.

What was the significance of the reference of the art teacher to socialism? Why was the history teacher so openly hostile to Franco Spain? Who hear overtones of revolution in the English teacher's discussion of the Grapes of Wrath? What was behind the praise of Soviet progress in metallurgy in the chemistry class? Was it not "subversive" for the teacher to cast doubt on the wisdom of the venture in Korea?

What happens under this law is typical of what happens in a police state. Teachers are under constant surveillance; their pasts are combed for signs of disloyalty; their utterances are watched for clues to dangerous thoughts. A pall is cast over the classrooms. There can be no real academic freedom in that environment. Where suspicion fills the air and holds scholars in line for fear of their jobs, there can be no exercise of the free intellect. Supineness and dogmatism take the place of inquiry. A "party line"—as dangerous as the "party line" of the Communists—lays hold. It is the "party line" of the orthodox view, of the conventional thought, of the accepted approach. A problem can no longer be pursued with impunity to its edges. Fear stalks the classroom. The teacher is no longer a stimulant to adventurous thinking; she becomes instead a pipeline for safe and sound information. A deadening dogma takes the place of free inquiry. Instruction tends to become sterile; pursuit of knowledge is discouraged; discussion often leaves off where it should begin.

This, I think, is what happens when a censor looks over a teacher's shoulder. This system of spying and surveillance with its accompanying reports and trials cannot go hand in hand with academic freedom. It produces standardized thought, not the pursuit of truth. Yet it was the pursuit of truth which the First Amendment was designed to protect. A system which directly or inevitably has that effect is alien to our system and should be struck down. Its survival is a real threat to our way of life. We need be bold and adventuresome in our thinking to survive. A school system producing students trained as robots threatens to rob a generation of the versatility that has been perhaps our greatest distinction. The Framers knew the danger of dogmatism; they also knew the strength that comes when the mind is free, when ideas may be pursued wherever they lead. We forget these teachings of the First Amendment when we sustain this law.

Of course the school systems of the country need not become cells for Communist activities; and the classrooms need not become forums for propagandizing the Marxist creed. But the guilt of the teacher should turn on overt acts. So long as she is a law-abiding citizen, so long as her performance within the public school system meets professional standards, her private life, her political philosophy, her social creed should not be the cause of reprisals against her. (53, pp. 392-94)

COMMENT   (See also comment with the next case following.)

As Justice Frankfurter insisted, this case was on speculative issues only, and not in response to any concrete situation in which a teacher had been removed by the board of regents. Had a teacher actually been removed, and had the teacher attacked the constitutionality of such removal, the holding of the Court could possibly have been different.

The decision, by the abstract nature of the facts upon which it was based, probably did not clearly either advance or retard attempts at establishing security through such legislation as New York's Feinberg law.

The following case was an actual controversy "between adversaries immediately affected." It should be noted, however, that in neither of the cases did the Court have under consideration the constitutionality of loyalty oaths per se.

AMDT. 1—RELIGION, FREE SPEECH, ETC.
Freedom of Speech (Loyalty Tests)
AMDT. 14—RIGHTS OF CITIZENS
Sec.   1—Due Process of Law

[21] TEACHERS' FREEDOM OF SPEECH AND LOYALTY OATHS

WIEMAN V. UPDEGRAF

344 U. S. 183, 73 Sup. Ct. 215 (1952)

The Supreme Court of the United States held invalid a state statute which prescribed loyalty oaths for certain public officers and employees, including teachers, as being in conflict with the due process clause of the Fourteenth Amendment to the federal Constitution.

Late in the same year that the Court held valid New York's Feinberg law, which exacted loyalty oaths from teachers, it ruled unanimously against an Oklahoma statute of similar purpose. This difference was not because the Court reversed itself, but only because the specific laws involved were found to be different. The constitutionality of loyalty oaths per se was not ruled upon in either of the cases.

Oklahoma required that each officer and employee of the state, counties, school districts, municipalities, public agencies, and public authorities swear to a loyalty oath within thirty days of taking office.

The portion of the oath found most objectionable by certain teachers was as follows:

> That I am not affiliated directly or indirectly . . . with the Communist Party, the Third Communist International, with any foreign political agency, party, organization or government or with any agency, party, organization or group whatever which has been officially determined by the United States attorney general or other authorized agency of the United States to be a Communist front or subversive organization; . . . that I will take up arms in the defense of the United States in time of war or national emergency, if necessary; that within five (5) years immediately preceding the taking of this oath (or affirmation) I have not been a member of . . . any agency, party, organization, association or group whatever which has been officially determined by the United States attorney general or other authorized agency of the United States to be a Communist front or subversive organization. . . .
> (160, pp. 215-16)

Thirteen employees of Oklahoma State Agricultural and Mechanical College did not take this oath within the thirty days allowed. Thereupon a citizen and taxpayer sought to enjoin disbursing officials from paying the thirteen employees. Through the Oklahoma courts the law was held constitutional but the thirteen appealed to the Supreme Court of the United States.

The appeal challenged the Oklahoma law on four points, declaring it to be a bill of attainder, an *ex post facto* law, an impairment of contracts held with the state, and, mainly, a violation of the "due process" clause of the Fourteenth Amendment.

The unanimous decision of the Supreme Court of the United States first reviewed three of its recent opinions on somewhat similar cases. In addition to the *Adler* case (53), just discussed, and the case of *Garner v. Los Angeles Board* (85) mentioned in connection with it, the Court referred to *Gerende v. Board of Supervisors* (37), an earlier case wherein a Maryland law requiring a loyalty oath of all candidates for elective office had been upheld, as had, indeed, the oath requirement in the other two cases. However, the Maryland law had been upheld only because the state court had interpreted the statute in question as requiring the candidates to swear that, in addition to not advocating violent overthrow of the government, they had not "knowingly" been members of any organization advocating such violence.

Justice Clark, who delivered the opinion of the Court, first takes the Oklahoma supreme court to task for not interpreting the Oklahoma oath in the light of the "knowingly" interpretation in the *Gerende* and *Garner* cases. The Justice, speaking of this failure of the Oklahoma supreme court, continued and said, in part:

This [action of the state supreme court] must be viewed as a holding that knowledge is not a factor under the Oklahoma statute. We are thus brought to the question . . . whether the due process clause permits a state in attempting to bar disloyal individuals from its employ to exclude persons solely on the basis of organizational membership, regardless of their knowledge concerning the organizations to which they belonged. For, under the statute before us, the fact of membership alone disqualifies. If the rule be expressed as a presumption of disloyalty, it is a conclusive one.

But membership may be innocent. A state servant may have joined a proscribed organization unaware of its activities and purposes. In recent years, many completely loyal persons have severed organizational ties after learning for the first time of the character of groups to which they belonged. . . .

. . . Yet under the Oklahoma Act, the fact of association alone determines disloyalty and disqualification; it matters not whether association existed innocently or knowingly. To thus inhibit individual freedom of movement is to stifle the flow of democratic expression and controversy at one of its chief sources. We hold that the distinction observed between the case at bar and . . . [the Garner, Adler and Gerende cases] is decisive. Indiscriminate classification of innocent with knowing activity must fall as an assertion of arbitrary power. The oath offends due process. . . . (160, pp. 218-19)

Certain of the Court's words in the *Adler* case had been cited in defense of the Oklahoma oath. In that case the Court had said that teachers "have no right to work for the state in the school system on their own terms," but teachers "may work for the school system upon reasonable terms laid down by the proper authorities of New York." To this Justice Clark now said:

. . . To draw from this language the facile generalization that there is no constitutionally protected right to public employment is to obscure the issue. . . .

. . . We need not pause to consider whether an abstract right to public employment exists. It is sufficient to say that constitutional protection does extend to the public servant whose exclusion pursuant to a statute is patently arbitrary or discriminatory. . . . (160, p. 219)

Justice Frankfurter in a concurring opinion spoke strongly for academic freedom. He said in part:

That our democracy ultimately rests on public opinion is a platitude of speech but not a commonplace in action. Public opinion is the ultimate reliance of our society only if it be disciplined and responsible. It can be disciplined and responsible only if habits of open-mindedness and of critical inquiry are acquired in the formative years of our citizens. The process of education has naturally enough been the basis of hope for the perdurance of our democracy on the part of all our great leaders, from Thomas Jefferson onwards.

To regard teachers— . . . from the primary grades to the university— as the priests of our democracy is therefore not to indulge in hyperbole.

It is the special task of teachers to foster those habits of open-mindedness and critical inquiry which alone make for responsible citizens, who, in turn, make possible an enlightened and effective public opinion. Teachers must fulfill their function by precept and practice, by the very atmosphere which they generate; they must be exemplars of open-mindedness and free inquiry. They cannot carry out their great and noble task if the conditions for the practice of a responsible and critical mind are denied to them. They must have the freedom of responsible inquiry, by thought and action, into the meaning of social and economic ideas, into the checkered history of social and economic dogma. They must be free to sift evanescent doctrine, qualified by time and circumstance, from that restless, enduring process of extending the bounds of understanding and wisdom, to assure which the freedoms of thought, of speech, of inquiry, of worship are guaranteed by the Constitution of the United States against infraction by national or state government. . . . (160, p. 221)

Justice Black, consistent with his dissent in the *Adler* case, likewise prepared a concurring opinion here. He added a warning when he said, in part:

. . . the present period of fear seems more ominously dangerous to speech and press than was that of the Alien and Sedition Laws. Suppressive laws and practices are the fashion. The Oklahoma oath statute is but one manifestation of a national network of laws aimed at coercing and controlling the minds of men. Test oaths are notorious tools of tyranny. . . .

Governments need and have ample power to punish treasonable acts. But it does not follow that they must have a further power to punish thought and speech. . . . Our own free society should never forget that laws which stigmatize and penalize thought and speech of the orthodox have a way of reaching, ensnaring and silencing many more people than at first intended. We must have freedom of speech for all, or we will in the long run have it for none but the cringing and the craven. . . . (160, p. 220)

COMMENT

It should perhaps be repeated that this decision did not reverse the Court's holding in the *Adler* case. In that case and the present one the Court dealt with specific legislation of different states. Had the Oklahoma statute in question permitted a teacher to swear that he had not "knowingly" joined any organization later declared subversive the Court would hardly have distinguished it from the *Garner*, *Adler*, and *Gerende* cases.

Inferences which may be drawn from the present case are that the Court can be expected to: (1) Refuse to countenance guilt by association. (2) Hold invalid those loyalty oaths which penalize teachers for innocent affiliation with organizations listed as subversive. (3) Uphold those loyalty oaths which penalize teachers knowingly affiliated with such organizations.

AMDT. 1—RELIGION, FREE SPEECH, ETC.
Freedom of Speech and the Press
AMDT. 14—RIGHTS OF CITIZENS
Sec.   1—Due Process of Law

[22] CENSORSHIP OF EDUCATIONAL MATERIALS OFFENSIVE TO RELIGIOUS GROUPS

BURSTYN V. WILSON

343 U. S. 495, 72 Sup. Ct. 777 (1952)

The Supreme Court of the United States held that under the First and Fourteenth Amendments to the federal Constitution the State of New York, acting through its Board of Education as censors, could not place a prior restraint on the showing of a motion picture found by the censors to be "sacrilegious."

This case involved certain school officials only because they held concurrent authority as censors over moving picture films shown in New York. Yet, since films afford instructional materials and a method increasingly utilized, the Court's decision may be of considerable import for education.

The New York censors were required to withhold the usual statutory license for films which they found were "obscene, indecent, immoral, inhuman, sacrilegious" or would have the effect of moral corruption or incitement to crime. When Roberto Rossellini's Italian production, *The Miracle*, was billed for showing, Catholics objected and the board denied a license on the ground that the film was "sacrilegious." This action and the statute under which it was taken were unsuccessfully challenged in New York courts. The matter was then pressed before the Supreme Court of the United States on the contention that the First and Fourteenth Amendments were violated. (65, pp. 778-79)

To an argument that motion picture films could create danger and evil for society, Justice Clark, who spoke for a unanimous Court observed that motion pictures did, indeed, like other means for public expression or communication of intelligence, raise the question of freedom and censorship but, again like those other means, motion pictures were subject to the same freedom. (65, pp. 780-81) The Court remarked that "the present case is the first to present squarely to us the question whether motion pictures are within the ambit of protection which the First Amendment, through the Fourteenth, secures to any form of speech or the press." (65, p. 780)

The Court then turned to an examination of the New York statute and viewed with disfavor the fact that the statute did not provide for punishment of actual, past offenses, but set up a "previous restraint" to be applied by censors "who judge the content of the words and pictures sought to be communicated." Previous restraints of this sort were, in the Court's view, "a form of infringement upon freedom of expression to be especially condemned." (65, p. 781)

In considering the meaning of the term "sacrilegious" as a basis for denying the license involved, the Court examined the New York court's interpretation that, as the word "religion" is "understood by the ordinary, reasonable person," no religion "shall be treated with contempt, mockery, scorn and ridicule."[22] This, said the Court's opinion, would give great latitude to the censors and great power to religious groups whose pressures would afford the censors their only guide. For, said the Court:

... In seeking to apply the broad and all-inclusive definition of "sacrilegious" given by the New York courts, the censor is set adrift upon a boundless sea amid a myriad of conflicting religious views with no charts but those provided by the most vocal and powerful orthodoxies. ... Under such a standard the most careful and tolerant censor would find it virtually impossible to avoid favoring one religion over another, and he would be subject to an inevitable tendency to ban the expression of unpopular sentiments sacred to a religious minority . . . the state has no legitimate interest in protecting any or all religions from views distasteful to them which is sufficient to justify prior restraints upon the expression of these views. It is not the business of government in our nation to suppress real or imagined attacks upon a religious doctrine, whether they appear in publications, speeches, or motion pictures. . . . (65, p. 782)

COMMENT

A commentary notes as significant the fact that, historically, those cases where previous restraints have been sanctioned involved "judicial, not administrative action," and goes on:

. . . The prime objective of the ban on previous restraints was to outlaw censorship accomplished by licensing. "The struggle for freedom of the press was primarily directed against the power of the licensor. It was against that power that John Milton directed his assault by his 'Appeal for the Liberty of Unlicensed Printing.' And the liberty of the press became initially the right to publish 'without a license what formerly could be published only with one'." Even today, a licensing requirement will bring judicial condemnation more surely than any other form of restriction. . . . (48, p. 787)

This same commentary notes that "in the case of radio broadcasting, however, where physical limitations make it impossible for everyone to utilize the medium of communication, the Court has thus far (1952) sanctioned a power of selective licensing;" but as for

---

[22]Justice Frankfurter, in a concurring opinion elaborates on the vagueness of the word "sacrilegious." (65, pp. 783-800)

moving pictures, although the Court has "until very recently held the State's power to license, and hence to censor, films intended for local exhibition to be substantially unrestricted,"[23] the 1948 decision in *United States v. Paramount Pictures* (151) and the decision here in the *Burstyn* case indicated a very different position. (48, pp. 787-88) These two cases have made it clear that movies are included in the "press" whose freedom the Constitution safeguards.

The alleged offensiveness of *The Miracle* to Catholics is a reminder that other more common forms of instructional material may likewise raise objections from a religious group or from a race.

Negroes have frequently protested, at least to teachers, a textbook's use of the terms "Rastus" or "Sambo," but these protests appear not to have been aired in courts.

Jews, however, have challenged in New York courts a school board's selection of *Oliver Twist* and *The Merchant of Venice* for classroom use (136). The objection was not that the books had been selected because they were anti-Jewish, but, rather, that use of the book tended to produce hatred of Jews.

In 1949 the New York court upheld the board and remarked that if each book selected must be "free from derogatory reference to any religion, race, country, nation or personality" the courts could expect that "endless litigation respecting many books would probably ensue." A reasonable test was, however, included along with a general statement on administrative freedom in the court's holding. This test was whether "a book has been maliciously written for the apparent purpose of promoting and fomenting a bigoted and intolerant hatred against a particular racial or religious group." The court continued:

. . . public interest in a free and democratic society does not warrant or encourage the suppression of any book at the whim of any unduly sensitive person or group of persons, merely because a character described in such a book as belonging to a particular race or religion is portrayed in a derogatory or offensive manner. The necessity for the suppression of such a book must clearly depend upon the intent and motive which has actuated the author in making such a portrayal. . . .

Educational institutions are concerned with the development of free inquiry and learning. The administrative officers must be free to guide teachers and pupils toward that goal. Their discretion must not be interfered with in the absence of proof of actual malevolent intent. . . . (136, p. 346)

---

[23]In 1915 in the case of *Mutual Film Corporation v. Hodges* (119) the Court upheld a Kansas statute forbidding motion pictures to be exhibited in the state unless first certified by the State Superintendent of Instruction as being moral and instructive.

SUMMARY: PART TWO

Answers by the Supreme Court of the United States to questions bearing on the First Amendment and affecting education.

Yes No

( ) (X) [9] *Vidal v. Girard's Executors* (1844). Was Girard's will, which established a college barring ministers and missionaries from its premises, derogatory to the Christian religion?

(X) ( ) [10] *Quick Bear v. Leupp* (1908). Was the payment of Indians' tribal funds in a contract effected by the Commissioner of Indian Affairs with a Catholic school valid?

(X) ( ) *Cochran v. Louisiana* (1930). Was the Louisiana statute which provided free textbooks out of public funds to private schools constitutional?

(X) ( ) [12] *Everson v. Board of Education* (1947). Was New Jersey's action in providing free transportation out of public funds for children attending Catholic parochial schools constitutional?

(X) ( ) [13] *Pearson v. Coale* (1933). Did the University of Maryland have the right to compel students to take military training?

(X) ( ) [14] *Hamilton v. Regents* (1934). Could the University of California make military training a condition for attendance, regardless of a student's contrary religious beliefs?

(X) ( ) [15] *Minersville School District v. Gobitis* (1940). Could the flag salute be made a condition of school attendance?

( ) (X) [16] *West Va. State Board of Education v. Barnette* (1943). Could the flag salute still be imposed as a condition of school attendance?

(X) ( ) [17] *McCollum v. Board of Education* (1948). Did the Champaign, Illinois, plan for "released time" religious instruction inside the schools amount to an establishment of religion?

( ) (X) [18] *Doremus v. Board of Education* (1952). Was a certain challenge of Bible reading in New Jersey schools a justiciable controversy?

( ) (X) [19] *Zorach v. Clauson* (1952). Did the New York City plan for "released time" religious instruction away from the schools amount to an establishment of religion?

(X) ( ) [20] *Adler v. Board of Education* (1952). Was New York's legislation barring from employment in its schools any member of an organization advocating overthrow of the government constitutional?

( ) (X) [21] *Wieman v. Updegraf* (1952). Was the form of the loyalty oath required by Oklahoma for teachers and others constitutional?

( ) (X) [22] *Burstyn v. Wilson* (1952). Could New York's board of education forbid the showing of a motion picture on the basis of a prior finding that the film was "sacrilegious"?

RECAPITULATION

Constitutionality of				*Yes*	*No*
A will excluding clerics and religious teaching...			[9]	1	0
Monetary concessions to religious schools.......	[10]	[11]	[12]	3	0
Military training in state universities...........		[13]	[14]	2	0
Flag-salute requirement in schools.............		[15]	[16]	1	1
"Released time" religious instruction..........		[19]	[17]	1	1
Bible reading in schools......................			[18]	1	0
Loyalty tests for teachers....................		[20]	[21]	1	1
Motion picture censorship...................			[22]	0	1
Federal action upheld			[10]	1	
State action upheld.......................	[11]	[12]	[13] [14]		
	[15]	[18]	[19] [20]	8	
Citizens upheld..........................	[9]	[16]	[17] [21]		
	[22]			5	

PART THREE

QUESTIONS ON RIGHTS OF
PERSONS RAISED UNDER THE
FOURTEENTH (AND FIFTH)
AMENDMENT

*Which means that persons challenged
some action as denying them "due
process of law" or—for Negro citizens
especially—"Equal protection of
the laws."*

11

POLICE POWER, LIBERTY, PROPERTY UNDER DUE PROCESS OF LAW

THE DUE PROCESS CLAUSE

However it may be regarded, there is little doubt that the Fourteenth Amendment of 1868 is one of the most important parts of the Constitution. Although much of it has lapsed into historical limbo—the parts dealing with ex-Confederates and the Civil War debts—the Amendment's first article has increased rather than diminished in significance. The portion which concerns us today reads:

No state shall make or enforce any law which shall abridge the privileges or immunities of citizens of the United States; nor shall any state deprive any person of life, liberty or property without due process of law; nor deny to any person within its jurisdiction the equal protection of the laws.

Taken at face value these words appear designed simply as a protection for the recently liberated Negro, but taken with the wisdom afforded by three-quarters of a century of history they appear designed for something quite different—a reversal of the Supreme Court's turn toward state's rights under Chief Justice Taney, and an effort to extend federal protection to corporations whose property

155

was threatened by state action.[24] This single sentence, Charles and Mary Beard have declared, "subdued the states for all time to the unlimited jurisdiction of the federal Supreme Court." (3, vol. 2, p. 114)

The Amendment's ostensibly straightforward language has, indeed, afforded much scope for judicial determination. The meaning of each of the terms—"person," "privileges or immunities," "life, liberty and property," "equal protection of the laws" and "due process of law" has received an immense amount of consideration by the Court. (48, pp. 963-1177)

At first the Court was reluctant to undertake the proffered task, declaring that it had no wish to become "a perpetual censor upon all State legislation," nor did it wish to "encourage Congress to take over," as it might under the fifth section of the amendment, "the regulation of all civil rights." Civil war and reconstruction had already sufficiently unsettled "the federal equilibrium." (48, p. XXIV)

Then, in 1884 in *Hurtado v. California* (101), the Court indicated that it was prepared to be persuaded, and the states "were put on notice that every species of State legislation, whether dealing with procedural or substantive rights, was subject to the scrutiny of the Court when the question of its essential justice is raised." (48, p. 974) About a generation was required to convert this into doctrine.

The key to the conversion was the meaning of the phrase, "due process of law," which appears in both the Fifth and Fourteenth Amendments and goes back to Article 39 of the *Magna Carta*. Until about 1890 this involved nothing more than matters of proper legal procedure,[25] for example, the right to trial under the due course and proper proceedings of the law. Thereafter the meaning of the term was extended until, today, the Court ordinarily decides any question involving the relation of governmental power to private rights by invoking "due process of law," i.e., "reasonable" law—reasonable as the Court sees it.

This newer, expanded meaning of the phrase resulted from the persistence of attorneys who gave the Court no peace in pressing for property rights. Whatever was done for "property" had to be done

---

[24]Eminent historians take different views on this matter. Professors Morison and Commager say: "That the framers of the Amendment anticipated any such interpretation of this article is highly improbable." (28, vol. 2, p. 40) Professor Faulkner maintains that the purpose was "to put the same prohibition on the states that the Fifth Amendment had placed upon the federal government." (20, p. 417) The Beards say that of two factions among the framers, one was "determined to take in the whole range of national economy." (3, vol. 2, p. 112)

[25]A conspicuous exception, apparently the only one by the Supreme Court, is found in Chief Justice Taney's decision in the Dred Scott case (138).

for "life and liberty," because the terms stood together in the phraseology of the Fourteenth Amendment. There, indeed, "life and liberty" are found to stand ahead of "property."

In 1890, in a railway rate case, *Chicago, M & St. P. R. Co. v. Minnesota* (69), the Court decided that rates fixed by a state agency were too low, and hence deprived a railroad of property without due process. Matters that had hitherto been legislative were becoming judicial.

It followed, then, that corporations, like other "persons," were protected in their "liberty" of acquiring property. By the same token, this liberty, safeguarded for artificial persons, had to be applied to natural persons at last, however slowly. As late as 1920 Justice Brandeis still had to plead: "I cannot believe that the liberty guaranteed by the Fourteenth Amendment includes only liberty to acquire and to enjoy property." (90, p. 131)

Finally, in 1923, in *Meyer v. Nebraska* (113), the Court affirmed the liberty of a foreign language teacher to teach, and "of parents to engage him so to instruct their children," and two years later, in *Pierce v. Society of Sisters* (128), the Court again held a state's restraint upon the liberty of parents to send their children to a school of their choice to be an unreasonable interference with private rights, hence a denial of due process.

AMDT. 14—RIGHTS OF CITIZENS

Sec.   1—Due Process of Law

Equal Protection of the Laws

Privileges and Immunities

[23] **CONTROL OVER SECRET SOCIETIES IN SCHOOLS**

WAUGH V. MISSISSIPPI UNIVERSITY

237 U. S. 589, 35 Sup. Ct. 720 (1915)

The Supreme Court of the United States upheld the competency of a state to enact legislation making attendance at the state university contingent upon renunciation of allegiance to a Greek letter fraternity, and declared that the legislation in question did not violate any right contained in the federal Constitution.

Litigation arising from proscriptions of high school fraternities or from expulsions because of fraternity activity at the high school level appears to have been common in lower courts.[26] The *Waugh* case involved the action of state university authorities, applying a state

---

[26]The action of school authorities has been sustained in all "fraternity cases" recorded, except one where a prohibition was held to be unreasonable. (41, pp. 233-34, 241-47)

statute, in refusing admission to a student whose fraternity affiliation had been established at a different school.

J. P. Waugh, a citizen of Mississippi applied for admission to the law department of Mississippi University. As a condition for admission he was shown a pledge on which, over signature, he would disavow allegiance to, or affiliation with, any of certain listed Greek letter fraternities, or any other fraternities unnamed. He discovered, too, that the pledge was not required of students previously in attendance at Mississippi, but only of transfer students. Earlier, while at Millsaps College, Mr. Waugh had become a member of Kappa Sigma, one of the fraternities specifically named on the pledge. He expressed a willingness to forego all fraternity activity short of foreswearing allegiance to Kappa Sigma. When the university remained adamant in demanding full compliance with the pledge, Mr. Waugh sued to have the law and the university order under it set aside. He alleged that his happiness and his property and property rights were infringed under the constitution of Mississippi and under the Fourteenth Amendment to the federal Constitution. The chancery court of Lafayette County decided in favor of Mr. Waugh, but the Supreme Court of Mississippi reversed the lower court. The Supreme Court of the United States then took the case on a writ of error. (157, p. 21)

Justice McKenna who delivered the opinion of the Court said, in part:

The statute is universal in its prohibitions. None of the named societies or others "of whatever name, or without name", are permitted to exist in the University; and no student who is a member of any of them is permitted to receive or compete for class honors nor contend for prizes or medals. To secure this result one of the orders of the trustees was directed.

But by another order of the trustees, a distinction is made. By it it is provided that the statute is not to be construed "to apply to students already entered, and who conduct themselves with that decorum always expected of Southern gentlemen". This order is assailed by plaintiff as a "clear discrimination between the 'ins' and 'outs', between those who were, at the time the statute was enacted, students in the University, and those who were not on that date members of the student body, and who might desire to be admitted as such." The contention is made much of by counsel and the order is denounced as irrational and arbitrary. But counsel overlook that it is an obvious principle of construction, and sometimes of justice, that laws are not to be construed retrospectively. The trustees regarded and followed the principle, and left undisturbed the students already in the University, admonishing them, however, that their honor would be regarded as pledged not to abuse the right or the indulgence. And whether it was a right or an indulgence,—whether required by the statute or accorded by the trustees,— it was based on an obvious and rational distinction, and the supreme court sustained its competence.

The next contention of complainant has various elements. It assails the statute as an obstruction to his pursuit of happiness, a deprivation of his property and property rights, and of the privileges and immunities guaranteed by the Constitution of the United States. Counsel have considered these elements separately and built upon them elaborate and somewhat fervid arguments, but, after all, they depend upon one proposition: whether the right to attend the University of Mississippi is an absolute or conditional right. It may be put more narrowly,—whether, under the Constitution and laws of Mississippi, the public educational institutions of the state are so far under the control of the legislature that it may impose what the supreme court of the state calls "disciplinary regulations."

To this proposition we are confined, and we are not concerned in its consideration with what the laws of other states permit or prohibit. Its solution might be rested upon the decision of the supreme court of the state. That court said: "The legislature is in control of the colleges and universities of the state, and has a right to legislate for their welfare and to enact measures for their discipline, and to impose the duty upon the trustees of each of these institutions to see that the requirements of the legislature are enforced; and when the legislature has done this, it is not subject to any control by the courts."

This being the power of the legislature under the Constitution and laws of the state over its institutions maintained by public funds, what is urged against its exercise to which the Constitution of the United States gives its sanction and supports by prohibition?

It is said that the fraternity to which complainant belongs is a moral and of itself a disciplinary force. This need not be denied. But whether such membership makes against discipline was for the state of Mississippi to determine. It is to be remembered that the University was established by the state, and is under the control of the state, and the enactment of the statute may have been induced by the opinion that membership in the prohibited societies divided the attention of the students, and distracted from that singleness of purpose which the state desired to exist in its public educational institutions. It is not for us to entertain conjectures in opposition to the views of the state, and annul its regulations upon disputable considerations of their wisdom or necessity. Nor can we accommodate the regulations to the assertion of a special purpose by the applying student, varying, perhaps, with each one, and dependent alone upon his promise.

This being our view of the power of the legislature, we do not enter upon a consideration of the elements of complainant's contention. It is very trite to say that the right to pursue happiness and exercise rights and liberty are subject in some degree to the limitations of the law, and the condition upon which the state of Mississippi offers the complainant free instruction in its University, that while a student there he renounce affiliation with a society which the state considers inimical to discipline, finds no prohibition in the 14th Amendment. . . . (157, pp. 722-23)

COMMENT

College-level students are frequently heard to remark that some regulation or disciplinary action of the school authorities is contrary to rights established under the Constitution. The foregoing decision should indicate that such student remarks, for the most part at least, are mistaken and based upon faulty knowledge of our federal system and of the powers of school authorities as either corporate or quasi-legislative agents. It is clear that the states can exact special requirements from those citizens who attend colleges supported or chartered by the states. The reasonableness of such special requirements is rarely questioned by the courts after the people have spoken through their legislature. As the Supreme Court said above: "It is not for us to entertain conjectures in opposition to the views of the state, and to annul its regulations upon disputable considerations of their wisdom or necessity." And the Court added that it was trite but true that "the right to pursue happiness and exercise rights and liberty are subject in some degree to the limitations of the law."

Although this decision was rendered in 1915, before the Court had given to the term "liberty" in the Fourteenth Amendment all the scope later granted, no discernible reason exists for supposing that the decision would be different today.

A lower court has held that membership in high-school secret societies may be forbidden by school officials even though all activities are away from school. However, school officials may not exercise authority over the matter during vacation periods, for it then passes into parental control (161). Otherwise, it appears that almost any regulation of school fraternities which is designed to provide a desirable social climate will be held reasonable by the courts. A recent example may be drawn from a 1952 decision of Oregon's supreme court which upheld the Portland school board's use of statutory authority to suppress all high-school organizations which the superintendent found to be serving less than the best interests of the pupils; moreover, the board was held to possess power to control admissions to, or separations from, organizations which it might permit to exist (64).

AMDT. 14—RIGHTS OF CITIZENS
Sec.   1—Due Process of Law
            Equal Protection of the Laws
            Privileges and Immunities

[24] COMPULSORY VACCINATION OF SCHOOL CHILDREN

ZUCHT V. KING

260 U. S. 174, 43 Sup. Ct. 24 (1922)

The Supreme Court of the United States held that a citizen could assert no constitutional right to have his child attend school without a certificate of vaccination as required by a city ordinance.

A mass of citations on cases in which citizens felt, mostly for religious reasons, that their personal liberties were infringed by compulsory vaccination statutes indicates that the issue is persistently questioned in lower courts. The Supreme Court has considered the matter in the case of *Jacobson v. Massachusetts* (106) decided in 1905 and again in this 1922 case directly involving school admission. In both cases the Court agreed with the generally consistent judgments of lower courts in holding that compulsory vaccination law enacted by a state or its local subdivisions is within the police power of the state, and that under such legislation this power can be exercised regardless of an epidemic.

In the present case, Rosalyn Zucht and A. D. Zucht, whom the court records as "her next friend" questioned as arbitrary an ordinance of the city of San Antonio, Texas, which provided that "no child or other person shall attend a public school or other place of education without having first presented a certificate of vaccination." (164, p. 24)

Because Rosalyn Zucht "did not have the required certificate and refused to submit to vaccination," public officials excluded her from a public school and "caused her to be excluded from a private school." Thereupon an injunction against enforcing the ordinance, a writ of mandamus to compel her admission, and damages were sought in her behalf. (164, p. 25)

Texas courts denied the plea and the case reached the Supreme Court of the United States on a writ in which, in the Court's words, "it is assigned as error that the ordinances violate the due process and equal protection clauses of the Fourteenth Amendment, and that as administered they denied to the plaintiff equal protection of the laws." (164, p. 25)

The Court rejected this contention in a decision by Justice Brandeis which said, in part:

. . . Long before this case was instituted *Jacobson v. Massachusetts*, 197 U. S. 11 . . . had settled that it is within the police power of a state to provide for compulsory vaccination. That case and others had also settled that a state may, consistently with the Federal Constitution, delegate to a municipality authority to determine under what conditions health regulations shall become operative. . . . (164, p. 25)

Here the Court cited opinions to show that "the municipality may vest in its officials broad discretion in matters affecting the application and enforcement of a health law," and continued:

. . . A long line of decisions by this Court had also settled that in the exercise of the police power reasonable classification may be freely applied, and that regulation is not violative of the equal protection clause merely because it is not all-embracing . . . we find in the record no question as to the validity of the ordinance sufficiently substantial to support the writ. . . . (164, p. 25)

COMMENT

The decision in the *Jacobson* and *Zucht* cases, as noted earlier, supports public officials in the enforcement of compulsory vaccination, even in the absence of an epidemic, provided statutory authority exists. In the absence of statutory authority it appears, however, that the state's power to require vaccination can be exercised only in the case of an epidemic, and the state courts have shown much marked disagreement as to what constitutes an epidemic.

Another question—one arising from parents' refusal to have their children vaccinated when authorities have required it, and the children have been barred from school—has brought from state courts similar disagreement as to whether the parents were in violation of compulsory attendance laws.

Adjudication of such questions as those just mentioned above, despite their persistence, has been limited to state courts where the state and local laws are interpreted. Since the Supreme Court of the United States has held compulsory vaccination to be an appropriate means by which public health and safety may be safeguarded and that the "manner in which this objective is to be accomplished is within the discretion of the State and its localities," provided no right in the federal Constitution is infringed (48, p. 1029), and since no infringement could be discovered in either the *Jacobson* or *Zucht* cases, it appears unlikely that other objectors to compulsory vaccination can persuade the Court to discover any.

AMDT. 14—RIGHTS OF CITIZENS
Sec.   1—Due Process of Law

[25] RIGHTS OF TEACHERS AND PARENTS IN THE MATTER OF FOREIGN LANGUAGE INSTRUCTION

MEYER V. NEBRASKA

262 U. S. 390, 43 Sup. Ct. 625 (1923)

The Supreme Court of the United States held that a state law which prohibited the teaching of foreign languages in private schools interfered with the liberty of parents to control and educate their children and with the liberty of teachers to follow their chosen occupation and did, therefore, violate the liberty guaranteed by the Fourteenth Amendment to the federal Constitution.

This case indicates a turning point in constitutional development. For, by the decision rendered here, the Court was clearly in the process of reconsidering the doctrine established in the *Slaughter House* cases (142) in 1873, shortly following the adoption of the Fourteenth Amendment. At that time the Court had ruled that the privileges and immunities clause of the amendment did not "federalize" or extend over the states those restraints imposed upon Congress by the Bill of Rights.

However, in various dissents during the years, certain Justices had insisted that one or another of the fundamental liberties written into the Constitution should, under the terms of the Fourteenth Amendment, also apply as restrictions upon the states. Then, here in the *Meyer* case the "Court began to exhibit clear evidence of its conversion to this broadened conception of the term 'liberty'." (14, p. 112) In the course of its decision the Court almost casually states that the problem is whether the Nebraska statute "unreasonably infringes the liberty guaranteed the plaintiff in error by the Fourteenth Amendment." The decision then proceeds to "denote" rather than to "attempt to define with exactness the liberty thus guaranteed."

By applying its new construction in this particular case the Court assumed the responsibility of deciding a contest between the rights of an individual and the principle of a state's right to determine its educational policies. This right of a state is usually said to rest upon its police power, a concept hardly definitive in case law, but regarded as a power residing in sovereignty and the necessary obligation to protect the welfare of society. In the exercise of this power each American state, through its legislature, is presumed to have established educational policies most socially appropriate to itself. Hence the Court is loath to restrict the discretion of the states. It did so here in the same reluctant terms as those sometimes appearing with lesser clarity in later decisions fraught with the more intense and socially complicated issues of religion and race. How far against individual rights the state may go in exercising the power to establish its educational, or any other, policies cannot be determined by abstraction. Only between details of rights, and only by the prevailing judicial opinion can boundary lines be drawn.

Meyer v. Nebraska, although perhaps less flagrant than the "Oregon case" (128) to follow, likewise arose from the growth of excessive nationalism nurtured in World War I. On April 9, 1919, "An Act Relating to the Teaching of Foreign Languages in the State of Nebraska" was approved. Penalties of fine or jail were provided for violations of the portions of the law following:

Section 1. No person, individually or as a teacher, shall, in any private, denominational, parochial or public school, teach any subject to any person in any language other than the English language.

Section 2. Languages, other than the English language, may be taught as languages only after a pupil shall have attained and successfully passed the eighth grade as evidenced by a certificate of graduation issued by the county superintendent of the county in which the child resides. (113, p. 626)

On May 25, 1920, Meyer, a teacher in a parochial school, taught German reading to a ten year old who, as would be expected of a child of that age, had not yet passed the eighth grade. Meyer was charged accordingly, but he contested, and continued to contest adverse decisions upward through the Nebraska courts to the Supreme Court of the United States. There an opinion in favor of Meyer was handed down. In the course of this opinion Justice McReynolds adverts to the findings of the Supreme Court of Nebraska. Quoted here from that point the decision said, in part:

The supreme court of the state affirmed the judgment of conviction, 107 Neb. 657. It declared the offense charged and established was "the direct and intentional teaching of the German language as a distinct subject to a child who had not passed the eighth grade", in the parochial school maintained by Zion Evangelical Lutheran Congregation, a collection of Biblical stories being used therefor. And it held that the statute forbidding this did not conflict with the Fourteenth Amendment, but was a valid exercise of the police power. The following excerpts from the opinion sufficiently indicate the reasons advanced to support the conclusion:

"The salutary purpose of the statute is clear. The legislature had seen the baneful effects of permitting foreigners, who had taken residence in this country, to rear and educate their children in the language of their native land. The result of that condition was found to be inimical to our own safety. To allow the children of foreigners who had emigrated here, to be taught from early childhood the language of the country of their parents was to rear them with that language as their mother tongue. It was to educate them so that they must always think in that language, and, as a consequence, naturally inculcate in them the ideas and sentiments foreign to the best interests of this country. The statute, therefore, was intended not only to require that the education of all children be conducted in the English language, but that, until they had grown into that language, and until it had become a part of them, they should not, in the schools, be taught any other language. The obvious purpose of this statute was that the English language should be and become the mother tongue of all children reared in this state. The enactment of such a statute comes reasonably within the police power of the state. . . .

"It is suggested that the law is an unwarranted restriction, in that it applies to all citizens of the state, and arbitrarily interferes with the rights of citizens who are not of foreign ancestry and prevents them, without reason, from having their children taught foreign languages in school. That argument is not well taken, for it assumes that every citizen finds himself restrained by the statute. The hours which a child is able to devote to study in the confinement of school are limited. It must have ample time for exercise or play. Its daily capacity for learning is comparatively small. A selection of subjects for its education, therefore, from among the many that might be taught, is obviously necessary. The legislature no doubt had in mind the practical operation of the law. The law affects few citizens except those of foreign lineage. Other citizens, in their selection of studies, except, perhaps, in rare instances have never deemed it of importance to teach their children foreign languages before such children have reached the eighth grade. In the legislative mind, the salutary effects of the statute no doubt outweighed the restriction upon the citizens generally, which, it appears, was a restriction of no real consequence."

[Here, after reviewing the state court's reasons, Justice McReynolds introduces the reasons of the Supreme Court by stating a broadened view of the Fourteenth Amendment and the liberties it may "federalize".]

The problem for our determination is whether the statute, as construed and applied, unreasonably infringes the liberty guaranteed to the plaintiff in error by the Fourteenth Amendment.

"No state . . . shall deprive any person of life, liberty, or property without due process of law."

While this court has not attempted to define with exactness the liberty thus guaranteed, the term has received much consideration, and some of the included things have been definitely stated. Without doubt, it denotes not merely freedom from bodily restraint, but also the right of the individual to contract, to engage in any of the common occupations of life, to acquire useful knowledge, to marry, establish a home and bring up children, to worship God according to the dictates of his own conscience, and, generally, to enjoy those privileges long recognized at common law as essential to the orderly pursuit of happiness by free men. . . . The established doctrine is that this liberty may not be interfered with, under the guise of protecting the public interest, by legislative action which is arbitrary or without reasonable relation to some purpose within the competency of the state to effect. Determination by the legislature of what constitutes proper exercise of police power is not final or conclusive, but is subject to supervision by the courts. . . .

The American people have always regarded education and acquisition of knowledge as matters of supreme importance, which should be diligently promoted. The Ordinance of 1787 declares:

"Religion, morality and knowledge being necessary to good government and the happiness of mankind, schools and the means of education shall forever be encouraged."

Corresponding to the right of control, it is the natural duty of the parent to give his children education suitable to their station in life; and nearly all the states, including Nebraska, enforce this obligation by compulsory laws.

Practically, education of the young is only possible in schools conducted by especially qualified persons who devote themselves thereto. The calling always has been regarded as useful and honorable,—essential, indeed, to the public welfare. Mere knowledge of the German language cannot reasonably be regarded as harmful. Heretofore it has been commonly looked upon as helpful and desirable. Plaintiff in error taught this language in school as part of his occupation. His right thus to teach and the right of parents to engage him so to instruct their children, we think, are within the liberty of the Amendment.

The challenged statute forbids the teaching in school of any subject except in English; also the teaching of any other language until the pupil has attained and successfully passed the eighth grade, which is not usually accomplished before the age of twelve. The supreme court of the state has held that "the so-called ancient or dead languages" are not "within the spirit or the purpose of the act." . . . Latin, Greek, Hebrew, are not proscribed; but German, French, Spanish, Italian, and every other alien speech are within the ban. Evidently the legislature has attempted materially to interfere with the calling of modern-language teachers, with the opportunities of pupils to acquire knowledge, and with the power of parents to control the education of their own.

It is said the purpose of the legislation was to promote civic development by inhibiting training and education of the immature in foreign tongues and ideals before they could learn English and acquire American ideals; and "that the English language should be and become the mother tongue of all children reared in this state." It is also affirmed that the foreign-born population is very large, that certain communities commonly use foreign words, follow foreign leaders, move in a foreign atmosphere, and that the children are thereby hindered from becoming citizens of the most useful type, and the public safety is imperiled.

That the state may do much, go very far, indeed, in order to improve the quality of its citizens, physically, mentally, and morally, is clear; but the individual has certain fundamental rights which must be respected. The protection of the Constitution extends to all,—to those who speak other languages as well as to those born with English on the tongue. Perhaps it would be highly advantageous if all had ready understanding of our ordinary speech, but this cannot be coerced by methods which conflict with the Constitution,— a desirable end cannot be promoted by prohibited means.

For the welfare of his ideal commonwealth, Plato suggested a law which should provide:

"That the wives of our guardians are to be common, and their children are to be common, and no parent is to know his own child, nor any child his parent . . . The proper officers will take the offspring of the good parents to the pen or fold, and there they will deposit them with certain nurses who dwell in a separate quarter; but the offspring of the inferior, or of the better when they chance to be deformed, will be put away in some mysterious, unknown place, as they should be."

In order to submerge the individual and develop ideal citizens, Sparta assembled the males at seven into barracks and intrusted their subsequent education and training to official guardians. Although such measures have been deliberately approved by men of great genius, their ideas touching the relation between individual and state were wholly different from those upon which our institutions rest; and it will hardly be affirmed that any legislature could impose such restrictions upon the people of a state without doing violence to both letter and spirit of the Constitution.

The desire of the legislature to foster a homogeneous people with American ideals, prepared readily to understand current discussions of civic matters, is easy to appreciate. Unfortunate experiences during the late war, and aversion toward every characteristic of truculent adversaries, were certainly enough to quicken that aspiration. But the means adopted, we think, exceed the limitations upon the power of the state, and conflict with rights assured to plaintiff in error. The interference is plain enough, and no adequate reason therefore in time of peace and domestic tranquility has been shown.

The power of the state to compel attendance at some school and to make reasonable regulations for all schools, including a requirement that they shall give instructions in English, is not questioned. Nor has challenge been made of the state's power to prescribe a curriculum for institutions which it supports. Those matters are not within the present controversy. Our concern is with the prohibition approved by the supreme court. Adams v. Tanner, 244 U. S. 590, 37 S. Ct. 662, 61 L. Ed. 1336, 1342, L.R.A. 1917F, 1163, Ann. Cas. 1917D, 973, pointed out that mere abuse incident to an occupation ordinarily useful is not enough to justify its abolition, although regulation may be entirely proper. No sudden emergency has arisen which renders knowledge by a child of some language other than English so clearly harmful as to justify its inhibition, with the consequent infringement of rights long freely enjoyed. We are constrained to conclude that the statute as applied is arbitrary, and without reasonable relation to any end within the competency of the state.

As the statute undertakes to interfere only with teaching which involves a modern language, leaving complete freedom as to other matters, there seems no adequate foundation for the suggestion that the purpose was to protect the child's health by limiting his mental activities. It is well known that proficiency in a foreign language seldom comes to one not instructed at an early age, and experience shows that this is not injurious to the health, morals, or understanding of the ordinary child.

The judgment of the court below must be reversed and the case remanded for further proceedings not inconsistent with this opinion. . . . (113, pp. 626-28)

COMMENT

The very narrow issue here—the right of a state to forbid the teaching of foreign languages in private schools—might too easily be overlooked through being served up among the impressive implications of the liberties that the Court declared more important, i.e., the liberty of a language teacher to teach and the liberty of parents to control and educate their children. There is, indeed, a tendency to regard such enunciations by the Court as mention of absolutes. Those who wish to regard them as absolutes should, however, note that the pragmatic definition remains in the hands of the Court, and that it avoids definition in terms of absolutes.

The decision makes clear that the power of a state over the curriculum in its tax-supported public schools was not questioned. The Court did in fact hint its approval of measures designed to forbid teaching in languages other than English. Possibly, had the Nebraska act merely required of all schools in the state the teaching in English of all subjects other than foreign languages, it might then have been sustained by the Court.

Four years later the Court again dealt with the matter of foreign languages, but in this Territory of Hawaii case, *Farrington v. Tokushige* (78), the constitutional as well as the social context was somewhat different.

The educational effects of the Nebraska and the Hawaii cases taken together appear to be that a state or territory may go very far in prescribing reasonable regulations for all schools and school offerings, whether in public or private institutions, but that the individual possesses certain fundamental rights which, except as they become harmful to the state must be respected. The Court spoke to much the same effect in an Oregon case which follows. There it was held that the state could not require its children to attend public schools.

Thus, the issue still remains somewhere along the disputed borderline where individual parents' rights in the education of their children may clash with a state's obligation to preserve itself and defend the rights of its other citizens.

A note may well be added here concerning the Tennessee "monkey trial" or the Scopes evolution case of 1927, probably the most widely publicized of all cases involving questions of legislative control over curriculum. The case arose when John Scopes, a high school biology teacher, deliberately violated a Tennessee statute forbidding the teaching of evolution. Scopes escaped penalty through a technicality but the law was upheld as being within the state's power. (It may be emphasized that this case was decided in the state courts and was never heard by the Supreme Court of the United States.) The opinion in the case included the following:

. . . [If certain school authorities] believe that the teaching of the Science of Biology has been so hampered by . . . [the statute in question] as to render such an effort no longer desirable, this course of study may be entirely omitted from the curriculum of our schools. If this be regarded as a misfortune, it must be charged to the legislature. . . . (137)

AMDT. 14—RIGHTS OF CITIZENS
Sec.   1—Due Process of Law
(AMDT. 1—RELIGION, FREE SPEECH, ETC.)
(An Establishment of Religion)
(The free exercise thereof)

[26] RIGHT OF ATTENDANCE AT PRIVATE SCHOOLS (THE OREGON CASE)

PIERCE V. SOCIETY OF THE SISTERS OF THE

HOLY NAMES OF JESUS AND MARY

(AND

PIERCE V. HILL MILITARY ACADEMY)

268 U. S. 510, 45 Sup. Ct. 571 (1925)

The Supreme Court of the United States held that an Oregon statute which required children of compulsory school age to attend *public* school was void because it violated the liberty guaranteed by the federal Constitution in that it denied parents the right to educate their children for purposes other than the state, and in that it deprived private schools of their property without due process of law.

Efforts to make the world safe for democracy in World War I included the cultivation of the seeds of excessive nationalism and intolerance. During the war and in the "normalcy" and "prosperity" that followed, these seeds bore noxious fruit in many fields. In the field of education, history became in some regions, as in Chicago under Mayor Thompson, truly a fable agreed upon, and the text books were revised accordingly. The teaching of certain foreign languages and the theory of evolution were extensively forbidden. Teachers were required to subscribe to loyalty oaths. A new Ku Kluxism flamed in fiery crosses, not only in the South but across the land from Massachusetts to Oregon. This new Klan adopted the spirit of the old nativist Know-Nothing-ism, and was no more anti-Negro than it was anti-Semitic and anti-Catholic. "Native, white, Protestant," was the slogan. It was in this context that the people of the state of Oregon acted against parochial and other nonpublic schools.

An initiative measure passed in Oregon on November 7, 1922, to become effective in 1926, required, with certain exemptions, that every parent, guardian, or other person having control of a child between the ages of eight and sixteen years, must send such child to public school in the district where he resided for the period during which school was held. (128, p. 572)

Two Oregon corporations, the Society of the Sisters of the Holy Names of Jesus and Mary and the Hill Military Academy sought and received from the District Court of the United States for the District of Oregon preliminary injunctions restraining the governor of Oregon (Pierce) and other state officials from enforcing the law. The two corporations argued that the law unreasonably interfered with the liberty of the parents and guardians to direct the upbringing of their children, and that it threatened with destruction their business and property, and in such respect violated the Fourteenth Amendment. (128, p. 572)

The State of Oregon appealed the action of the district court in granting the injunctions. An opinion in favor of the two corporations or schools was rendered in 1925.

Justice McReynolds delivered the opinion of the Court. He said, in part:

No question is raised concerning the power of the State reasonably to regulate all schools, to inspect, supervise and examine them, their teachers and pupils; to require that all children of proper age attend some school, that teachers shall be of good moral character and patriotic disposition, that certain studies plainly essential to good citizenship must be taught, and that nothing be taught which is manifestly inimical to the public welfare.

The inevitable practical result of enforcing the Act under consideration would be destruction of appellees' primary schools, and perhaps all other private primary schools for normal children within the State of Oregon.

Under the doctrine of Meyer v. Nebraska, 262 U. S. 390, we think it entirely plain that the Act of 1922 unreasonably interferes with the liberty of parents and guardians to direct the upbringing and education of children under their control. . . .

The fundamental theory of liberty under which all governments in this Union repose excludes any general power of the State to standardize its children by forcing them to accept instruction from public teachers only. The child is not the mere creature of the State; those who nurture him and direct his destiny have the right, coupled with the high duty, to recognize and prepare him for additional obligations.

Appellees are corporations and therefore, it is said, they cannot claim for themselves the liberty which the Fourteenth Amendment guarantees. Accepted in the proper sense, this is true . . . But they have business and property for which they claim protection. These are threatened with destruction through the unwarranted compulsion which appellants are exercising over present and prospective patrons of their schools. And this court has gone very far to protect against loss threatened by such action. . . .

Appellees asked protection against arbitrary, unreasonable and unlawful interference with their patrons and the consequent destruction of their business and property. . . .

The suits were not premature. The injury to appellees was present and very real, not a mere possibility in the remote future. If no relief had been possible prior to the effective date of the Act, the injury would have become irreparable. Prevention of impending injury by unlawful action is a recognized function of courts of equity. . . . (128, pp. 573-74)

COMMENT

The foregoing decision only indirectly defends religious liberty and the right of parents to educate their children in schools where religious instruction is a part of the curriculum. The First Amendment and its guarantee of religious liberty is, therefore, in a sense supported by the decision, but, to repeat, only indirectly. A secular private school as well as a parochial school was involved in the case. The decision as rendered held the Oregon statute to be a denial of due process of law under the Fourteenth Amendment by the fact that it deprived the schools of their business and property, and denied to parents their "freedom to direct the upbringing and education" of their children by sending them to either parochial or secular private schools.

Insofar as the Court may have considered the Fourteenth Amendment as a basis for a broadened conception of liberty, it strengthened a trend begun two years earlier in the case of *Meyer v. Nebraska* (113).

The Court had, of course, made clear by its answers to the questions raised that the states may not require children to be educated in public schools so long as the needs of the state for developing an intelligent and competent citizenry are met by other schools maintaining required educational standards. A related question—do children have to be educated at school or may parents comply with the state's interest by providing instruction in some manner away from school—has never been answered by the Supreme Court. Traditionally and generally the legislative and judicial view appears to be that the state's interest is adequately served if the child receives a certain amount of instruction from parents or tutors. However, there are qualified views, one being that the public interest cannot be efficiently or practically insured where the state is burdened by having to supervise units so small, and another being that to deny the child the group activities and social experience provided by schools is to deny him a practical equivalent in education. Possibly the Supreme Court will sometime be called upon to answer this question, and in answering it to say what, in its view, constitutes "a school." The Court's statement in *Meyer v. Nebraska* (113) that "The power of the State to compel attendance at some school and to make reasonable regulations for all schools . . . is not questioned" may contain an ambiguity, but it would seem to be one affording very limited scope to counsel for parental rights asserted in a clash at the borderline between the rights of the individual and the powers of the state. Thus, while both the Meyer case and the present case sustained and gave definition to certain rights of parents over the education of their children, the powers of the state were also given a definition which might be applied to limit the rights of the individual and the traditional degree of family control.

AMDT. 5—RIGHTS OF PERSONS
—Due Process of Law

[27] **RIGHT OF ATTENDANCE AT FOREIGN LANGUAGE SCHOOLS**

FARRINGTON V. TOKUSHIGE

273 U. S. 284, 47 Sup. Ct. 406 (1927)

(AND

STAINBACK V. MO HOCK KE LOK PO)

336 U. S. 368, 69 Sup. Ct. 606 (1949)

The Supreme Court of the United States, interpreting federal statutes which extended the guarantee of due process of law to the Territory of Hawaii, held invalid a law by the territorial legislature designed to restrict attendance at foreign language schools, the Court declaring that the law went beyond reasonable regulation and deprived parents (Orientals) of the right to educate their children without undue interference.

During those same years following World War I in which Nebraska tried to restrict the teaching and the use of foreign languages by schools within the state, a similar attempt was made by the legislature of the Territory of Hawaii. The problem in Hawaii, if the problem be admitted, was made more grave by the large Oriental population.

Beginning with an act of 1920, and extending through others in 1923 and 1925, the territorial legislature sought to limit foreign language schools and provided penalties to be imposed on teachers and others for violations of the acts. (78, pp. 406, 408) Apparently the schools felt no great restraint until after passage of the act of 1925. By that year the territory held 163 foreign language schools, nine of them Korean, seven of them Chinese and the remainder Japanese. The value of the school property was about $250,000 and the support was by about 5,000 people. (78, p. 406) The territorial officials then moved against these schools through measures which have been digested by Justice McReynolds:

On June 1, 1925, the department of public instruction adopted, and the Governor approved, certain regulations which undertook to limit the pupils who might attend foreign language schools to those who regularly attended some public school or approved private school, or had completed the eighth grade, or were over 14 years of age; also, to designate the text-books which foreign language schools should use in their primary grades. . . . (78, p. 408)

Japanese parents thereupon sought to enjoin the territorial officials from enforcing the regulations which, it was contended, would deprive them of their liberty and property without the due process of law guaranteed by the Fifth Amendment to residents of a territory subject to the control of Congress. The United States District Court granted the injunction sought, and this action being affirmed by the Circuit Court of Appeals, the case went to the Supreme Court of the United States on a writ of certiorari. There, in reviewing the facts, the Court quoted from the affidavit made by Mr. T. Iwanaga as part of the motion for the injunction. The affidavit included the following:

That in the schools referred to in said bill, which are conducted for each grade for one hour for each school day, nothing contrary to American history and American institutions and principles of democracy is taught, the instruction being confined to the speaking, reading, and writing of the Japanese language. . . .

That in the schools represented by plaintiffs there are about 12,400 pupils and said schools employ about 192 teachers; that said teachers are paid and said schools are maintained from voluntary contributions and from the fees of the children attending said schools; that the provisions of said Act 152 of the Sessions Law of 1925 are so drastic that the parents of children will be afraid to pay tuition fees and other persons will be afraid to contribute to the funds of said schools lest they be subjected to the pains and penalties provided in said act; and that, therefore, unless immediate relief is afforded by this honorable court, the said schools will be unable to pay the teachers' salaries and the expenses of conducting said schools will be utterly destroyed. (78, p. 408)

The Court next considered the Attorney General's description of litigation which had arisen from the efforts to limit such foreign language schools, and noted that he "does not disavow purpose to enforce all provisions of the challenged act and regulations." An affidavit by the superintendent of public instruction suggested that the supporters of the foreign language schools could contribute without fear; also, that compliance with the acts would not, as the Court understood the superintendent, "prevent the operation of schools which conduct kindergartens; and that the elimination of kindergartens would not materially affect them." The Court goes on to quote the superintendent in support of the decision to be rendered against the territory. The superintendent said:

That instruction in said Japanese language schools is not and cannot be confined to the speaking, reading and writing of the Japanese language, but extends to many subjects and even in so far as it is intended to have for its object the speaking, reading and writing of said language, the teaching of that is and must be largely through the medium of stories whether of history or fiction and in other ways than the mere teaching of letters and words and sentences. . . .

That, in the opinion of this affiant, the parents of children will not because of the provisions of said Act 152 be afraid to pay tuition fees nor will other persons be afraid to contribute to the funds of such schools and this affiant denies that said schools will, unless immediate relief is afforded by this honorable court, be unable to pay the teachers' salaries and the expenses of conducting said schools, and denies that the property of plaintiffs in said schools will be utterly or at all destroyed. (78, p. 408)

At this point Justice McReynolds who delivered the opinion of the Court said, in part:

The foregoing statement is enough to show that the School Act and the measures adopted thereunder go far beyond mere regulation of privately supported schools, where children obtain instruction deemed valuable by their parents and which is not obviously in conflict with any public interest. They give affirmative direction concerning the intimate and essential details of such schools, intrust their control to public officers, and deny both owners and patrons reasonable choice and discretion in respect of teachers, curriculum and text-books. Enforcement of the act probably would destroy most, if not all, of them; and, certainly, it would deprive parents of fair opportunity to procure for their children instruction which they think important and we cannot say is harmful. The Japanese parent has the right to direct the education of his own child without unreasonable restrictions; the Constitution protects him as well as those who speak another tongue. . . . (78, pp. 408-09)

COMMENT

The Fifth Amendment as a restriction on Congress protects the inhabitants of territories from denial of due process of law just as the Fourteenth Amendment protects the inhabitants of states. Possibly, however, such protection extends only to such "incorporated" territories as Hawaii and Alaska, and not to the various "unincorporated" territories such as American Samoa.[27]

STAINBACK v. MO HOCK KE LOK PO

Following World War II the Territory of Hawaii was again involved in litigation from efforts to regulate the teaching of foreign languages.

A corporation and others sought to enjoin the territory from applying the restrictions of Act 104, Section 7, of its legislature, to prevent the teaching of Chinese to their children. This statute, as the United States District Court held in granting an injunction, would have barred home instruction in the Chinese language; for any instruction in any foreign language was forbidden before a child had been in attendance at the first four grades of public school. A rationale of defense for the law was built upon the legislature's finding that chil-

---

[27]For the Philippine Islands, a Philippine statute which prohibited Chinese merchants from keeping accounts in Chinese was held unconstitutional in 1926 under the Fifth Amendment because the guarantee of due process of law had been extended to the Philippines even though the islands were not exactly a territory of the United States. (*Yu Cong Eng v. Trinidad*) (162)

dren of average intelligence did not do as well with courses taught in English if they were subjected to instruction in another language during their formative years. The judges of the district court noted that a substantial number of above-average children were accordingly barred from exploiting their superiority where they chose to apply it toward foreign language study. *Meyer v. Nebraska* (113) was cited to show that the right of parents to educate their children in a foreign language was guaranteed by the Fifth and Fourteenth Amendments. The court added that the capacity to teach was God-given and not subject to limitation by the state, except where the public morals or safety were endangered. Moreover, held the court, the right to teach is a property right—the more so when done for compensation. And as for the fact that corporations could not claim the liberty guaranteed to natural persons by the Constitution (see the *Berea College* case (58)), the court declared that corporations did have property rights and property for which they could demand security from undue interference. (116, p. 865)

This *Stainback* case (actually two parallel cases) was taken to the Supreme Court on appeal by the governor of the territory but was turned back on procedural grounds (144). Non-authoritative information indicates that Hawaiian children of primary school age were, in 1954, freely attending foreign language schools.

12

SEGREGATION BY RACE IN SCHOOLS AND EQUAL PROTECTION OF THE LAWS

SEGREGATION IN SCHOOLS AND THE "SEPARATE BUT EQUAL" DOCTRINE

The test of dominant Western Civilization may lie in its treatment of races and cultures. The treatment currently accorded those racial and cultural minorities found within the geographical area of that civilization evokes something less than confidence that a satisfactory solution to the minority problem will be found.

The efforts of the United States, the paramount power in the West, toward a solution are probably more successful than critics asserting communist ideology know or will allow. However that may be, one aspect of the problem—segregation of Negroes into separate and often inferior schools—has produced one of the most bitter educational issues ever to face the nation; and because public-school systems are not only responsive to, but productive of, dominant social influences in the American communities of which they are parts, the school practice with respect to segregation and discrimination is probably of pivotal importance in the whole problem.

Although other minorities[28] are sometimes painfully involved by

[28]Indians, Mexicans, and Orientals are, of course, subjected to discrimination. Jews may be added in consideration of admissions policies in some colleges and professional schools.

176

the attitudes of the dominant whites, it is the Negro who comprises, in point of overwhelming numbers, the most severely handicapped group. Also, his involvement has been most dramatic.

In 1857, Chief Justice Taney handed down the Dred Scott decision which declared that the Constitution had never contemplated citizenship for Negroes who, whether freeborn or slaves, were, therefore, ineligible for citizenship (138). But within eight years all the millions who had been slave joined the thousands who had been free, and within eleven years the millions and thousands together became citizens when the Fourteenth Amendment rectified the deficiency in the original Constitution.

This Amendment, adopted in 1868, was, like the reconstruction acts of the previous year, the retaliation by Radical Republican leaders, against President Johnson for his veto of an 1866 bill to expand the Freedmen's Bureau, a federal agency previously established to aid and educate the former slaves. Thence, for nearly a decade while the Negro's friends in Congress ruled the South through military governors, the southern Negro enjoyed perhaps the greatest rise in status of any such sizable group in all history. Then the rise stopped and receded as abruptly as it had begun.

With federal troops withdrawn from the South following the disputed presidential election of 1876, the southern states were as free as the others to deal with the Negro as they wished. The consequence was a return to the Black Codes through which the South, in the period between defeat and the reconstruction acts of 1867, had sought to render freedom for the Negro as meaningless as possible.

Yet the southern states could no longer make the teaching of Negroes to read and write an offense punishable by fine or imprisonment as many of them had before the Civil War. (25, pp. 661, 664-66, 669-70) Although white southerners could seek to intimidate teachers of Negroes as they had in the immediate postwar period (25, pp. 676-79), the forces loosed by the war and the reconstruction were against them and beyond them. The Freedmen's Bureau had established "hundreds of schools and enrolled several hundred thousand pupils," and at the same time "the new constitutions of the reconstructed states made provision for free public education for blacks as well as for whites." (28, vol. 2, pp. 20-21) By the time of President Hayes' inauguration in 1877, there were "about six hundred thousand Negroes in Southern elementary and secondary schools" and "several normal and industrial schools, such as Hampton and Tuskegee, had been established and

Howard, Fisk, and Atlanta Universities were giving instruction in higher education." (28, vol. 2, p. 21)

To destroy such developments for Negro education was no longer feasible, but the Southerner (and, certainly, many Northerners since) was determined to prevent commingling of the races in schools. In seeking to fit this determination to the total pattern of conflicting national attitudes, the practical solution was to take great care in authorizing and requiring separate schools for black and white. Less care could be devoted to seeing that the two races were equally well served in the schools provided.

Recent practice of racial separation in the public schools has ranged from segregation combined with discrimination in many southern states and the District of Columbia, through local option with segregation commonly at the lower levels only in border states, to the wholly indiscriminate assignment of students and teachers, regardless of race, in some northern cities. Yet, while the phrase "segregated schools" may properly evoke another phrase, "the South," such association proves oversimplified. On May 17, 1954, when the Court held segregation in the public schools unconstitutional, the District of Columbia and seventeen states required that Negroes and whites attend separate schools. Four of these states were "border states" and one was "western." In four more states, all western, segregated schools were optional.[29] As will be indicated shortly, segregated schools have not only been maintained until relatively recent times in some parts of the "North" but it was a decision by a judge in a Massachusetts court a century ago which first upheld segregated schools.

Laws and practices meant to segregate the races in schools, like the laws designed to segregate them in the location of their homes and in the use of public conveyances, have provided a vast amount of litigation under the "equal protection" clause of the Fourteenth

---

[29]*Segregation required*:

Alabama	Louisiana	South Carolina
Arkansas	Maryland	Tennessee
Delaware	Mississippi	Texas
Florida	Missouri	Virginia
Georgia	North Carolina	West Virginia
Kentucky	Oklahoma	The District of Columbia

Segregation optional:
Arizona
Kansas
New Mexico
Wyoming

Harry S. Ashmore's *The Negro in the Public Schools* (2, p. 2) contains a map which shows the foregoing and also those states in which segregation was prohibited and those in which there was no specific legislation on the matter.

Amendment. Many of these cases reached the Supreme Court, but, so far as the public schools are concerned, the Court long avoided a decision dealing directly with segregation. However, in cases involving higher education, beginning in 1938, the Court came increasingly closer to doing so. Then, during the 1952 and 1953 terms the Court allowed extended hearings upon five cases arising from lower schools which did involve the issue in such fashion that a decision speaking directly upon segregation could hardly be avoided. In the course of these hearings the Court asked attorneys for both sides, and the United States Attorney General's office as well, whether the framers of the Fourteenth Amendment intended to abolish segregation in the schools. (45, p. 16)

Whatever the framers of the Fourteenth Amendment may have thought of segregation, it has, of course, been widely practiced and almost as widely supported by state and local authority. Its validity has long been sustained by the Supreme Court, under the "separate but equal" doctrine. This doctrine was confirmed in 1896 by the Court's decision in *Plessy v. Ferguson* (129), a common carrier case that has become the guide to those who defend the legality of segregation measures, whether on railroads, at places of amusement, or in hotels, or restaurants, or schools.

A rationale in case law for the concept that such segregation did not violate the equal protection clause of the Fourteenth Amendment, so long as equal facilities were made available to both races, had, however, risen long before the *Plessy* case in 1896, or, even before the Fourteenth Amendment was framed. Indeed, the "separate but equal" doctrine took its rise under Massachusetts' chief justice Shaw in 1849. (48, p. 1163)

In this case, *Roberts v. City of Boston* (135) Charles Sumner spoke in behalf of Sarah Roberts, a Negro child who sought admission to a "white" school—a school but eight hundred feet from her doorstep, whereas the "colored" school was 2,100 feet distant. In an eloquent but unsuccessful argument Sumner maintained that to require Sarah Roberts to walk the greater distance because of her race denied to her the equality in fact which was guaranteed her by the state's bill of rights in its declaration that all citizens were born equal. But the state's chief justice rejected the argument that segregation by race constituted discrimination. He went on to say that the school authorities had only exercised reasonable powers in providing substantially equal but separate schools. He added that if such schools fostered prejudice and odious distinctions of caste, the situation was "not created by law and probably cannot be changed by law."[30] Thus, as Harry S. Ashmore points out in *The Negro and the Schools*, Charles Sumner and chief justice Shaw explored views "not substantially different from those that were to be heard in state and federal courts a hundred years later." (2, pp. 3-4)

Additional perspective on the matter of segregated schools is afforded by attention to the fact that highest courts in some northern states long upheld the practice—as late as 1900 in the Brooklyn, New York, public schools (126) and in the Indianapolis public schools as late as 1926 (95). Shortly after these cases both New York and Indiana enacted statutes designed to end the practice. In Ohio, statutory prohibition of segregated public instruction also existed prior to May 17, 1954, when the Court held the practice unconstitutional; yet in September, 1954, Negro parents were reported as having sought an injunction against segregation of their children in the schools of Hillsboro, Ohio (33).

At first the Supreme Court of the United States refused to sanction the "separate but equal" doctrine. In 1873, in considering the case of Catherine Brown, a Negro woman who had been ejected from a "white" car in a train from Alexandria, Virginia, to Washington, the Court ruled that separate accommodations, even if identical, were not equal under the Constitution (155).

Then, in 1878 in the case of *Hall v. DeCuir* (96), the Court decided that a state law, which prohibited segregation of passengers according to race on Mississippi river steamers, was unconstitutional under the commerce clause because the statute placed an undue burden on interstate commerce. Yet, at the same time the Court observed that where equal facilities were provided, segregation in schools did not conflict with the Fourteenth Amendment. This dictum appears to have been made law by subsequent decisions in lower federal courts.

Thus, some time before the Supreme Court heard its first case involving a race contest over schools, the dictum was available as restated by the Court in *Plessy v. Ferguson*. This significant case arose in Lousiana in 1892 when Homer Plessy, one-eighth Negro, took a seat in a "white" railroad car. He refused to comply with orders to give up the seat and was taken from the train to jail. The issue considered by the Court was whether the Louisiana statute which required equal but separate railroad accommodations denied equal protection of the laws. In the Court's opinion it did not. In the course of the decision the observation was made that: "If one race be inferior

---

[30] in 1855 abolitionists succeeded in having the segregation upheld in this Massachusetts case eliminated by statute. (2, p. 4)

to the other socially, the Constitution of the United States cannot put them on the same plane." Moreover, the contention that "the enforced separation of the two races stamps the colored race with a badge of inferiority" was dismissed by the Court with the observation that: "If this be so, it is not by reason of anything found in the [Louisiana] act, but solely because the colored race chooses to put that construction upon it" (129). Justice Harlan, however, in considering the same case, held the problem in different light. In a dissenting opinion, he maintained that "in the view of the Constitution, in the eye of the law, there is in this country no superior, dominant, ruling class of citizens. There is no caste system here. Our Constitution is color blind" (129).

Although many Court opinions have held segregation to be valid, it could, in Professor Cushman's words, be "valid only if the 'separate' accommodations for the two races are 'equal' ", but:

. . . In common usage there are no degrees of equality; things or conditions are either equal or they are not equal. But the Supreme Court has not taken this view. It has held, rather, that equality in accommodations means not exact or mathematical equality, but only "substantial" equality. In earlier cases the Court was extremely lenient in construing what "equality" required in the segregated school system of the south. . . . It looked as though the Negro was not only to be segregated, but must also be content with very inferior accommodations and services under that segregation. (14, pp. 182-83)

It was in the attitude just indicated, and conforming to the doctrine stated in *Plessy v. Ferguson* that the Court, in 1899, decided the case of *Cumming v. County Board of Education* (72), the first case involving race and public schools. Not until 1914, in the case of *McCabe v. Atchison, Topeka and Santa Fe Ry. Co.* (110) did the Court begin to construe "equality" more strictly, and not until 1938, in the case of *Missouri ex rel. Gaines v. Canada* (115), was this stricter view of "equality" applied by the Court to a contest involving schools.

AMDT. 14—RIGHTS OF CITIZENS
Sec.   1—Equal Protection of the Laws

[28] SCHOOL AUTHORITIES MAY TEMPORARILY SUSPEND FOR ECONOMIC REASONS THE NEGRO HIGH SCHOOL ALONE

CUMMING V. COUNTY BOARD OF EDUCATION
175 U. S. 528, 24 Sup. Ct. 197 (1899)

The Supreme Court of the United States sustained the action of county authorities in Georgia in supporting a high school for white children while providing no such school for Negro children.

Richmond County, Georgia, had for a time maintained high schools for both white and Negro children. Later, on the plea of economic necessity, the county school board suspended the Negro school but continued the "white" school. Thereupon Negro parents and taxpayers sued the school board to enjoin it from maintaining a high school for the white children without maintaining a similar school for the Negro children. The school board contested the action, but the county superior court, though granting the injunction sought by the Negroes, suspended the order until the state supreme court should consider the case. The supreme court of Georgia reversed the lower court and the Negroes then took their case to the Supreme Court of the United States on a writ of error. (72, pp. 197-98)

Justice Harlan, who, dissenting in *Plessy v. Ferguson* had asserted our Constitution to be "color blind," here delivered the opinion of the unanimous Court. He said, in part:

. . . [The Negroes] complain that the board of education used the funds in its hands to assist in maintaining a high school for white children without providing a similar school for colored children. The substantial relief asked is an injunction that would either impair the efficiency of the high school provided for white children or compel the board to close it. . . . The board had before it the question whether it should maintain, under its control, a high school for about 60 colored children or withhold the benefits of education in primary schools from 300 children of the same race. . . .

We are not permitted by the evidence in the record to regard that decision as having been made with any desire or purpose on the part of the board to discriminate against any of the colored school children of the county on account of their race. But if it be assumed that the board erred in supposing that its duty was to provide educational facilities for the 300 colored children who were without an opportunity in primary schools to learn the alphabet and to read and write, rather than to maintain a school for the benefit of the 60 colored children who wished to attend a high school, that was not an error which a court of equity should attempt to remedy by an injunction that would compel the board to withhold all assistance from the high school maintained for white children.

If, in some appropriate proceedings instituted directly for that purpose, the plaintiffs had sought to compel the board of education, out of the funds in its hands or under its control, to establish and maintain such a high school for colored children, and if it appeared that the board's refusal to maintain such a school was in fact an abuse of its discretion and in hostility to the colored population because of their race, different questions might have arisen in the state court.

. . . Under the circumstances disclosed, we cannot say that this action of the state court [in finding against the Negro parents] was within the meaning of the Fourteenth Amendment, a denial by the state to the plaintiffs and to those associated with them of the equal protection of the laws, or of any privileges belonging to them as citizens of the United States. We may add that, while all admit that the benefits and burdens of public taxation must be shared by citizens without discrimination against any class on account of their race, the education of the people in schools maintained by state tax-ation is a matter belonging to the respective states, and any interference on the part of federal authority with the management of such schools cannot be justified, except in the case of a clear and unmistakable disregard of rights secured by the supreme law of the land. We have here no such case to be determined. . . . (72, pp. 200-201)

COMMENT

The foregoing may be interpreted as an uncomfortable expression by Justice Harlan to the effect that the record on which the decision had to be based was not one which afforded application of actual justice, and that the question of "separate but equal" was so clumsily presented as to be scarcely apparent. He seems to suggest to the Negroes that they could have made a more effective approach, not, as they had, by seeking the injunction which would have reduced or removed education for whites without giving it to Negroes, but by first seeking an order requiring the school authorities to establish a school for Negro children and then, had the authorities refused and the refusal appeared arbitrary, the "different questions" might have arisen.[31]

The Court clearly expresses a reluctance, often repeated in decisions involving other matters touching on education, to interfere with the states' powers to manage their own schools, and does so, of course, in explanation of the stand taken.

When the powers of the states and the Court's reluctance are con-sidered within the social contexture existing at the century's end the decision is not unexpected. Therefore, if nearly forty years later, the willingness of the Court to find in the *Gaines* case that constitutional rights, which (to the layman) may appear no more "clear and un-mistakable" as violations than those considered here, had been vio-lated, is an indication that the whole social context, including consti-

---

[31]This interpretation is not inconsistent with certain facts about Justice John Marshall Harlan. He had been a Colonel of infantry on the Union side during the Civil War. In 1877, President Hayes appointed him to the Supreme Court where, like his namesake, he served for more than three decades. His opinions were generally forceful, and comparatively liberal in attitude. Dissenting in *Plessy v. Ferguson* in 1896 he spoke of Louisiana's statutory segregation on trains and continued:

". . . If laws of like character should be enacted in the several states of the Union, the effect would be in the highest degree mischievous. Slavery as an institution tolerated by law would, it is true have disappeared from our country, but there would remain a power in the states, by sinister legislation, to interfere with the full enjoyment of the blessings of freedom; to regulate civil rights, common to all citizens, upon the basis of race; and to place in a condition of legal inferiority a large body of American citizens. . . ." (129, p. 1148)

tutional law, had changed. And if Justice Harlan regretted that his decision had to take the form it did, it is perhaps the more ironic that it proved the first of a series extending over several decades in which the Court sustained the "separate but equal" doctrine for schools.

Between this case and the *Gaines* case (115) two others are to be considered. The first of these, the *Berea College* case (58) involves not segregation in public schools but the right of a state to impose segregation on a chartered private school.

AMDT. 14—RIGHTS OF CITIZENS
Sec.   1—Citizens of the United States
ART.   1—LEGISLATIVE DEPT.
Sec.   10—Powers Denied to the States
Cl.   1—Obligation of Contracts

[29] SEGREGATED INSTRUCTION MAY BE IMPOSED ON A CHARTERED PRIVATE SCHOOL

BEREA COLLEGE V. COMMONWEALTH
OF KENTUCKY
211 U. S. 45, 29 Sup. Ct. 33 (1908)

The Supreme Court of the United States upheld a state statute which prohibited educational corporations from giving instruction to mingled white and Negro students.

Berea College is a coeducational, non-denominational institution with only a year or two less than a century of history behind it. Notable for its program of student self-support and of manual work as a specific feature of the curriculum, the school admitted both white and Negro students and treated them without discrimination. The college was chartered by the state.

In 1904 the legislature of Kentucky acted to prohibit mixing of the races in schools by a statute of which the following is a part:

Sec. 1. That it shall be unlawful for any person, corporation or association of persons to maintain or operate any college, school or institution where persons of the white and negro races are both received as pupils for instruction; and any person or corporation who shall operate or maintain any such college, school or institution shall be fined $1000, and any person or corporation who may be convicted of violating the provisions of this act, shall be fined $100 for each day they may operate said school, college or institution, after such conviction. (58, p. 33)

The fourth section of the act forbade any one institution from teaching the races separately, unless in branches more than twenty-five miles apart. (58, p. 36)

Berea College was indicted in the fall of the same year the legislation was passed, and on trial was found guilty and fined the prescribed one-thousand-dollar penalty. This judgment was affirmed by the court of appeals of the state. That court did strike out the twenty-five mile requirement of the fourth section because it "violates the limitations upon the police power" and "is unreasonable and oppressive." (58, p. 36) Berea College refused to accept the otherwise adverse holding of the state court and the case was taken to the Supreme Court of the United States on a writ of error.

Justice Brewer, with Justice Harlan dissenting, delivered the opinion of the Court, which said, in part:

> There is no dispute as to the facts. That the act does not violate the constitution of Kentucky is settled by the decision of its highest court, and the single question for our consideration is whether it conflicts with the Federal Constitution. The Court of Appeals discussed at some length the general power of the State in respect to the separation of the two races. It also ruled that "the right to teach white and negro children in a private school at the same time and place is not a property right. Besides, appellant as a corporation created by this State has no natural right to teach at all. Its right to teach is such as the State sees fit to give to it. The State may withhold it altogether, or qualify it." Allgeyer v. Louisiana, 164 U. S. 578.
>
> Upon this we remark that when a state court decides a case upon two grounds, one Federal and the other non-Federal, this court will not disturb the judgment if the non-Federal ground, fairly construed, sustains the decision. Murdock v. City of Memphis, 20 Wall. 590, 636; Eustis v. Bolles, 150 U. S. 361; Giles v. Teasley, 193 U. S. 146, 160; Allen v. Arguimbau, 198 U. S. 149.
>
> Again, the decision by a state court of the extent and limitation of the powers conferred by the State upon one of its own corporations is of a purely local nature. In creating a corporation a State may withhold powers which may be exercised by and cannot be denied to an individual. It is under no obligation to treat both alike. In granting corporate powers the legislature may deem that the best interests of the State would be subserved by some restriction, and the corporation may not plead that in spite of the restriction it has more or greater powers because the citizen has. "The granting of such right or privilege [the right or privilege to be a corporation] rests entirely in the discretion of the State, and, of course, when granted, may be accompanied with such conditions as its legislature may judge most befitting to its interests and policy." Home Ins. C. v. New York, 134, U. S. 594, 600; Perine v. Chesapeake & Delaware Canal Co., 9 How. 172, 184; Horn Silver Mining Co. v. New York, 143 U. S. 305-312. The act of 1904 forbids "any person, corporation or association of persons to maintain or operate any college", etc. Such a statute may conflict with the Federal Constitution in denying to individuals powers which they may rightfully exercise, and yet, at the same time, be valid as to a corporation created by the State. . . . (58, p. 34)

COMMENT

In addition to the material quoted, the Court's opinion also related to another matter which a commentator who cites the case has phrased as follows:

> Is the right which is reserved by a State to "amend" or "alter" a charter without restriction? When it is accompanied, as it generally is, by the right to "repeal", one would suppose that the answer to this question was self-evident. None the less, there are a number of judicial dicta to the effect that this power is not without limit, that it must be exercised reasonably and in good faith, and that the alterations made must be consistent with the scope of the grant, etc. . . . (48, pp. 343-44)

Courts have held that "person" under the Fourteenth Amendment may include artificial persons, i.e., corporations. The *Berea College* case makes clear, however, that under the meaning of the same amendment, citizens of the United States "must be natural and not artificial persons; a corporate body is not a citizen of the United States." (48, p. 965)

The keynote of the decision, so far as it concerned segregation, lay in the lines which the Supreme Court quoted from the state court's ruling that "the right to teach white and Negro children in a private school at the same time and place is not a property right;" and that a corporation "has no natural right to teach at all," but only such right as the state "sees fit to give it." (58, p. 34)

This holding in the *Berea College* case of 1908, when added to that in the *Cumming* case of 1899, left the issue of segregation standing thus: Public school authorities maintaining segregation could avoid serving both races equally on the plea of economic necessity, and a state could forbid persons and private schools from instructing white and Negro pupils at the same time and place.[32] Thereafter the question of race and schools was not to appear before the Court until nineteen years later when a Chinese child found herself somehow between the whites and Negroes.

It should be noted that in the *Berea College* case, as in the *Alston* case (56 and 55) to be reviewed later in this chapter, the "separate but equal" doctrine was not involved. Property rights and a legal application of the phrase "citizens of the United States" were at issue. The case did, of course, obviously relate to segregation, though not in public schools.

---

[32]Early in 1950 the Kentucky legislature modified the 1904 act to permit admission of Negroes to institutions offering work beyond high school level, provided school authorities approved and comparable work was not available at the Kentucky State College for Negroes. (9, p. 91)

AMDT. 14—RIGHTS OF CITIZENS
Sec.   1—Equal Protection of the Laws
Due Process of Law

[30] A CHINESE CHILD MAY BE CLASSIFIED AS COLORED FOR SCHOOL SEGREGATION PURPOSES

GONG LUM V. RICE

275 U. S. 78, 48 Sup. Ct. 91 (1927)

The Supreme Court of the United States held that the action of Mississippi school authorities in assigning a Chinese child, who was born a citizen of the United States, to a "colored" school did not deny the child equal protection of the laws when equal facilities for white and colored were provided.

Martha Lum, of pure Chinese descent and a native-born citizen of the United States, was denied admittance to Mississippi "white" schools. The availability of "colored" schools in Bolivar County, where she resided, was pointed out to her, but she chose to bring a mandamus action against the school authorities to compel them to admit her to the "white" school. (93, pp. 91-92)

The school authorities contested issuance of the writ but the trial court overruled them by granting Martha Lum's petition. The school authorities then appealed to the Mississippi supreme court. That court's finding was against Martha Lum. In an opinion which cited section 207 of the Mississippi constitution of 1890, providing that "separate schools shall be maintained for children of the white and colored races," the state court held this to mean that Martha Lum as a member of the Mongolian or yellow race could not be classified as white. The state supreme court went on to include in its opinion the following:

The legislature is not compelled to provide separate schools for each of the colored races, and unless and until it does provide such schools, and provide for segregation of the other races, such races are entitled to have the benefit of the colored public schools. Under our statutes a colored public school exists in every county and in some convenient district, in which every colored child is entitled to obtain an education. These schools are within the reach of all the children of the state, and the plaintiff does not show by her petition that she applied for admission to such schools. On the contrary, the plaintiff takes the position that, because there are no separate public schools for Mongolians, she is entitled to enter the white public schools in preference to the colored public schools. . . .

If the plaintiff desires she may attend the colored public schools of her district, or, if she does not so desire, she may go to a private school. The compulsory school law of this state does not require the attendance at a public school, and a parent under the decisions of the Supreme Court of the United States has a right to educate his child in a private school if he so desires.[33] But the plaintiff is not entitled to attend a white public school. (93, p. 92)

On this adverse finding Martha Lum's case was carried to the Supreme Court of the United States. There, in an opinion by Chief Justice Taft, the Court cited the paragraph quoted above. Additional material from the Mississippi supreme court's finding was quoted and examined in an effort to reconcile "averments" in Martha Lum's petition with the statement by the state supreme court that "colored schools are maintained in every county."

The differences asserted by the contenders concerned the availability of schools near Martha Lum's home. The discrepancy needed examination in order that the Court could determine whether Martha Lum's parents, as taxpayers, were denied their rights under due process of law.

Upon examination the Court found that any apparent contradiction in the statements of the two parties "seems to be explained" by the state's description of a system of districts not co-extensive for the "white" and "colored" schools. (93, p. 93)[34] After dealing with this difficulty to the advantage of the state the Court proceeded.

Chief Justice Taft, in delivering the opinion of the Court, said, in part:

The case then reduces itself to the question whether a state can be said to afford to a child of Chinese ancestry, born in this country and a citizen of the United States, the equal protection of the laws, by giving her the opportunity for a common school education in a school which receives only colored children of the brown, yellow or black races.

The right and power of the state to regulate the method of providing for the education of its youth at public expense is clear. [Here the case of Cumming v. County Board of Education is cited and quoted in support]. . . .

The question here is whether a Chinese citizen of the United States is denied equal protection of the laws when he is classed among the colored races and furnished facilities for education equal to that offered to all, whether white, brown, yellow, or black. Were this a new question, it would call for very full argument and consideration; but we think that it is the same question which has been many times decided to be within the constitutional power of the state Legislature to settle, without intervention of the federal courts under the federal Constitution. . . .

In Plessy v. Ferguson, 163 U. S. 537, 544, 545, 16 S. Ct. 1138, 1140, 41 L. Ed. 256, in upholding the validity under the Fourteenth Amendment of a statute of Louisiana requiring the separation of the white and colored races in railway coaches, a more difficult question than this, the court, speaking of permitted race separation, said:

---

[33]The reference here appears to be to the 1923 decision in *Meyer v. Nebraska* (113) and the 1925 decision in *Pierce v. Society of Sisters* (128).

[34]The system of districting described looks like gerrymandering.

"The most common instance of this is connected with the establishment of separate schools for white and colored children, which has been held to be a valid exercise of the legislative power even by courts of states where the political rights of the colored race have been longest and most earnestly enforced."

The case of Roberts v. City of Boston, supra [5 Cush., Mass., 198], in which Chief Justice Shaw, of Supreme Judicial Court of Massachusetts, announced the opinion of that court upholding the separation of colored and white schools under a state constitutional injunction of equal protection, the same as the Fourteenth Amendment, was then referred to, and this court continued:

"Similar laws have been enacted by Congress under its general power of legislation over the District of Columbia (Rev. Stat. D. C. sections 281, 282, 283, 310, 319), as well as by the Legislatures of many of the states, and have been generally, if not uniformly, sustained by the courts"—citing many of the cases above named.

Most of the cases cited arose, it is true, over the establishment of separate schools as between white pupils and black pupils; but we cannot think that the question is any different, or that any different result can be reached, assuming the cases above cited to be rightly decided, where the issue is as between white pupils and the pupils of the yellow races. The decision is within the discretion of the state in regulating its public schools, and does not conflict with the Fourteenth Amendment. . . . (93, pp. 93-94)

COMMENT

By the foregoing the Court had reaffirmed the doctrine laid down in *Cumming v. County Board of Education* that federal interference with a state's management of its schools "cannot be justified, except in the case of a clear and unmistakable disregard of rights secured by the supreme law of the land." Thus, the Court again refused to question segregation of races in the schools as conflicting with any rights within its purview.

Moreover, just as the Court, by its handling of the *Berea College* case had left no doubt that it santioned laws expressly requiring white and Negro children to be educated in separate schools, the right of the state to do as it saw fit in classifying citizens into "white" and "colored" for school purposes was now confirmed.

It looked as though the "colored" races would have to grow reconciled to segregation and its concomitant of generally inferior schools. (14, p. 183) Then, with the *Gaines* case (115) eleven years after the *Gong Lum* case the court showed a disposition to view certain long-standing inequalities in educational facilities maintained by states as "clear and unmistakable disregard of rights secured by the supreme law of the land."

Two reasons for the change can be suggested in most general terms.

One of these may have risen in the changing social and political milieu of the depression and the New Deal.

The other and more specific reason lay in the calculated campaign against segregation in schools and elsewhere by the National Association for the Advancement of Colored People under the guidance of its counsel, Charles Houston, and a group of attorneys he had trained while Dean of the Howard University law school. (45, p. 19) The fact that three of the five cases involving race and schools which were to be decided by the Court following the *Gong Lum* case rested on facts of discrimination and segregation in law schools was probably no accident. Here was a setting well designed for the Justices' personal insight and appreciation of inequalities.

With a measure of success in cases involving higher education the Negroes could then appeal to favorable precedent in bringing before the Court inequalities existing at lower-school levels. This they proceeded to do, and their success was demonstrated by the two decisions of May 17, 1954.

AMDT. 14—RIGHTS OF CITIZENS
Sec.   1—Equal Protection of the Laws

[31] EQUAL OPPORTUNITY FOR A LEGAL EDUCATION MUST BE PROVIDED WITHIN A STATE'S OWN BORDERS

MISSOURI EX REL GAINES V. CANADA
305 U. S. 337, 59 Sup. Ct. 232 (1938)

The Supreme Court of the United States declared that a state could insure equal protection of the laws only within its own jurisdiction, and hence could not maintain equality of opportunity for the legal education of its qualified Negroes through the expedient of paying their tuition at law schools outside the state.

In this case, as in the preceding, the Court avoided discussion of the constitutionality of segregation itself. Nevertheless, the Court's declaration that the state could not fulfill its obligation to afford equal educational facilities to a Negro student by paying his tuition at an out-of-state school, makes the decision here a landmark in the history of Negro education.

Lloyd L. Gaines, a citizen of Missouri, was graduated in 1935 from Lincoln University, an institution maintained for Negroes by the state. The university did not include a law school. Gaines, upon seeking to enter the University of Missouri law school, was referred by its registrar to the president of Lincoln University who pointed out a portion of the Revised Statutes of Missouri (1929), which read:

Sec. 9622. *May arrange for attendance at university of any adjacent state—Tuition fees.*—Pending the full development of the Lincoln University, the board of curators shall have the authority to arrange for the attendance of negro residents of the state of Missouri at the university of any adjacent state to take any course or to study any subjects provided for at the state university of Missouri and which are not taught at the Lincoln University and to pay the reasonable tuition fees for such attendance; provided that whenever the board of curators shall deem it advisable they shall have the power to open any necessary school or department. (115, p. 233)

Gaines refused to seek the aid available under the statute, but he did seek from the courts a writ of mandamus to compel the University of Missouri to admit him. He contended that such admission had been denied solely because he was a Negro. The University of Missouri agreed that Gaines' "work and credits at the Lincoln University would qualify him for admission to the School of Law at the University of Missouri if he were found otherwise eligible," but that to admit a Negro was "contrary to the constitution, laws and public policy of the state." (115, p. 233)

The state circuit court refused to grant Gaines' petition and the state supreme court upheld the lower court. The case was then taken to the United States Supreme Court on a writ of certiorari. The Supreme Court denied the university's right to exclude Gaines, holding that an unconstitutional discrimination within the state could not be cured by providing opportunities where the jurisdiction of the state did not extend. The Court added that the action of the curators of the University of Missouri was clearly state action; that although the authorities of Lincoln university had some discretion in extending to Missouri Negroes offerings equal to those at the University of Missouri, the absence of sufficient mandate to Lincoln University authorities made the state responsible for the inequality of opportunity in legal education facilities. (115, p. 237)

Chief Justice Hughes in delivering the Court's opinion, said in part:

. . . we must regard the question whether the provision for the legal education in other states of negroes resident in Missouri is sufficient to satisfy the constitutional requirement of equal protection, as the pivot upon which this case turns.

The state court stresses the advantages that are afforded by the law schools of the adjacent states, Kansas, Nebraska, Iowa and Illinois, which admit non-resident negroes. . . .

We think that these matters are beside the point. The basic consideration is not as to what sort of opportunities other states provide, or whether they are as good as those in Missouri, but as to what opportunities Missouri itself furnishes to white students and denies to negroes solely upon the ground of color. The admissibility of laws separating the races in the enjoyment of privileges afforded by the state rests wholly upon the quality of the privileges which the laws give to the separated groups within the state. The question here is not of a duty of the state to supply legal training, or of the quality of the training which it does supply, but of its duty when it provides such training to furnish it to the residents of the state upon the basis of an equality of right. By the operation of the laws of Missouri a privilege has been created for white law students which is denied to negroes by reason of their race. The white resident is afforded legal education within the state; the negro resident having the same qualifications is refused it there and must go outside the state to obtain it. That is a denial of the equality of legal right to the enjoyment of the privilege which the state has set up, and the provision for the payment of tuition fees in another state does not remove the discrimination.

The equal protection of the laws is "a pledge of the protection of equal laws" . . . Manifestly, the obligation of the state to give the protection of equal laws can be performed only where its laws operate, that is, within its own jurisdiction. It is there that the equality of legal right must be maintained. . . . We find it impossible to conclude that what otherwise would be an unconstitutional discrimination, with respect to the legal right to the enjoyment of opportunities within the state, can be justified by requiring resort to opportunities elsewhere. That resort may mitigate the inconvenience of the discrimination but cannot serve to validate it.

Nor can we regard the fact that there is but a limited demand in Missouri for the legal education of negroes as excusing the discrimination in favor of whites. . . .

Here, petitioner's right was a personal one. It was as an individual that he was entitled to the equal protection of the laws, and the state was bound to furnish him within its borders facilities for legal education substantially equal to those which the state there afforded for persons of the white race, whether or not other negroes sought the same opportunity.

It is urged, however, that the provision for tuition outside the state is a temporary one,—that it is intended to operate merely pending the establishment of a law department for negroes at Lincoln University. While in that sense the discrimination may be termed temporary, it may nevertheless continue for an indefinite period by reason of the discretion given to the curators of Lincoln University and the alternative of arranging for tuition in other states, as permitted by the state law as construed by the state court, so long as the curators find it unnecessary and impracticable to provide facilities for the legal instruction of negroes within the state. In that view, we cannot regard the discrimination as excused by what is called its temporary character. . . .

. . . We are of the opinion that . . . petitioner was entitled to be admitted to the law school of the state university in the absence of other and proper provision for his legal training within the state. . . . (115, pp. 236-38)

COMMENT

Two years before this decision was handed down a very similar case had been decided in Maryland where Donald Murray, a citizen and an Amherst graduate, was denied admission to the law school of the university because he was a Negro.[35] He was later admitted when the highest Maryland court held that if the races were to be separated the facilities must be equal. This court went on to observe that a scholarship to another state would increase Murray's expense and cost him the opportunity of specializing in the law of his home state. (23, p. 182)

Although neither of the latter points were expressly included by the Supreme Court of the United States in the *Gaines* decision, a point quite close to the last was made by Chief Justice Vinson in his decision on the *Sweatt* (146) case in 1950. Therein it was noted that a segregated law school in Texas "excludes" the greater portion of the white attorneys and most of the judges and jurors with whom a Negro lawyer practicing in Texas would deal. (146, p. 850)

To return to the *Gaines* case, the decision did not, of course, prevent states maintaining segregation from continuing to provide out-of-state scholarships to Negroes who were willing to accept them.

Similarly, as the developments in the *Sipuel* (141) and *Sweatt* (146) cases show, at least some such states were persuaded to provide Negroes only makeshift arrangements for professional training, and then only when a specifically applied court case impelled them to it.

Although the Court held in the *Gaines* case that the Missouri provision for paying a Negro's out-of-state tuition was discriminatory, the Court failed to say exactly why, and thereby left to the states a possible means of keeping their own graduate and professional schools for whites alone. This they could possibly do by sharing in the support of regional schools.

However, the fact that fourteen southern states did enter into a compact for pooling their resources to provide educational facilities in centers open to both races (25, pp. 633-35) appears to have had little, if any, relationship to the Court's decisions on segregation

---

[35]Thurgood Marshall, today's eminently successful counsel for the National Association for the Advancement of Colored People had found a few years earlier that no law school in Maryland would admit him. He thereupon enrolled in all-Negro Howard University in Washington where Charles Houston, then the law dean and later the counsel for Gaines, "looked on Howard as a self-destroying force: He wanted it to turn out a battery of able Negro lawyers who would one day accomplish the abolition of segregation, and so make Howard obsolete." Marshall has since won many segregation cases, including the *Alston* case and the *Sweatt* case. (45, p. 19) His greatest reward as counsel before the Court was in Chief Justice Warren's two decisions of May 17, 1954, at last declaring segregation in public schools to be unconstitutional.

issues.[36] That the compact followed by a few weeks the 1948 decision in the *Sipuel* case (141) which held that a state must provide an equal legal education for Negroes as soon as for whites, was probably coincidence and conceived not as a counter to the Court's stricter construction of the separate but equal doctrine; but rather as a response to plain economic considerations. As a move to counter the Court's stricter construction the compact would probably not have proved enduringly effective. For, without Chief Justice Warren's decision on May 17, 1954, declaring segregation in the public schools unconstitutional, the question whether Negroes' rights under the equal protection clause were met by providing them regional schools supported by the public funds of several states while those states still kept their own schools "white" would undoubtedly have reached the Supreme Court. Two considerations would have appeared in connection with the question. First, unless the states provided a generous system of graduated compensation, it might still have been held that a Negro directed to a regional school was discriminated against by virtue of greater expense to him. This, it will be remembered, was a point in the state court decision for Maryland mentioned above. The second point is also related to a factor which appeared in the Maryland court's decision and in the *Sweatt* decision (146) by the Supreme Court as well—that to require a Negro to attend a regional law school would deny him the specialization and the associations advantageous to a member of the bar in a particular state. Similar considerations would, of course, have applied to equality in training for other professions. Indeed it is possible that these questions may yet receive attention from the Court in a case actually or ostensibly not involving race.

Of the cases combining race and education which the Court did decide after 1927, all but the most recent involved professions, and of these all except two involved training for the law. The first of the two exceptions concerned a teacher already established in his profession. The Court refused to grant certiorari and by so doing decided the case, which follows.

---

[36]Harry S. Ashmore's, *The Negro and the Schools*, says that "the plan was denounced by many Negro leaders as a device for preserving segregation at the university level." Evidence to refute the view is presented in a statement by the Southern Regional Education Board that it is not the "purpose that the regional program shall serve any state as a legal defense for avoiding responsibilities under existing state and federal laws and court decisions." Indeed, according to Ashmore, when Maryland, in 1949, directed a Negro student to a regional center for certain education which the state maintained at its own university, the regional board intervened against the state and assisted the Negro student in securing a court order for admission to the university. (2, pp. 36-37)

AMDT. 14—RIGHTS OF CITIZENS
Sec.   1—Equal Protection of the Laws
Due Process of Law

[32] WHITE AND COLORED PUBLIC SCHOOL TEACHERS SIMILARLY SITUATED AND QUALIFIED MUST BE PAID EQUAL SALARIES

ALSTON V. SCHOOL BOARD OF THE CITY OF NORFOLK

311 U. S. 693, 61 Sup. Ct. 75 (1940)

The Supreme Court of the United States denied a petition for a writ of certiorari and thereby sustained the United States Circuit Court of Appeals in a judgment holding that a disparate salary schedule for equally qualified and similarly assigned Negro and white teachers violated due process and equal protection of laws under the Fourteenth Amendment.

In this Virginia case Melvin O. Alston, a Negro public school teacher, contended that since he was equally situated and qualified with white teachers he was discriminated against in being paid less salary. He hoped to show that the practice of paying lower salaries to Negroes was "violative of the 'due process' and 'equal protection' clauses of the Fourteenth Amendment." Therefore, he sought "an injunction restraining defendants from making any distinction on the ground of race and color in fixing the salaries of public school teachers in Norfolk."

The United States District Court dismissed the case on the ground that:

. . . Alston and the School Board were the only necessary parties to the cause and that Alston had waived such constitutional rights as he was seeking to enforce by having entered into a written contract with the School Board to teach for a year at the price fixed in the contract. . . . (55, p. 994)

Alston's case was thereupon carried to the Circuit Court of Appeals where the three judges reduced the matter to the following questions, here paraphrased:

(1) Was an unconstitutional discrimination shown by the school board in fixing Alston's salary?
(2) Were Alston's rights infringed by such discrimination?
(3) Had Alston waived his right to complain of the discrimination by signing a contract with the school board? (55, p. 994)

The judges then considered these questions and held that:

(1) The discrimination shown was unconstitutional.
(2) Alston's rights were infringed.
(3) The fact that Alston had signed a contract for a specified sum did not prevent redress. (55, pp. 995-97)

In connection with the answer to the first and second questions, Judge Parker, speaking for the court said, in part:

That an unconstitutional discrimination is set forth in these paragraphs hardly admits of argument. The allegation is that the state, in paying for public services of the same kind and character to men and women equally qualified according to standards which the state itself prescribes, arbitrarily pays less to Negroes than to white persons. This is as clear a discrimination on the ground of race as could well be imagined and falls squarely within the inhibition of both the due process and the equal protection clauses of the Fourteenth Amendment. As was said by Mr. Justice Harlan in Gibson v. Mississippi, 162 U. S. 565, 591, 16 S. Ct. 904, 910, 40 L. Ed. 1075: "Underlying all of those decisions is the principle that the constitution of the United States, in its present form, forbids, so far as civil and political rights are concerned, discrimination by the general government, or by the states, against any citizen because of his race. All citizens are equal before the law. The guaranties of life, liberty, and property are for all persons, within the jurisdiction of the United States, or of any state, without discrimination against any because of their race. Those guaranties, when their violation is properly presented in the regular course of proceedings, must be enforced in the courts, both of the nation and of the state, without reference to considerations based upon race." . . . (55, pp. 995-96)

The Supreme Court of the United States refused a petition for a writ of certiorari to review the case (56) and thereby affirmed the holding of the lower court, the Circuit Court of Appeals, Fourth District, earlier in 1943.

COMMENT

In Professor Cushman's words: "If the rule of the Alston case were to be effectively enforced throughout the south, the effect upon Negro education can hardly be overestimated." (14, p. 183)

The administration of equal-pay laws appears quite difficult, even where no race issue is involved—should the home economics supervisor be paid the same salary as the supervisor of the program for handicapped children? The answer lies in a multitude of factors often difficult to equate on a rating scale.

Indeed, the ambiguity available to administrators in applying rating scales has been pointed out by Negro teachers in Florida. In a 1945 case (133) Hubert C. Reynolds and others alleged that although local school officials had, in 1941, abolished separate pay scales based upon race, the current rating system generally resulted in consistently less pay for Negro teachers. The federal district court did not find the discrimination complained of, but the following was included in its opinion:

. . . We recognize, too, that equal protection may be denied, not only by arbitrary discrimination in legislation, or in quasi-legislation such as this Board's establishment of schedules of classification and the resulting salaries, but also by administration "with an evil eye and an unequal hand". . . . (133, p. 756)

In a similar case arising in Arkansas, Negro teachers were successful in their complaint. In 1945 the United States circuit court of appeals, in *Morris v. Williams* (117), reversed the federal district court and upheld Susie Williams in her contention that she and other Negro teachers in Little Rock were being discriminated against in a salary differential ostensibly based upon other factors but actually based solely upon race. The court found that the board of directors and the superintendent were, in fact, illegally "maintaining a policy, usage and custom of discriminating against the colored teachers," and that such was done "solely on account of race or color." (117, p. 709)

Three years later, in 1948, a federal district court in Virginia heard the case of *Freeman v. County School Board* (83), wherein a Negro teacher sought to show that he and others received less salary than comparable white teachers. The court noted that the "rating of the various teachers is suggested by the Division Superintendent and adopted by the Board," and that the superintendent testified that he "endeavors to give consideration to the qualifications of various individuals based upon his knowledge and observation of teachers." "Upon its face," said the federal judge, this procedure "appears fair and reasonable." Then he adds:

At the hearing I was favorably impressed with the arrangement. However, upon analysis I have reached the conclusion that as applied it is not free of discrimination. (83, pp. 169)

Factors in the court's analysis and judgment against the school board included the absence of any examinations upon which to base the ratings, the inability of a busy superintendent to personally rate a large number of principals and teachers and, particularly, the evidence that while only 27 per cent of the white teachers held degrees, 96 per cent of them received salaries above the minimum, whereas 52 per cent of the Negro teachers held degrees, yet only 36 per cent of them received above the minimum salary. (83, pp. 169-70)

It should, perhaps, be emphasized that neither the *Alston* case nor the three just mentioned were questions on the "separate but equal" doctrine. The same constitutional clauses were involved but the issue was not segregation.

AMDT. 14—RIGHTS OF CITIZENS
Sec.   1—Equal Protection of the Laws

[33] OPPORTUNITY FOR A LEGAL EDUCATION MUST BE PROVIDED ONE RACE AS SOON AS ANOTHER

SIPUEL V. OKLAHOMA BOARD OF REGENTS
332 U. S. 631, 68 Sup. Ct. 299 (1948)
(AND
FISHER V. HURST)
333 U. S. 147, 68 Sup. Ct. 389 (1948)

The Supreme Court of the United States held that under the equal protection clause of the Fourteenth Amendment the State of Oklahoma must provide for Negro applicants a legal education equal to that afforded white students in its state schools, and must do so for one race as soon as for another.

This case, it will be noted, is very similar to the *Gaines* case which preceded it by a decade.

In 1946, after the University of Oklahoma Law School, the only institution for legal training supported by the state, had refused admission to Ada Louis Sipuel solely because she was a Negro, a petition for a writ of mandamus was filed in her behalf. The Oklahoma courts refused to grant the writ, but on appeal to the Supreme Court of the United States the state courts were reversed and the ruling in the *Gaines* case was reaffirmed. In a per curiam opinion in January, 1948, the Court said, in part:

. . . [Ada Louis Sipuel] is entitled to secure legal education afforded by a state institution. To this time it has been denied her although during the same period many white applicants have been afforded legal education by the State. The State must provide it for her in conformity with the equal protection clause of the Fourteenth Amendment and provide it as soon as it does for applicants of any other group. . . . (141, p. 299)

The state court had attempted to distinguish this case from the *Gaines* case by holding that because Ada Sipuel had not given advance warning of her intent to apply for admission to law school, the state had therefore been unable to provide separate facilities for legal education; hence she was not discriminated against. This contention the Supreme Court rejected.

The Court had again avoided a specific ruling on segregation, but the decision that Oklahoma must provide a legal education for applicants of one race as soon as for another appeared to mean that the state would have to admit Ada Sipuel to its existing law school, or admit no one, or establish a separate law school overnight. Each of these three alternatives was attempted by various state authorities.

The Oklahoma Board of Regents voted to admit qualified Negroes to those professional schools at the university not provided at the State College for Negroes; while Oklahoma's attorney general expressed doubt that a mandate from the Supreme Court of the United States would prevail over the state's constitution and statutes requiring segregation in its public schools; and the supreme court of Oklahoma ordered the trial court to carry out the mandate of the Supreme Court of the United States, but within limits of the Oklahoma constitutional provisions and statutes on segregation. Accordingly, the trial court gave the Board of Regents a choice of enrolling Ada Sipuel in the first-year class of the university's law school or of enrolling no one of either race in the class until equal facilities to provide a legal education for Negroes were ready; but if such equal facilities were made available, Ada Sipuel would not then be enrolled in the university. Thereupon the Board of Regents designated space in the state capitol as a "law school" and provided a faculty of three for Ada Sipuel "and all others similarly situated," but she refused to attend a school manifestly below the standards for law school accreditation. (51, pp. 144-48)

She then sought to compel state compliance with the decision of the Supreme Court of the United States and petitioned for a writ of mandamus to that end. In the interval between her two cases Ada Sipuel had become Mrs. Fisher. Hence her part of the title in the new case, *Fisher v. Hurst* (80). In this new case the Court again rendered a per curiam decision. Mrs. Fisher's petition was denied by the Court's holding that the Oklahoma trial court had not departed from its mandate. The Court added that it saw nothing in the events since its earlier decision to raise the issue of the right of a state to comply with the equal protection clause through segregated schools. The decision was not, however, unanimous. Justice Murphy believed that the question of the trial court's evasion of the Supreme Court's mandate should be more thoroughly examined, while Justice Rutledge insisted that the state court had circumvented the equal protection requirement by including only the first-year class in its order. The result of this, said the Justice, might still allow white students to enjoy facilities denied the black. He added that the original mandate envisaged "equality in fact, not in legal fiction." (80, p. 391)

In the *Sweatt* (146) and *McLaurin* (112) decisions handed down in June, 1950, the Court did demand more of the "fact" and less of the "fiction."

AMDT. 14—RIGHTS OF CITIZENS
Sec.   1—Equal Protection of the Laws

[34] FACILITIES AND SERVICES FOR A LEGAL EDUCATION MUST BE TRULY EQUAL

SWEATT V. PAINTER

339 U. S. 629, 70 Sup. Ct. 848 (1950)

The Supreme Court of the United States found that a separate law school provided for Texas Negroes did not afford them a legal education equivalent to that afforded other races by the state, and held that the equal protection clause of the Fourteenth Amendment required the University of Texas Law School to admit a qualified Negro.

Decisions in both this and the *McLaurin* case were rendered by the Court on June 5, 1950. Until May 17, 1954, they were the latest involving race and education.

In prospect the *Sweatt* case offered promise that the broad issue of the constitutionality of statutes requiring segregation for professional training might be resolved, but Chief Justice Vinson, in rendering the decision, alluded to the Court's traditional reluctance to consider constitutional issues "except in the particular case before it" and therewith kept the issue narrow. Accordingly, the state of Texas was disappointed when the Court refused to reaffirm the ruling in *Plessy v. Ferguson* (101) that a requirement for separate but equal facilities did not violate the Fourteenth Amendment. At the same time, attorneys for the colored Texan, Hemon Sweatt, were disappointed by the Court's concurrent refusal to abandon the same 1896 ruling. Nevertheless, Sweatt was ordered admitted to the University of Texas Law School and he and his race saw the Court's definition of the meaning of "substantially equal" come to stand much closer to "truly equal."

Speaking for a unanimous Court Chief Justice Vinson traced the history of the case in delivering the opinion, here quoted in part:

In the instant case, petitioner filed an application for admission to the University of Texas Law School for the February, 1946, term. His application was rejected solely because he is a Negro. Petitioner thereupon brought this suit for mandamus against the appropriate school officials, respondents here, to compel his admission. At that time, there was no law school in Texas which admitted Negroes.

The State trial court recognized that the action of the State in denying petitioner the opportunity to gain a legal education while granting it to others deprived him of the equal protection of the laws guaranteed by the Fourteenth Amendment. The court did not grant the relief requested, however, but continued the case for six months to allow the State to supply substantially equal facilities. At the expiration of the six months, in December, 1946, the court denied the writ on the showing that the authorized university officials had adopted an order calling for the opening of a law school for Negroes the following February. While petitioner's appeal was pending, such a school was made available, but petitioner refused to register therein. The Texas Court of Civil Appeals set aside the trial court's judgment and ordered the cause "remanded generally to the trial court for further proceedings without prejudice to the right of any party to this suit." . . .

The University of Texas Law School, from which petitioner was excluded, was staffed by a faculty of sixteen full-time and three part-time professors, some of whom are nationally recognized authorities in their field. Its student body numbered 850. The library contained over 65,000 volumes. Among the other facilities available to the students were a law review, moot court facilities, scholarship funds, and Order of the Coif affiliation. The school's alumni occupy the most distinguished positions in the private practice of the law and in the public life of the State. It may properly be considered one of the nation's ranking law schools.

The law school for Negroes which was to have opened in February, 1947, would have had no independent faculty or library. The teaching was to be carried on by four members of the University of Texas Law School faculty, who were to maintain their offices at the University of Texas while teaching at both institutions. Few of the 10,000 volumes ordered for the library had arrived; nor was there any full-time librarian. The school lacked accreditation.

Since the trial of this case, respondents report the opening of a law school at the Texas State University for Negroes. It is apparently on the road to full accreditation. It has a faculty of five full-time professors; a student body of 23; a library of some 16,500 volumes serviced by a full-time staff; a practice court and legal aid association; and one alumnus who has become a member of the Texas Bar.

Whether the University of Texas Law School is compared with the original or the new law school for Negroes, we cannot find substantial equality in the educational opportunities offered white and Negro law students by the State. In terms of number of the faculty, variety of courses and opportunity for specialization, size of the student body, scope of the library, availability of law review and similar activities, the University of Texas Law School is superior. What is more important, the University of Texas Law School possesses to a far greater degree those qualities which are incapable of objective measurements but which made for greatness in a law school. Such qualities, to name but a few, include reputation of the faculty, experience of the administration, position and influence of the alumni, standing in the community, traditions and prestige. It is difficult to believe that one who had a free choice between these law schools would consider the question close.

Moreover, although the law is a highly learned profession, we are well aware that it is an intensely practical one. The law school, the proving ground for legal learning and practice, cannot be effective in isolation from the individuals and institutions with which the law interacts. Few students and no one who has practiced law would choose to study in an academic vacuum, removed from the interplay of ideas and the exchange of views with which the law is concerned. The law school to which Texas is willing to admit petitioner excludes from its student body members of the racial groups which number 85% of the population of the State and include most of the lawyers, witnesses, jurors, judges and other officials with whom petitioner will inevitably be dealing when he becomes a member of the Texas Bar. With such a substantial and significant segment of society excluded, we cannot conclude that the education offered petitioner is substantially equal to that which he would receive if admitted to the University of Texas Law School. . . . (146, pp. 849-50)

[The Court goes on to cite *Shelley v. Kraemer* (140), the *Sipuel* (141) and the *Gaines* (115) cases, and continues:]

In accordance with these cases, petitioner may claim his full constitutional right: legal education equivalent to that offered by the State to students of other races. Such education is not available to him in a separate law school as offered by the State. We cannot, therefore, agree with respondents that the doctrine of Plessy v. Ferguson, 163 U. S. 537 (1896), requires affirmance of the judgment below. Nor need we reach petitioner's contention that Plessy v. Ferguson should be reexamined in the light of contemporary knowledge respecting the purposes of the Fourteenth Amendment and the effects of racial segregation. . . .

We hold that the Equal Protection Clause of the Fourteenth Amendment requires that petitioner be admitted to the University of Texas Law School. The judgment is reversed and the cause is remanded for proceedings not inconsistent with this opinion. . . . (146, pp. 850-51)

COMMENT

The Chief Justice, in making a point of the fact that the University of Texas Law School "possesses to a far greater degree those qualities which are incapable of objective measurement but which make for greatness in a law school," thereby shifted the Court's interpretation of the term "substantially equal" to a position much closer to the ordinary connotation associated with equality in fact.

New, so far as the Supreme Court's consideration of this matter is concerned, was the point that the Negro law school "excludes" the great preponderance of the population of Texas and consequently, the professional associates with whom a Negro graduate would have to deal when practicing law in Texas.

Still, it should be emphasized the court did not abandon the separate but equal rule, nor did it define separate but equal facilities. The law schools involved were merely held to be less than equal.

Nevertheless, the implications of this opinion are large, and they become the greater when the *McLaurin* opinion, which was handed down at the same time, is also considered. The *McLaurin* case follows.

AMDT. 14—RIGHTS OF CITIZENS
Sec.   1—Equal Protection of the Laws

[35] **AN ENROLLED GRADUATE STUDENT MUST NOT BE**
SEGREGATED IN A STATE UNIVERSITY

MC LAURIN V. OKLAHOMA STATE REGENTS

339 U. S. 637, 70 Sup. Ct. 851 (1950)

The Supreme Court of the United States held that the enforced segregation measures imposed by the state university upon a Negro admitted to its
graduate school were a handicap to the pursuit of effective graduate work,
and denied the equal protection guaranteed by the Fourteenth Amendment.

Following the *Gaines* case (115) in 1938 a state supporting segregation could be required to provide equal facilities for a legal education
within its own borders. Then, in 1948, the *Sipuel* case (141) required
that a state provide opportunity for a legal education to one race as
soon as another. Next, the *Sweatt* case (146) of 1950 required that the
facilities for legal education provided the races should be truly equal.

Here, in the *McLaurin* case (112), the issue raised was whether a
state, after having enrolled a Negro in its university, could treat him
differently than other students solely because of his race.

The student involved, G. W. McLaurin, was an experienced teacher
of mature years when he applied for admission to the graduate school
of the University of Oklahoma in 1948. He already held a master's
degree and contemplated a program leading to a doctorate in education.

The school denied McLaurin admission under an Oklahoma
statute which made it a misdemeanor for authorities to permit whites
and Negroes to attend the same school. Thereupon he sought an
injunction on the ground that the state statute and the action of the
school authorities under it was unconstitutional and denied him equal
protection of the laws. The United States District Court, in terms
mindful of the *Sipuel* case, held that the state was indeed required to
afford him the education he sought as soon as for any other group,
and that the statutes of which he complained were unconstitutional
and void to the extent that they denied him admission. The District
Court then stated its assumption that Oklahoma would follow constitutional mandates. It refused the injunction but at the same time
maintained jurisdiction in order to secure McLaurin the protection
to which he was entitled. (112, p. 852)

Accordingly, the Oklahoma legislature did amend the statutes to
allow admission of Negroes to those courses of study in "white" schools
which were not available in Negro schools, but provided that the

instruction should be given "upon a segregated basis." McLaurin was thereupon granted admission "subject to 'such rules and regulations as to segregation as the President of the University shall consider to afford Mr. G. W. McLaurin substantially equal educational opportunities as are afforded to other persons seeking the same education at the Graduate College.' " (112, p. 853)

Chief Justice Vinson again spoke for the unanimous court. The opinion, quoted from the point in which it describes McLaurin's conditional admission, said, in part:

. . . Thus he was required to sit apart at a designated desk in an anteroom adjoining the classroom; to sit at a designated desk on the mezzanine floor of the library, but not to use the desks in the regular reading room; and to sit at a designated table and to eat at a different time from the other students in the school cafeteria.

To remove these conditions, appellant filed a motion to modify the order and judgment of the District Court. That court held that such treatment did not violate the provisions of the Fourteenth Amendment and denied the motion. This appeal followed.

In the interval between the decision of the court below and the hearing in this Court, the treatment afforded appellant was altered. For some time, the section of the classroom in which appellant sat was surrounded by a rail on which there was a sign stating, "Reserved For Colored", but these have been removed. He is now assigned to a seat in the classroom in a row specified for colored students; he is assigned to a table in the library on the main floor; and he is permitted to eat at the same time in the cafeteria as other students although here again he is assigned to a special table.

It is said that the separations imposed by the State in his case are in form merely nominal. McLaurin uses the same classroom, library and cafeteria as students of other races; there is no indication that the seats to which he is assigned in these rooms have any disadvantage of location. He may wait in line in the cafeteria and there stand and talk with his fellow students, but while he eats he must remain apart.

These restrictions were obviously imposed in order to comply, as nearly as could be, with the statutory requirements of Oklahoma. But they signify that the State, in administering the facilities it affords for professional and graduate study, sets McLaurin apart from the other students. The result is that appellant is handicapped in his pursuit of effective graduate instruction. Such restrictions impair and inhibit his ability to study, to engage in discussions and exchange views with other students, and, in general, to learn his profession.

Our society grows increasingly complex, and our need for trained leaders increases correspondingly. Appellant's case represents, perhaps, the epitome of that need, for he is attempting to obtain an advanced degree in education, to become, by definition, a leader and trainer of others. Those who will come under his guidance and influence must be directly affected by the education he receives. Their own education and development will necessarily suffer to the extent that his training is unequal to that of his classmates. State-imposed restrictions which produce such inequalities cannot be sustained.

It may be argued that appellant will be in no better position when these restrictions are removed, for he may still be set apart by his fellow students. This we think irrelevant. There is a vast difference—a Constitutional difference—between restrictions imposed by the state which prohibit the intellectual commingling of students, and the refusal of individuals to commingle where the state presents no such bar. . . .

The removal of the state restrictions will not necessarily abate individual and group predilections, prejudices and choices. But at the very least, the state will not be depriving appellant of the opportunity to secure acceptance by his fellow students on his own merits.

We conclude that the conditions under which this appellant is required to receive his education deprive him of his personal and present right to the equal protection of the laws. See Sweatt v. Painter, 339 U. S. We hold that under these circumstances the Fourteenth Amendment precludes differences in treatment by the state based upon race. Appellant, having been admitted to a state-supported graduate school, must receive the same treatment at the hands of the state as students of other races. . . . (112, pp. 853-54)

COMMENT

In four decisions since 1937, those on the *Gaines*, *Sipuel*, *Sweatt*, and *McLaurin* cases, the Court had not abandoned the rule laid down in *Plessy v. Ferguson* in 1896: That segregation is no violation of equal protection of the laws under the federal Constitution, provided the separate facilities are equal. Clearly, however, as a review of the four decisions against the background afforded by earlier cases demonstrates, the Court had progressively given stricter definition to the term, "equality."[37] Thus, in the *McLaurin* decision the Court went about as far as it could go in assuring equality for Negro graduate students without abolishing segregation itself. As for segregation itself, the Court had each time found a narrower ground for its ruling and so had avoided that issue in every opinion rendered.

Soon, however, five more cases reached the Court and all appeared to present segregation as the direct issue. Since schools below the college level were involved, it was conjectured that even if the Court once again found other grounds upon which to decide, application of the tone and trend of the late decisions involving higher education to southern elementary and high-school systems would effect changes much more profound.

---

[37]This has been just as notably true in recent cases involving segregation or discrimination elsewhere than in schools, e.g., the Court's 1948 holding in *Shelley v. Kraemer* (140) that state enforcement of private covenants forbidding the transfer of real estate to persons of a certain race or color constitute a denial of equal protection of the laws. Likewise, in 1950, in *Henderson v. United States* (99) the Court held that segregation in an interstate railroad dining car was unlawful. In this case, apparently for the first time, an attorney for the United States asked that the separate but equal doctrine be overruled.

AMDT. 14—RIGHTS OF CITIZENS
Sec.   1—Equal Protection of the Laws
AMDT. 5—RIGHTS OF PERSONS
Due Process of Law

[36] " 'SEPARATE BUT EQUAL' HAS NO PLACE" IN PUBLIC EDUCATION

BROWN V. BOARD OF EDUCATION
OF TOPEKA (KANSAS)
347 U. S. 483, 74 Sup. Ct. 686 (1954)

[37] BOLLING V. SHARPE, (DISTRICT
OF COLUMBIA)
347 U. S. 497, 74 Sup. Ct. 693 (1954)

The Supreme Court of the United States held segregation by race in the public schools a violation of Constitutional prohibitions applicable to the states under the Fourteenth Amendment and to the District of Columbia under the Fifth Amendment.

In the seventeen years preceding June, 1950, the Supreme Court settled that states supporting segregated public education would have to establish an equality more than merely nominal.[38] The Court had not, however, needed to re-examine its 1896 doctrine of "separate but equal" during the period because, in each case decided, the states were unable to demonstrate that they maintained equality in fact in university education for both Negroes and whites.

Thus, while states might continue to provide equal but separate facilities for the two races, the task was proving a formidable if not a well-nigh impracticable one at the university level alone. Moreover, the trend of the Court's recent decisions involving segregated schools could be interpreted as heralding some other, which, in the not-too-distant future, might clearly spell a beginning of the end to the practice itself. Yet in many states supporting segregated schools, authorities appear to have made sincere efforts to adjustment at all levels with the Court's late holdings, and by making Negro schools actually equal, to insure as well as they might against possible desegregation. Meanwhile, lower federal courts, although somewhat understanding of the practical problems connected with attempts to establish true equality in segregated school systems, had taken their cue from the Supreme Court's closer scrutiny of the separate facilities provided. The language of educators, especially the terminology peculiar to those who surveyed and evaluated public schools, grew familiar in judicial chambers and unless local school authorities could show that they

---

[38]See the cases dated 1938 and later on preceding pages, especially the *Gaines*, *Sipuel*, and *Sweatt* cases.

were making reasonable efforts to reduce inequality, the federal courts were inclined to grant injunctions or issue orders asked by the Negroes asserting they were discriminated against.

Still, as would be expected, the Negroes were not everywhere successful. By the fall of 1952 four cases which originated in federal courts with the holdings adverse to the Negroes had reached the Supreme Court from grade and high schools in Kansas, South Carolina, Virginia, and the District of Columbia. In a fifth case which originated in a Delaware court the Negroes had prevailed and the state had appealed. The nature of these five cases, argued together before the Court in December, 1952, gave attorneys for the Negroes a favorable opportunity to challenge segregated schools in such fashion that the Court could hardly avoid a re-examination of the "separate but equal" doctrine.

THE FIVE CASES[39]

DELAWARE

Gebhart v. Belton. (86, p. 688) Negro parents asserted substantial inequalities in the local separate schools and sought from a state court an order for the admission of their children to the nearest "white" school. The inequalities being demonstrated, the court held that the Negro children were being denied equal educational opportunity, and ordered the children admitted to the "white" school, but only for so long as the inequalities remained. School authorities appealed this decision to the Delaware supreme court. There it was upheld—not because the court questioned the "separate but equal" doctrine, but because of its view that a child could not lawfully be denied available educational opportunity while waiting for authorities to make the "separate" truly "equal." The authorities then appealed to the Supreme Court of the United States on the question of a reasonable time allowance for removing the inequalities.

KANSAS

Brown v. Board of Education of Topeka. (63, p. 687) Negro parents, although here readily conceding substantial equality of the separate schools provided by the local board, charged in a federal district court that segregation was, nevertheless, socially and psychologically damaging to their children and a denial of "equal protection of the laws." The court fully agreed with the contention that the segregation was damaging, but, since no inequalities in services and facilities of the separate schools had been shown, segregation was upheld in ac-

---

[39]Harry S. Ashmore, *The Negro and the Schools* (2, pp. 99-102) contains a more extensive digest of these cases.

cordance with existing Supreme Court rulings. The Negro parents appealed.

SOUTH CAROLINA

Briggs v. Elliott. (61, p. 687) Negro parents sought from a federal court an order which would end in their district the segregated schools existing under statute. They demonstrated to the court that the schools were unequal, and argued that, in any event, the statute denied "equal protection of the laws." The court upheld the constitutionality of the statute, but ordered the inequalities removed and a progress report rendered at the end of six months. An appeal by the parents was taken to the Supreme Court where, because it was not heard until after the six months had passed, the case was merely returned to the lower court for action indicated from an examination of the progress report. The lower court found the progress to be satisfactory. The parents conceded the satisfactory progress but still questioned the constitutionality of segregation itself and again appealed to the Supreme Court.

VIRGINIA

Davis v. County School Board. (73, p. 687) This case is much like the South Carolina case above. Negro parents, questioning the constitutionality of a segregation statute, asked a federal court to either order their children admitted to a "white" school or to order the inequalities in the separate schools ended. The court's decision was, in effect, the same as in the South Carolina case except that the inequalities were to be removed with "dispatch." Thereupon the Negro parents pressed the view that any delay in substantial equality of educational opportunity denied their children the "equal protection of the laws" guaranteed by the Fourteenth Amendment. Appeal on that basis was made to the Supreme Court.

DISTRICT OF COLUMBIA[40]

Bolling v. Sharpe. (59, p. 694) This case was contested under the Fifth rather than the Fourteenth Amendment. Negro parents argued with school authorities the intent of Congress' statutes and appropriations acts in providing and approving segregated schools for the District. Counsel for the school authorities moved, and the court

---

[40]An earlier District of Columbia case, *Carr v. Corning* (67), decided in 1950 by the Court of Appeals for the District had refused to enjoin segregation. This decision held that neither the first ten Amendments nor the Fourteenth prohibited segregated grade and high schools where facilities were equal. Moreover, said the court, the fact that the same years which saw the freeing of the slaves and the adoption of the Fourteenth Amendment also saw Congress providing for segregated schools in the District, was an indication that the Fourteenth Amendment was not directed at segregation.

granted, dismissal of the case because no issue of actual inequality had been presented. The parents then appealed to the Supreme Court. They maintained that segregation in public schools was unconstitutional and that the dismissal by the lower court should, therefore, be reversed and a decision rendered on the segregation issue.

SOME ARGUMENTS AND ATTITUDES

As has been indicated, these cases all raised the constitutional issue of segregation as such. The five were argued together before the Supreme Court in December, 1952. No quick decision was forthcoming and in June, 1953, a reargument was ordered for the next December, with all parties prepared to answer certain questions which may be reduced from two columns of print to the following:

(1.) Did Congress and the state legislatures intend to abolish segregation in the schools by ratifying the Fourteenth Amendment?

(2.) If not, does the amendment afford scope for congressional or judicial action against segregation today?

(3.) If segregation is to be abolished, must the order require immediate compliance or can the process be accomplished gradually? (62, p. 1114 and 37, p. 10)

To the first question the Court received three answers. Negro attorney Thurgood Marshall, of the National Association for the Advancement of Colored People and one of counsel for the South Carolina and Virginia appellants, asserted that the Fourteenth Amendment did clearly intend to abolish segregation in the schools. John W. Davis, perhaps the pre-eminent constitutional lawyer, spoke for South Carolina and said that the amendment clearly bore no such intent. He included a quotation from Disraeli in a warning to the Court: "No man will treat with indifference the principle of race. It is the key of history." Speaking for the United States in its position as a "friend of the Court," Assistant Attorney General J. Lee Rankin held the evidence inconclusive, but asserted that the United States favored the end of segregated schools on other grounds. (45, p. 16)

The stand, similar to this, now taken by the Eisenhower administration had been held by the Truman administration at the previous hearings. (35, p. 1)

In response to the second and third questions the United States Attorney General's office said that the state courts could be directed to end segregation "forthwith," then added that the broad implications of such a ruling would make a transition period necessary. In connection with such transition period the brief suggested: "There is no single formula or blueprint which can be universally applied in all areas where existing school segregation must be ended." (36, p. 3)

Appointment of a special master to referee the process of readjustment was also suggested.

Against this somewhat middle-of-the-road position which, however, supported the Negroes in answer to the second question, the contending states made various arguments.

In the South Carolina and Virginia cases, which were practically identical and which arose in states where segregation was mandatory, the only apparent difference in the briefs was that while Virginia gave an impression that it viewed a ruling against segregation as "enforceable," South Carolina insisted that if the Court did possess power to alter the intent of the framers of the Fourteenth Amendment, it could abolish segregation only on a case-by-case, district-by-district basis. Kansas, which permitted segregation by local option and which was said to be the only state in which the services and physical facilities in schools provided the two races were actually equal, contended that the question of segregation under such circumstances was not a constitutional matter, and that although "segregation may not be the ethical or political ideal," its abolition "is not within the judicial power." Delaware, a state with statutes making segregation mandatory but where a lower court had ordered Negroes admitted to "white" schools until truly equal facilities were established, insisted in terms much like those of Kansas that "it is not within the judicial power to give the amendment a meaning directly contrary to that given by its framers." (37, p. 10)

The case from the District of Columbia demanded a difference in attention. There Congress makes the local law and the school authorities interpreted an act of 1862 as requiring that segregated public schools be maintained. This case, therefore, arose under the Fifth Amendment's limitation upon the powers of Congress rather than under the Fourteenth Amendment's limitation upon the powers of the states. One sphere of government had not proceeded much ahead of the other in the matter of segregated schools.

Perhaps the best indication of the direction in which the Court was expected to move in these cases was afforded by the anticipatory actions of the legislatures of South Carolina and Georgia. Both states began measures enabling discontinuance of public schools and transfer of state support to "private" school systems. Statements by James F. Byrnes and Herman Talmadge, the governors of the two states, declared that they were prepared to use such powers if segregation was outlawed in state institutions. (37, p. 10; and 35, p. 1) Such threat did not, of course, appear in the record, but possible reference to it was made by the Negroes who suggested: "This Court cannot be intimidated." (37, p. 10) Yet, as Harry S. Ashmore (2) has pointed out, while some who debated the issue of segregation in or out of the Court often spoke as if they faced Armageddon, others felt that it could "turn out to be no more than one more milestone in the long road the Negro has traveled since he was brought to this continent in chains." (2, pp. 132-33) The same author goes on to quote Ralph McGill, editor of the Atlanta *Constitution* who, writing in the days during which the Georgia legislature was working out the measure mentioned above, said:

What the various state legislatures are doing, as they busy themselves with plans to carry on school segregation without legal compulsion, is admitting segregation by law is finished . . . either this year, next or within the next few to come. . . .

As a matter of fact, segregation has been on its way out for a good long time and has been breaking down at the edges for more than a generation. . . . Two great forces have been at work on segregation and the problem of race. One is secular, the other religious. The Christian of today cannot help but wince at the full implications, and the jarring clash of his creed, with discrimination against any person because of color. . . . Christianity cannot well afford to be on the wrong side of a moral force, as it was in some areas when it defended slavery.

The other influence is secular. Segregation implies inferiority. There are those who argue that it does not. But those segregated believe it does. . . . Across two great wars now we, along with other free peoples, have preached the rights of men everywhere to be free and equal—we have encouraged long-oppressed peoples to rise. . . .

. . . Segregation is on the way out and he who tries to tell the people otherwise does them great disservice. The problem of the future is how to live with the change. (2, p. 133)

In sum, then, the Court, sitting amidst conflicting and changing attitudes, faced more than the immediate issue of the constitutionality of segregation in public schools. Perhaps no decision in three generations past had been so long pondered by the Court and so thoughtfully awaited by such large groups of people within the nation, and abroad. Implicated in the decision and provocative of great ramifications were four broadly apparent points:

(1) Social: The effect of desegregation in schools upon a still-segregated society.

(2) Federal: The effect upon the Constitution through sharpened questioning of how far the United States may go in imposing its will upon a minority of sovereign states, and of how far those states may go in making legal and practical resistance.

(3) Political: The effect on domestic party and regional alignments, but more especially, the effect upon our position in foreign affairs where "racial discrimination furnishes grist for the Communist propaganda mills."

(4) Educational: The effect upon efficient schooling of the rising generation.

Nearly a year and a half after the first arguments had been heard the Court finally spoke in two rather brief opinions, one for the state cases and the other for the District of Columbia. In the state cases it was held that historical evidence on the intent of those who framed and adopted the Fourteenth Amendment was "inconclusive" with regard to segregation. Accordingly, since the record showed that the schools in the four states were equal or were "being equalized," the Court was obliged to re-examine the "separate but equal" doctrine and decide the effect of segregation itself on public education.

Available to the Court in deciding the state cases was the Fourteenth Amendment's requirement that the states shall guarantee "equal protection of the laws." In the District of Columbia case the Court could only avail itself of the Fifth Amendment's requirement that Congress shall guarantee "due process of law"; for, the Constitution does not expressly guarantee equal protection to persons under the federal government.

On May 17, 1954, Chief Justice Warren delivered the unanimous opinions of the Court. Spelling epitaphic lines for the proximate close of an era in American history, he said:

(BROWN V. BOARD OF EDUCATION)

These cases come to us from the States of Kansas, South Carolina, Virginia, and Delaware. They are premised on different facts and different local conditions, but a common legal question justifies their consideration together in this consolidated opinion.

In each of the cases, minors of the Negro race, through their legal representatives, seek the aid of the courts in obtaining admission to the public schools of their community on a non-segregated basis. In each instance, they had been denied admission to schools attended by white children under laws requiring or permitting segregation according to race. This segregation was alleged to deprive the plaintiffs of the equal protection of the laws under the Fourteenth Amendment. In each of the cases other than the Delaware case, a three-judge federal district court denied relief to the plaintiffs on the so-called "separate but equal" doctrine announced by this Court in Plessy v. Ferguson, 163 U. S. 537. Under that doctrine, equality of treatment is accorded when the races are provided substantially equal facilities, even though these facilities be separate. In the Delaware case, the Supreme Court of Delaware adhered to that doctrine, but ordered that the plaintiffs be admitted to the white schools because of their superiority to the Negro schools.

The plaintiffs contend that segregated public schools are not "equal" and cannot be made "equal," and that hence they are deprived of the equal protection of the laws. Because of the obvious importance of the question presented, the Court took jurisdiction. Argument was heard this Term on certain questions propounded by the Court.

Reargument was largely devoted to the circumstances surrounding the adoption of the Fourteenth Amendment in 1868. It covered exhaustively consideration of the Amendment in Congress, ratification by the states, then existing practices in racial segregation, and the views of proponents and opponents of the Amendment. This discussion and our own investigation convince us that, although these sources cast some light, it is not enough to resolve the problem with which we are faced. At best, they are inconclusive. The most avid proponents of the post-War Amendments undoubtedly intended them to remove all legal distinctions among "all persons born or naturalized in the United States." Their opponents, just as certainly, were antagonistic to both the letter and the spirit of the Amendments and wished them to have the most limited effect. What others in Congress and the state legislatures had in mind cannot be determined with any degree of certainty.

An additional reason for the inconclusive nature of the Amendment's history, with respect to segregated schools, is the status of public education at that time. In the South, the movement toward free common schools, supported by general taxation, had not yet taken hold. Education of white children was largely in the hands of private groups. Education of Negroes was almost non-existent, and practically all of the race were illiterate. In fact, any education of Negroes was forbidden by law in some states. Today, in contrast, many Negroes have achieved outstanding success in the arts and sciences as well as in the business and professional world. It is true that public education had already advanced further in the North, but the effect of the Amendment on Northern States was generally ignored in the congressional debates. Even in the North, the conditions of public education did not approximate those existing today. The curriculum was usually rudimentary; ungraded schools were common in rural areas; the school term was but three months a year in many states; and compulsory school attendance was virtually unknown. As a consequence, it is not surprising that there should be so little in the history of the Fourteenth Amendment relating to its intended effect on public education.

In the first cases in this Court construing the Fourteenth Amendment, decided shortly after its adoption, the Court interpreted it as proscribing all state-imposed discriminations against the Negro race. The doctrine of "separate but equal" did not make its appearance in this Court until 1896 in the case of Plessy v. Ferguson, supra, involving not education but transportation. American courts have since labored with the doctrine for over half a century. In this Court, there have been six cases involving the "separate but equal" doctrine in the field of public education. In Cumming v. County Board of Education, 175 U. S. 528, and Gong Lum v. Rice, 275 U. S. 78, the validity of the doctrine itself was not challenged. In more recent cases, all on the graduate school level, inequality was found in that specific benefits enjoyed by white students were denied to Negro students of the same educational qualifications. Missouri ex rel. Gaines v. Canada, 305 U. S. 337; Sipuel v. Oklahoma, 332 U. S. 631; Sweatt v. Painter, 339 U. S. 629; McLaurin v. Oklahoma State Regents, 339 U. S. 637. In none of these cases was it necessary to re-examine the doctrine to grant relief to the Negro plaintiff. And in Sweatt v. Painter, supra, the Court expressly reserved decision on the question whether Plessy v. Ferguson should be held inapplicable to public education.

In the instant cases, that question is directly presented. Here, unlike Sweatt v. Painter, there are findings below that the Negro and white schools involved have been equalized, or are being equalized, with respect to buildings, curricula, qualifications and salaries of teachers, and other "tangible" factors. Our decision therefore, cannot turn on merely a comparison of these tangible factors in the Negro and white schools involved in each of the cases. We must look instead to the effect of segregation itself on public education.

In approaching this problem, we cannot turn the clock back to 1868 when the Amendment was adopted, or even to 1896 when Plessy v. Ferguson was written. We must consider public education in the light of its full development and its present place in American life throughout the Nation. Only in this way can it be determined if segregation in public schools deprives these plaintiffs of the equal protection of the laws.

Today, education is perhaps the most important function of state and local governments. Compulsory school attendance laws and the great expenditures for education both demonstrate our recognition of the importance of education to our democratic society. It is required in the performance of our most basic public responsibilities, even service in the armed forces. It is the very foundation of good citizenship. Today it is a principal instrument in awakening the child to cultural values, in preparing him for later professional training, and in helping him to adjust normally to his environment. In these days, it is doubtful that any child may reasonably be expected to succeed in life if he is denied the opportunity of an education. Such an opportunity, where the state has undertaken to provide it, is a right which must be made available to all on equal terms.

We come then to the question presented: Does segregation of children in public schools solely on the basis of race, even though the physical facilities and other "tangible" factors may be equal, deprive the children of the minority group of equal educational opportunities? We believe that it does.

In Sweatt v. Painter, supra, in finding that a segregated law school for Negroes could not provide them equal educational opportunities, this Court relied in large part on "those qualities which are incapable of objective measurement but which make for greatness in a law school." In McLaurin v. Oklahoma State Regents, supra, the Court, in requiring that a Negro admitted to a white graduate school be treated like all other students, again resorted to intangible considerations: "... his ability to study, to engage in discussions and exchange views with other students, and, in general, to learn his profession." Such considerations apply with added force to children in grade and high schools. To separate them from others of similar age and qualifications solely because of their race generates a feeling of inferiority as to their status in the community that may affect their hearts and minds in a way unlikely ever to be undone. The effect of this separation on their educational opportunities was well stated by a finding in the Kansas case by a court which nevertheless felt compelled to rule against the Negro plaintiffs:

"Segregation of white and colored children in public schools has a detrimental effect upon the colored children. The impact is greater when it has the sanction of the law; for the policy of separating the races is usually interpreted as denoting the inferiority of the Negro group. A sense of inferiority affects the motivation of a child to learn. Segregation with the sanction of law, therefore, has a tendency to retard the educational and mental development of Negro children and to deprive them of some of the benefits they would receive in a racial[ly] integrated school system."

Whatever may have been the extent of psychological knowledge at the time of Plessy v. Ferguson, this finding is amply supported by modern authority. Any language in Plessy v. Ferguson contrary to this finding is rejected.

We conclude that in the field of public education the doctrine of "separate but equal" has no place. Separate educational facilities are inherently unequal. Therefore, we hold that the plaintiffs and others similarly situated for whom the actions have been brought are, by reason of the segregation complained of, deprived of the equal protection of the laws guaranteed by the Fourteenth Amendment. This disposition makes unnecessary any discussion whether such segregation also violates the Due Process Clause of the Fourteenth Amendment.

Because these are class actions, because of the wide applicability of this decision, and because of the great variety of local conditions, the formulation of decrees in these cases presents problems of considerable complexity. On reargument, the consideration of appropriate relief was necessarily subordinated to the primary question—the constitutionality of segregation in public education. We have now announced that such segregation is a denial of the equal protection of the laws. In order that we may have the full assistance of the parties in formulating decrees, the cases will be restored to the docket, and the parties are requested to present further argument on Questions 4 and 5 previously propounded by the Court for the reargument this Term.[1] The Attorney General of the United States is again invited to participate. The Attorneys General of the states requiring or permitting segregation in public education will also be permitted to appear as *amici curiae* upon request to do so by September 15, 1954, and submission of briefs by October 1, 1954. (63, pp. 687-93)

(BOLLING V. SHARPE)

This case challenges the validity of segregation in the public schools of the District of Columbia. The petitioners, minors of the Negro race, allege that such segregation deprives them of due process of law under the Fifth

---

[1](*Footnote by the Court.*)

"4. Assuming it is decided that segregation in public schools violates the Fourteenth Amendment

"(*a*) would a decree necessarily follow providing that, within the limits set by normal geographic school distributing, Negro children should forthwith be admitted to schools of their choice, or

"(*b*) may this Court, in the exercise of its equity powers, permit an effective gradual adjustment to be brought about from existing segregated systems to a system not based on color distinction?

"5. On the Assumption on which question 4 (*a*) and (*b*) are based, and assuming further that this Court will exercise its equity powers to the end described in question 4 (*b*),

"(*a*) should this Court formulate detailed decrees in these cases;

"(*b*) if so, what specific issues should the decrees reach;

"(*c*) should this Court appoint a special master to hear evidence with a view to recommending specific terms for such decrees;

"(*d*) should this Court remand to the courts of first instance with directions to frame decrees in these cases, and if so, what general directions should the decrees of this Court include and what procedures should the courts of first instance follow in arriving at the specific terms of more detailed decrees?"

Amendment. They were refused admission to a public school attended by white children solely because of their race. They sought the aid of the District Court for the District of Columbia in obtaining admission. That court dismissed their complaint. We granted a writ of certiorari before judgment in the Court of Appeals because of the importance of the constitutional question presented.

We have this day held that the Equal Protection Clause of the Fourteenth Amendment prohibits the states from maintaining racially segregated public schools. The legal problem in the District of Columbia is somewhat different, however. The Fifth Amendment, which is applicable in the District of Columbia, does not contain an equal protection clause as does the Fourteenth Amendment which applies only to the states. But the concepts of equal protection and due process, both stemming from our American ideal of fairness, are not mutually exclusive. The "equal protection of the laws" is a more explicit safeguard of prohibited unfairness than "due process of law," and, therefore, we do not imply that the two are always interchangeable phrases. But, as this Court has recognized, discrimination may be so unjustifiable as to be violative of due process.

Classifications based solely upon race must be scrutinized with particular care, since they are contrary to our traditions and hence constitutionally suspect. As long ago as 1896, this Court declared the principle "that the Constitution of the United States, in its present form, forbids, as far as civil and political rights are concerned, discrimination by the General Government, or by the States, against any citizen because of his race." And in Buchanan v. Warley, 245 U. S. 60, the Court held that a statute which limited the right of a property owner to convey his property to a person of another race was, as an unreasonable discrimination, a denial of due process of law.

Although the Court has not assumed to define "liberty" with any great precision, that term is not confined to mere freedom from bodily restraint. Liberty under law extends to the full range of conduct which the individual is free to pursue, and it cannot be restricted except for a proper governmental objective. Segregation in public education is not reasonably related to any proper governmental objective, and thus it imposes on Negro children of the District of Columbia a burden that constitutes an arbitrary deprivation of their liberty in violation of the Due Process Clause.

In view of our decision that the Constitution prohibits the states from maintaining racially segregated public schools, it would be unthinkable that the same Constitution would impose a lesser duty on the Federal Government. We hold that racial segregation in the public schools of the District of Columbia is a denial fo the due process of law guaranteed by the Fifth Amendment to the Constitution.

For the reasons set out in Brown v. Board of Education, this case will be restored to the docket for reargument on Questions 4 and 5 previously propounded by the Court.

It is so ordered.

Case restored to the docket for reargument on question of appropriate decree. (59, pp. 694-95)

COMMENT

After more than half a century the Court conceded the absurdity in its "separate but equal" doctrine. To hold that where services and facilities were equal, Negroes were no more handicapped, no more discriminated against than were whites by requirements for separate schools was to ignore the socio-historical context in which the two races have had their being in the United States. Such holding may have satisfied a theoretical test, but not the test of experience by the minority race. Numbers of the majority race who may not deny "prejudice" must, nevertheless, have felt a certain relief when the Court abandoned such fiction.

It is to be noted from the decisions that the Court did not order its decree settled "on notice." Instead it held open for reargument by interested parties in October, 1954,[41] the questions of whether Negro children shall "forthwith be admitted to schools of their choice," or whether the Court may "permit an effective gradual adjustment" toward desegregation; and if the latter alternative is decided upon, how the decree is to be carried out. Perhaps the precise and ultimate answers to these questions will be bitterly fought, and some compulsion to obey the Court's ultimate order may yet be required. But, to consider the sanction of the Constitution, and behind it the prestige of the Court, is to suggest that the words already spoken by the Chief Justice contain sufficient force. Fortunately, "gradual adjustment" need not be unconstitutional if the process can be justified as the solution to educational problems apart from any question of race.

Yet, whatever the legal details or the time required for complete de-

---

[41]Before the reargument was heard Justice Jackson had died. The hearing was therefore postponed until the Court would be again at full roster. A new Justice Harlan, grandson of the old, was confirmed in March, 1955, and the hearings were scheduled for April 11, 1955. Then, on May 31, 1955, the brief, unanimous ruling on how integration shall be carried out was read by Chief Justice Warren. Requiring "all deliberate speed" but imposing no deadline, the order included the following:

"All provisions of federal, state, or local law requiring or permitting" racial segregation in public schools "must yield" to the May 17, 1954, decisions that such segregation is unconstitutional.

Federal District Courts, "because of their proximity to local conditions" are delegated to supervise the process of desegregation, being guided by "equitable principles" and the "public interest"; but, "it should go without saying that the vitality of constitutional principles cannot be allowed to yield simply because of disagreement with them." The district courts shall require of school authorities "a prompt and reasonable start toward full compliance" with the 1954 decisions. However, if school authorities demonstrate that they have made a start in good faith but are hampered by problems of "administration, school plant, transportation, personnel, revision of school districts, local law and regulations" the courts may grant "additional time." (75 Sup. Ct. 753-57)

Clearly, the order is unequivocal in its requirement that segregation come to an end. Although that end remains perhaps scores upon scores of court cases away, it can hardly be avoided in our government of law.

segregation, the burden of its accomplishment will rest most squarely upon educators for years to come. Removal of differences in appropriations for separate schools and the tangible things associated with them will place upon administrators and teachers the responsibility for developing necessary attitudes for the future out of the current difficult relationships.

For the present, some specific indications from events at the opening of schools in the fall of 1954 may be of interest. The twenty-one states which, with the District of Columbia, were affected by the Court's opinions in May, reacted in one or another of three general ways. For the first, the western states of Arizona, Kansas, and New Mexico, where optional segregation had been provided and actually practiced, indicated full compliance with the Court's opinion (32, p. 6E), but Kansas planned a two year period in which to complete integration. (39, p. 13) Similarly, the border states of Delaware, Maryland, Missouri, and West Virginia, with the District of Columbia, showed that they apparently regarded the issue as settled by beginning integration in some of their schools. (32, p. 6E) One southern state, Tennessee, appeared to have a comprehensive plan for integration. This plan, which was expected in a brief the state would file as a "friend of the Court," was reported as scheduling gradual desegregation, starting with the first grade and moving progressively with the passage of each year through the other grades. The District of Columbia began various adjustments toward integration which were expected to be completed in the fall of 1955. (39, p. 13)

From the fringe areas of segregated schools some remarkable individual reactions to the matter were reported. In the southern Ohio town of Hillsboro a separate elementary school for Negroes appears to have been maintained in a state where segregation was prohibited under law. There the city engineer, later adjudged sane but possessed of "some unusual and strong ideas," set fire to the Negro school in hope of burning it down and thereby forcing the authorities to order immediate integration. Firemen saved the building and the Negro children had to attend a school "slightly charred." (7, p. 14) In once-segregated Hobbs, New Mexico, a minister who likewise seems to have possessed certain unusual and strong ideas, protested integration on the ground that the children of Noah had been segregated by God. This expression and an accompanying threat of violence was effectively met by a presumably non-scriptural warning from the local district attorney. Temporal law prevailed and the schools opened quietly. (30, p. 1; and 1, pp. 91-92)

Such incidents, contrasting with the general good temper and order

exhibited at the opening of schools in the fall, seasoned the otherwise rather commonplace cataloging of beginning integration. In
October, however, bad feeling and disorder did flare, notably in
Baltimore and in Washington, D. C., but when school people and
peace officers promptly and explicitly made clear that integration
would be continued the disturbances stopped. (40, pp. 78-79; and
38, p. 50) Delaware's larger cities reported no disturbances as integration began; but in Milford, where less than a dozen Negroes had
been enrolled in the high school, a situation developed which attracted much attention. There a certain Bryant Bowles, head of a
"National Association for the Advancement of White People," aroused
racial feeling with which the school board compromised by trans-
porting the Negroes to school in an adjacent community. (40, pp.
78-79; 38, p. 50; 15, p. 43) In West Virginia various student "strikes"
and parent "boycotts" appear to have stayed desegregation in some
communities.

But for all such disturbances, the early reports of good order appear
to have reflected the general acceptance of integration in the border
states.

A second grouping within the twenty-one states affected by the
Court's opinions appeared, with local exceptions, to be marking time
while waiting for the Court's next move. These states were: Arkansas,
Alabama, Florida, Kentucky, North Carolina, Oklahoma, Texas,
and Virginia. (32, p. 6E; and 39, pp. 13-14)

A third grouping, the four states of Georgia, Louisiana, Mississippi,
and South Carolina, took measures designed either for legal avoid-
ance or the imposition of prolonged delay upon desegregation as it
might be finally decreed by the Court. (31, p. 2E) South Carolina,
in March, 1954, ended a two-year process of amending its constitutional requirement for a public school system. Its legislature was
given discretionary power to eliminate the public system in favor of
"private" schools where the Court's opinions would not reach. Similar state constitutional amendments enabling disestablishment of
public schools were approved by Georgia (by a narrow margin) in
November, 1954, and by Mississippi the next month. (34, p. 31;
18, p. 52; 27, p. 42) In November also, Louisiana approved a state
constitutional amendment designed to continue segregated public education by placing the practice within the state's police power "to
promote and protect the public health, morals, better education and
the peace and good order and not because of race." (34, p. 31) Such
reliance on the Tenth Amendment and the powers it reserves to the

states was regarded by "many Louisianians . . . solely as an expression of sentiment, not a legal bar to integration." (18, p. 52)

It would, indeed, seem unlikely that the Supreme Court could view the Louisiana action as other than an inadmissable pretext. However, it does appear possible for Georgia, Mississippi, and South Carolina or any other state to place their public schools under control of individuals or private corporations and thereby beyond the reach of the Fourteenth Amendment which, it will be remembered, puts prohibitions on the states but does not forbid an individual to do anything. Even so, states employing this strategy might find themselves entangled by questions on the illegal use of taxpayer's money. Moreover, the Supreme Court did not allow resort to "private" status in a related matter which was tested in the 1953 case of *Terry v. Adams* (147). There the Texas Jaybird Association had argued that it was an entirely private political organization which, because unconnected with the state, could exclude anyone from its polls for any reason, including race. The Court was not misled and refused to uphold the subterfuge. Moreover, since Chief Justice Warren's decisions hinged on the points that segregation based on race is conducive to feelings of inferiority, and that such feelings operate for unfavorable learning situations, the value of any segregated schooling may be questioned. Hence, the Court may have to apply to private as well as to public schools the principle that segregation is bad!

Perhaps the strongest reason for anticipating failure in attempts to make one-time public education private has nothing directly to do with courts or statutes or constitutions; it lies in the American tradition of a public school system. Editor Hodding Carter of the Greenville, Mississippi, *Delta Democrat-Times* reflected the strength of this tradition in commenting upon his state's approval of its notion for abolishing public schools. He observed,

Someday . . . curious and shocked Americans will ask history and each other who were these angry and fearful people who reacted so unwisely to a doubtful threat as to be willing to relinquish to politicians the decision as to whether their hard-gained public-school systems should endure or die. . . . Neither do we believe that any county's school system should be permitted to be abolished by a simple majority of the legislature. Man and boy, we've seen too often how simple that majority can be. (27, p. 42)

Amendment of state constitutions to permit abandonment of public schools may be viewed as unnecessary by some who are determined to defeat desegregation. Terrorism by Citizens' Councils in the pattern of Ku Kluxism may yet be the result in some areas.   Gerrymandering, an old resource in American politics, has been mentioned as available, at least for urban school districting. By taking advantage of the prevalent concentration of the two races into separate residential areas, attendance boundaries could be drawn to keep the school children separated accordingly. Social and economic patterns might support this expedient to a degree or for a time but not entirely nor in the long run. The people would move and, as the Court made clear in 1948 in the case of *Shelley v. Kraemer* (140), no race may be legally confined to a specified residential area.

Those who are determined to maintain segregated schools will persist with strategems, many of which are now unpredictable; and the federal courts will counter these strategems by actions of their own, some of which may be equally unpredictable.

Southern publicists and commentators, reviewing whatever suggestions for defeating or postponing integration, seem generally to conclude that the end of legal segregation in their schools will not produce the revolution predicted by some who attacked and some who defended the practice, but that it will produce an acceleration of processes long at work, regionally and nationally. Harry S. Ashmore, editor of *The Arkansas Gazette* of Little Rock, has pointed to this conclusion (2, p. 135) and offers a reminder that only in the school districts directly involved in the five cases on public-school segregation could integration be flatly ordered. In the other "11,173 districts" where segregation has been legal and usually practiced "any change will be voluntary until and unless individual suits are brought against each." Ashmore goes on to observe that "this in itself guarantees a rather lengthy transition period," and he also notes that although the Court began in 1938 to "enunciate the new points of law which led to the admission of Negroes to the graduate schools of southern universities," five such universities "still remain inviolate and the number of Negro students on the de-segregated campuses still may be counted in hundreds." (2, p. 134) He concludes a chapter on "The South and the Issue" with the following:

In the long sweep of history the abandonment of *Plessy* by the Supreme Court may be written down as the point at which the South cleared the last turning in the road to reunion—the point at which finally, and under protest, the region gave up its peculiar institutions and accepted the prevailing standards of the nation at large as the legal basis for its relationship with its minority race. This will not in itself bring about any great shift in Southern attitudes, nor even any far-reaching immediate changes in the pattern of biracial education. But it clearly re-defines the goal the Southern people, white and Negro, are committed to seek in the way of democracy. (2, p. 139)

SUMMARY: PART THREE

Answers by the Supreme Court of the United States to questions involving the rights of citizens under the Fourteenth (and Fifth) Amendment and touching on education.

A. *Due Process of Law—Other than Segregation Issues*

Yes No

(X) ( ) [23] *Waugh v. Mississippi University* (1915). Could the university make attendance contingent upon renunciation of allegiance to a fraternity?

(X) ( ) [24] *Zucht v. King* (1922). Could a child be prohibited from attending school without the certificate of vaccination required by a city ordinance?

( ) (X) [25] *Meyer v. Nebraska* (1923). Could the state forbid the teaching of foreign languages in private schools?

( ) (X) [26] *Pierce v. Society of Sisters* (1925). Could Oregon require that all children attend public schools only?

( ) (X) [27] *Farrington v. Tokushige* (1927). Could the state (territory) forbid teaching or subjects in foreign language schools without showing that the state was harmed?

RECAPITULATION

State action upheld .... [23] [24]...... 2
Citizen upheld............................... [25] [26] [27]...... 3

B. *Equal Protection of the Laws—Segregation Issues*

Yes No

( ) (X) [28] *Cumming v. County Board* (1899). Did Georgia authorities maintaining a high school for white girls have to maintain such a school for Negro children?

( ) (X) [29] *Berea College v. Commonwealth of Kentucky* (1903). In a state which required segregation in schools could a private school give instruction to mingled races?

( ) (X) [30] *Gong Lum v. Rice* (1927). Was the classification of a Chinese-American child as a member of the colored races in Mississippi's segregated schools unconstitutional?

(X) ( ) [31] *Gaines v. Canada* (1938). Was Missouri required to maintain equal opportunity for a legal education within its own borders where its own laws could insure its obligation to its citizens?

(X) ( ) [32] *Alston v. School Board* (1940). Was an equally qualified and similarly employed Negro entitled to an equal salary with the white teachers in Norfolk, Virginia?

(X) ( ) [33] *Sipuel v. University of Oklahoma* (1948). Was the state, in the practice of segregation, required to provide facilities for a legal education to one race as soon as another?

(X) ( ) [34] *Sweatt v. Painter* (1950). Was Texas, where the opportunities for a legal education were judged unequal, required therefore to admit a Negro to its University Law School?

(X) ( ) [35] *McLaurin v. Oklahoma* (1950). Was the state university's imposition of segregation measures upon an enrolled Negro student a denial of equal protection of the laws?

(X) ( ) [36] *Brown v. Board of Education*, [37] *Bolling v. Sharpe* (1954). Was segregation by race in public schools unconstitutional in violating the Fourteenth Amendment in states and the Fifth Amendment in the District of Columbia?

RECAPITULATION

State action upheld...................... [28] [29] [30]...... 3
Citizen upheld .... [31] [32] [33] [34]
[35] [36] [37]...... 7

13

SUMMARY AND CONCLUSION

Of the decisions in which the Supreme Court of the United States has touched on education, thirty-seven have been presented. The cases in which these decisions were handed down arose over the years from 1819 to 1954, but the greater portion appeared within the last fifty years—indeed, within the last twenty-five.

This accelerating number of cases resulted, in general, from the growing complexity of the nation's social order and from an increasing trend toward centralization of its government. More specifically, it resulted from the Court's expansion of the "due process of law" concept after 1890, and, beginning in the twenties, from the willingness of the Court to absorb the federal Bill of Rights into the Fourteenth Amendment.

TABLE II

RESULTS IN THE CASES PRESENTED
ON SUPREME COURT DECISIONS AFFECTING EDUCATION

Constitutional Point Questioned	No. of Cases	Fed. Supremacy Asserted in:	State or Fed. Action Upheld in:	Citizens Upheld in:
ART. 1 or AMDT. 10	8	4 (of 4 cases)	3 (of 4 cases)	1 (of 4 cases)
AMDT. 1	14		9 (of 14 cases)	5 (of 14 cases)
AMDTS. 5 & 14 (except race)	5		2 (of 5 cases)	3 (of 5 cases)
AMDTS. 5 & 14 (race only)	10		3 (of 10 cases)	7 (of 10 cases)
	37	4 (of 4 cases)	17 (of 33 cases)	16 (of 33 cases)

224

In the foregoing pages, the cases have been presented against the background of constitutional context and development, where some of them make notable exhibits.

In the pages to follow, the meaning of each decision is summarized in a sentence or so, and placed under its proper heading in terms of effect upon persons or agencies directly concerned in the schools. Following this summary certain conclusions will be offered.

RIGHTS OF PARENTS AND STUDENTS

CONTESTS RESULTING IN POSITIVE EXPRESSIONS OF RIGHTS

1908 [10]

In declaring that a contract involving Indian tribal funds and in behalf of petitioning Indian parents, made by the Commissioner of Indian Affairs with a Catholic school, did not violate the constitutional injunction against an establishment of religion, the Court said that it could not "concede the proposition that Indians cannot be allowed to use their own money to educate their own children in the schools of their own choice because the government is necessarily undenominational." *Quick Bear v. Leupp*.

1923 [25]

In applying a similar view, an attempt by Nebraska's legislature to forbid the teaching of modern languages, except English, in any private denominational, parochial, or public school to any child who had not passed the eighth grade was invalidated by the Court in an opinion which found arbitrary the restraint of a foreign language teacher's right to teach and "of parents to engage him so to instruct their children." *Meyer v. Nebraska*.

1925 [26]

Arbitrary restraints were considered with a similar result when, an Oregon statute which required compulsory education of all children aged eight to sixteen in *public schools* was held invalid. In the course of its opinion the Court said: "The fundamental theory of liberty under which all governments in this Union repose excludes any general power of the State to standardize its children by forcing them to accept instruction from public teachers only. The child is not the mere creature of the state; those who nurture him and direct his destiny have the right, coupled with the high duty, to recognize and prepare him for additional obligations." *Pierce v. Society of Sisters*.

1927 [27]

Proceeding in the same vein, an act of the legislature of the Territory of Hawaii designed to limit attendance at language schools maintained by Orientals was held unconstitutional, the Court declaring that enforcement of the act "would deprive parents of fair opportunity to procure for their children instruction which they think important and we cannot say is harmful. The Japanese parent has the right to direct the education of his own child without unreasonable restriction; the Constitution protects him as well as those who speak another tongue." *Farrington v. Tokushige.*

1930 [11]

As for concessions to religious groups, the right granted sectarian and other private schools to receive free textbooks from public funds under a Louisiana statute was upheld in a Supreme Court decision which sanctioned the "child benefit theory" by quoting the words of the lower court approvingly. The lower court had said that the sectarian and private schools "are not the beneficiaries," rather, it is "the school children and the state alone who are beneficiaries." *Cochran v. Louisiana.*

1947 [12]

This theory and the practice under it was expanded by a finding that, Catholic parochial school children can constitutionally receive free bus transportation from public funds by authority provided in a New Jersey statute. The majority of a sharply divided Court held that the state had done "no more than provide a general program to help parents get their children, regardless of their religion, safely and expeditiously to and from accredited schools." The Court also noted that: "It is much too late to argue that legislation intended to facilitate the opportunity of children to get a secular education serves no public purpose." *Everson v. Board of Education.*

1953 [22]

Turning to a question of censorship, a New York statute under which the board of education had refused to license the showing of a motion picture viewed as "sacrilegious," was held by the Court to violate the First Amendment's guarantee of freedom of "speech" and "the press." The Court declared that "the state has no legitimate interest in protecting any or all religions from views distasteful to them which is sufficient to justify prior restraints upon these views." *Burstyn v. Wilson.*

DECISIONS INVOLVING RIGHTS ASSERTED BY PARENTS OR STUDENTS BUT NOT AFFIRMING SUCH RIGHTS

1915 [23]

A student could assert no constitutional right to attend the University of Mississippi without complying with a requirement that he foreswear allegiance to, or affiliation with, a Greek letter fraternity. *Waugh v. Mississippi University.*

1922 [24]

Likewise, a parent could assert no constitutional right to have his child attend school without first presenting the certificate of vaccination required by an ordinance of the city of San Antonio, Texas. *Zucht v. King.*

1933 [13] and 1934 [14]

Somewhat similarly, in two cases students were unable to claim any constitutional rights to attend state universities free of the requirement that they take military training. *Pearson v. Coale*, and, especially, *Hamilton v. Regents of the University of California.*

RIGHTS OF TEACHERS

CONTESTS TOUCHING PROPERTY RIGHTS AND PERSONAL FREEDOMS

1923 [25]

In finding invalid a Nebraska statute which forbade the teaching of modern languages other than English to any child who had not passed the eighth grade, the Court held that a teacher did have a constitutional right to follow his chosen profession or calling. In declaring that to deprive a teacher of such right was to deny due process, the right of a teacher to teach was labeled a property right. The Court remarked: "Practically, education of the young is only possible in schools conducted by especially qualified persons who devote themselves thereto." *Meyer v. Nebraska.*

1937 [6]

Turning to another type of question, reduction of teachers' salaries—notwithstanding their tenure status—by action of a school board under a New Jersey statute, was upheld by the Court on the grounds that by the law and practice prevailing in the state, the rights which the teachers asserted were essentially statutory (not contractual), hence subject to the will of the legislature. *Phelps v. Board of Education.*

1938 [7]

In a related matter, a dismissed teacher was found by the Court to have established a contractual relationship with the state of Indiana, which the legislature could not impair by repealing the tenure law which had applied in the school where the teacher formerly taught. The Court observed that "a legislative enactment may contain provisions which, when accepted as a basis of action by individuals, become contracts between them and the State or its sub-division within the protection of Article I, Section 10," of the federal Constitution. *Indiana ex rel. Anderson v. Brand.*

1937 [8]

In the previous year, however, an Illinois statute, which reduced the payments to be made to retired teachers *wholly out of public funds* under earlier legislation, was held by the Court not to be a violation of the contract clause in the federal Constitution because the relationship established under the earlier legislation had been but an implementation of policy and intended only as such. This points up a distinction between a pension system supported wholly by public funds and a retirement system supported through joint contributions. *Dodge v. Board of Education of Chicago.*

1940 [32]

As for a matter related more to race than to teachers as such, a Negro teacher paid less salary than similarly situated and equally qualified white teachers was held by a circuit court of appeals to be discriminated against in violation of the "due process" and "equal protection" clauses of the Fourteenth Amendment; this, despite the fact that the teacher had signed a contract for the salary of which he complained. The Supreme Court refused a petition to review the case and thereby affirmed the holding of the lower court. *Alston v. School Board of the City of Norfolk.*

1952 [20]

Turning to a question of freedom of speech, New York's Civil Service Law, as implemented by the Feinberg law which makes ineligible for employment in the public schools of the state any member of an organization advocating overthrow of the government by unlawful means, and which establishes criteria for measuring the loyalty of teachers, was upheld by the Court in a six-to-three decision. *Adler v. Board of Education.*

1952 [21]

A few months later in a somewhat similar case, an Oklahoma statute requiring loyalty oaths of public officers and employees, including teachers, was invalidated unanimously by the Court on the ground that the required oath would disqualify all those who were or had been members of a proscribed organization, regardless of whether the fact of association "existed innocently or knowingly." Therefore, the Court declared, "The oath offends due process." *Wieman v. Updegraf.*

RIGHTS OF RACES IN SCHOOLS

CONTESTS IN STATES MAINTAINING SEGREGATED SCHOOLS

1899 [28]

The Court applied the "separate but equal" doctrine to public schools and accepted the defense of a Georgia county maintaining segregated schools that it could not afford to provide a high school for Negro children, although it did provide such a school for white children. *Cumming v. County Board of Education.*

1908 [29]

Speaking of race and a private school, a Kentucky statute which required segregation in a chartered college by forbidding instruction to mingled white and Negro students was upheld by the Court, which, quoting the words of a lower court approvingly, said that a chartered corporation's "right to teach is such as the State sees fit to give it. The State may withhold it altogether, or qualify it." *Berea College v. Commonwealth of Kentucky.*

1927 [30]

Also, county school authorities acting under a Mississippi statute were held by the Court to be exercising power within the competency of the state in classifying as "colored" for school purposes a Chinese child born a citizen of the United States, and assignment of such child to a "colored" school did not deny "due process" when equal facilities for education were provided both white and colored races. *Gong Lum v. Rice.*

1938 [31]

Then, beginning a new trend, the Court held, in a Missouri case, that the state could insure equal facilities to the races and equal protection of the laws only within its own borders where its own laws applied, and hence could not maintain equal opportunity for the legal education of its qualified Negroes by paying their tuition at law schools outside the state. *Missouri ex rel. Gaines v. Canada.*

1940 [32]

Having made the turning, and when action of a Virginia school board in paying a disparate salary to white and Negro teachers who were similarly qualified and situated was held by the Circuit Court of

Appeals to be a denial of "due process" and of "equal protection," the Supreme Court refused to review the case and thereby affirmed the judgment. *Alston v. School Board of the City of Norfolk.*

1948 [33]

Returning again to a case involving segregation and a prospective law student, Oklahoma was required, under the equal protection clause, to provide Negro applicants a legal education equal to that afforded whites, and to do so for one race as soon as for another. *Sipuel v. Oklahoma Board of Regents.*

1950 [34]

Soon, in an equally explicit decision, the Court found that a separate law school for Texas Negroes did not afford them a legal education equivalent to that provided whites, and declared that the equal protection clause required that the University of Texas Law School admit a qualified Negro applicant. *Sweatt v. Painter.*

1950 [35]

Then, pressing deeper and considering discrimination in a school the University of Oklahoma was declared to be in violation of the "equal protection" clause by imposing discriminatory rules upon an enrolled Negro student doing graduate work in the school of education. *McLaurin v. Oklahoma State Regents.*

1954 [36]

Finally, in two "landmark" opinions, after prolonged hearings on cases from four states in which Negro parents of public school children challenged the constitutionality of segregation itself in such schools, the Court concluded that " 'separate but equal' has no place in public education" and held segregated public school children to be denied the "equal protection of the laws" guaranteed by the Fourteenth Amendment. In doing so the Court quoted approvingly the words of a Kansas court which had viewed segregated schools as conducive to feelings of inferiority in the Negro group, and "a sense of inferiority" as affecting "the motivation of a child to learn." *Brown v. Board of Education of Topeka.*

1954 [37]

At the same time in a parallel case, segregation by race in the public schools of the District of Columbia was held violative of the "due process of law" guaranteed by the Fifth Amendment to persons under the federal government. *Bolling v. Sharpe.*

POWERS OF SCHOOL AUTHORITIES

CONTESTS AFFIRMING OR RESTRAINING RIGHTS OR POWERS OF
PUBLIC SCHOOL AUTHORITIES IN FISCAL MATTERS

Cases [10], [11], and [12] above affirm the power of public school
authorities to make monetary concessions to religion out of public
funds. Cases [6], [7], and [8] bear on salaries and pensions. Items
below, variously involve the finances of public schools.

1859 [2]

A state enjoying a federal grant of school lands was upheld by the
Court in its right to withhold additional funds derived from tax
moneys and other sources from those schools benefiting directly from
the grants until such time as other schools were on a parity with
them and equality of educational opportunity had been established
in the state. The decision declared that the complainants had "no
right to call upon this court to interfere with the power exercised by
the State Legislature in laying and collecting taxes, and in appropriating them for educational purposes at its discretion." *Springfield Township v. Quick.*

1899 [28]

In affirming state action, the Court accepted the defense of a southern
county maintaining segregated schools that it could not afford to
provide a high school for Negro children, although it did provide
one for white children. *Cumming v. County Board of Education.* (Other
"segregation cases" may also be considered for affects upon the cost
of maintaining "separate but equal" school systems. See *Rights of
Races in Schools.*)

1933 [4]

Federal supremacy was asserted by the Court when it held that a
state university, although furthering one of its functions by import-
ing scientific apparatus for use in its educational department, must
nevertheless pay the federal import duties. In the words of the Court:
"To permit the states and their instrumentalities to import commodities for their own use, regardless of the requirements imposed by
Congress, would undermine if not destroy, the single control which
it was one of the dominant purposes of the Constitution to create."
University of Illinois v. United States.

1938 [5]

Likewise state universities which hold athletic contests as an integral
part of, and in financial support of, the state's function and program

for public education cannot thereby create circumstances in which the federal excise taxes on admissions to the contests do not apply. The Court held that: "If it be conceded that the education of its prospective citizens is an essential governmental function . . . it does not follow that if the State elects to provide the funds . . . by conducting a business, the application of the avails in aid of necessary governmental functions withdraws the business from the field of Federal taxation." *Allen v. Regents of the University System of Georgia.* In this case, and in the one preceding, the recourse open to the universities was through persuasion of Congress to modify the statutes. Congress did largely eliminate the tax on admissions to collegiate athletic contests by an act approved March 31, 1954.

CONTESTS FOR THE MOST PART AFFIRMING POWERS OF SCHOOL AUTHORITIES IN MATTERS INVOLVING RIGHTS OF CITIZENS

1915 [23]

Mississippi University authorities were held by the Court to have infringed in no constitutional meaning upon a student's happiness or upon his property or property rights by making his admission to the university law department contingent upon his compliance with a statute requiring renunciation of affiliation with, or allegiance to, a Greek letter fraternity. The right to attend the university was declared not an absolute right, but a conditional right, and the legislature was judged fully competent to impose disciplinary regulations for the government of the state's schools. *Waugh v. Mississippi University.*

1933 [13]

Somewhat similarly, the University of Maryland was sustained in its right to compel male students to take military training as a condition for admission. Such was the holding of a lower court. The Supreme Court, "for want of a substantial federal question" refused to hear the case and thereby sustained the judgment. *Pearson v. Coale.*

1934 [14]

The following year the Supreme Court decided expressly that the University of California was wholly within its rights in denying admission to male students who refused on religious grounds to take military training. The Court held that the students involved were not being compelled to attend the university and that "the Fourteenth Amendment as a safeguard of 'liberty' [does not confer] the right to be students in the university free from the obligation to take military training as one of the conditions of attendance." *Hamilton v. Regents of the University of California.*

1940 [15]

The religious issue appeared again where a Pennsylvania school board's rule making participation in the flag salute a condition for school attendance was upheld eight-to-one by the Court. *Minersville School District v. Gobitis.*

1943 [16]

Then, within three years, the Court reversed itself on this question and a rule by West Virginia's state board of education requiring participation in the flag salute and the pledge of allegiance as a condition for school attendance was invalidated, six-to-three, as an invasion of "the sphere of intellect and spirit which it is the purpose of the First Amendment of our Constitution to reserve from all official control." *West Virginia State Board of Education v. Barnette.*

1948 [17]

Another matter involving religion is still somewhat ambiguous, for, the plan of "released time" religious instruction, as sanctioned by the Champaign, Illinois, schools, wherein occurred religious teaching in the public school buildings during public school time, was held invalid because, contrary to the prohibition in the First (and Fourteenth) Amendment to the Constitution it amounted to an establishment of religion. *Illinois ex rel. McCollum v. Board of Education.*

1952 [19]

A plan of similar purpose but somewhat different practice, the plan of "released time" religious instruction, prevailing by action of the school board of the City of New York under authority of a state statute, and providing such instruction during public school time, but off public school premises and with a minimum of school administrative assistance, was held valid as not being in conflict with the prohibition against an establishment of religion. *Zorach v. Clauson.* The type plan sustained here was more common than that found unconstitutional in the *McCollum* case.

1952 [18] and 1954

Another aspect of religion in public schools was challenged, but, the Court refused, on jurisdictional grounds, to question a New Jersey statute which required certain Bible reading in public schools and hence sustained the right of the state to continue the requirement. *Doremus v. Board of Education.* Nor would the Court review a decision of the highest New Jersey court which had enjoined Gideons International from distributing copies of the New Testament through the public schools to children who secured the written request of their parents. *Tudor v. Board of Education.*

Cases [25], [26], and [27] under "Rights of Parents and Students" record additional cases in which rights of citizens rather than powers of school authorities were upheld.

RIGHTS OF NONPUBLIC SCHOOLS

CONTESTS TOUCHING ON CHARTERS, A WILL, AND INSTRUCTION
BY CORRESPONDENCE

1819 [1]

A charter granted to Dartmouth College was in the nature of a contract which the state legislature could not alter or revoke without the consent of the college. Such charters, said the Court, were protected by the prohibition in the federal Constitution against the impairment of the obligation of contracts. *Trustees of Dartmouth College v. Woodward.*

1908 [29]

Many years later, however, the charter of Berea College was held by the Court to be a grant of right or privilege which "rests entirely in the discretion of the State, and, of course, when granted, may be accompanied with such conditions as its legislature may judge most befitting to its interest and policy." (Dicta indicate that where a state has reserved the right to alter or amend a charter, the exercise of such right must be reasonable and in good faith so that the object and scope of the grant will not be destroyed.) In this decision the Court declared that chartered corporations enjoy only those rights granted to artificial persons and not the rights enjoyed by natural persons who are citizens of the United States. *Berea College v. Commonwealth of Kentucky.*

1844 [9]

Long ago the provisions of a will under which an endowed school would give no sectarian instruction and would bar ecclesiastics, ministers, and missionaries, even as visitors, from setting foot on its premises were not questioned by the Court. It declared itself "satisfied" that there was nothing in such provisions "inconsistent with the Christian religion," or "opposed to any known policy of the State of Pennsylvania." *Vidal v. Girard's Executors.*

1910 [3]

A different question, instruction by a correspondence school or the transmission of intelligence by mail across state lines and the contracts relating to such transmission, was declared by the Court to be interstate commerce within the meaning of the federal Constitution, and not to be obstructed or unnecessarily encumbered by the states. *International Text-Book Co. v. Pigg.*

CONCLUSION

The ultimate wisdom of the delegates to the Convention of 1787 may be reflected in the points upon which the Constitution it produced is silent. Such silence has, in part, enabled the Supreme Court to develop its stature and to render decisions which are not only legal decisions, for the Court does not merely say "yes" or "no" to the legality of legislative enactments and constitutional provisions.

Still, if that were all the Court did, its power to direct the course of law, including the law affecting education, would clearly exist. But the Court does more.

Unlike almost all other public servants, the Justices must give reasons for their official actions at the moment of performance. Thus there is a need for premises, a need for understanding national aspirations and goals, and a need for a definite philosophy. This philosophy, in the democratic process, cannot be the Court's alone. It must also be ours. If the Court's philosophy is sometimes less or more than ours, or that of legislatures or school officials, a situation for a new balancing or a new structuring within the conceptual design of our education may be established.

Yet, in deference to the fact that public education remains a state and local function, the Court has repeatedly expressed its reluctance to take the responsibility for interfering with state educational policy or practice, even when the rise of constitutional questions compelled it.

Only in cases where school authorities have argued state function against federal supremacy has the Court consistently held against the state contention, as Table II and cases [1], [3], [4], and [5] will show. The first of these, the *Dartmouth College* case of 1819 appears to have had well-nigh immeasurable effect upon constitutional and economic development of the nation, but perhaps less effect upon the development of schools than is sometimes credited. It has been suggested that reasons exist for the view that the development of schools within the United States could well have followed much the same pattern without the decision in the *Dartmouth College* case.

Except for the matter of segregation in schools, the Court's decisions have not, outside the question of federal supremacy, moved with any consistency to either side, in cases where the powers of a state or the actions of state agents have been challenged through a question bearing on education. Possibly one such decision, *Springfield Township v. Quick*, 1859, which upheld the Indiana practice of utilizing funds derived from a federal grant of land for purposes of school equalization, marks the greatest influence by the Court upon education in the nineteenth century.

It is in decisions involving personal rights and property rights of the individual, with the preponderance of such cases falling in the period since World War I, that the Court has most frequently dealt with questions affecting education.

Three cases, [6], [7], and [8], which arose during the depression years, if taken together, involve matters of teachers' tenure, contracts, and retirement. The conclusion from them is threefold: (1) The mere holding of a teaching position does not establish a contractual obligation, (2) the language and the intent of a governing statute will determine whether teacher's rights are statutory or contractual, but (3) after teachers' services have once been rendered an implied contract arises, except in the case of pensions paid retired teachers from funds derived exclusively from public sources.

In considering questions, [10], [11], and [12], as to whether the use of public funds for the education of Indians, and for free textbooks and bus transportation might advance sectarian interests and, thereby, amount either to an establishment of religion, or to depriving citizens of their property without due process of law, the Court has given development to the "child benefit" theory in upholding such expenditures of funds. The "child benefit" theory means, in briefest terms, that in the view of court, the interest of the state in equal educational opportunity for all its children transcends a too literal application of constitutional restraints. In the *Everson* case, 1947, the latest and most significant of the three, the Court, while upholding free bus transportation from public funds for parochial school children, voiced a broad constitutional doctrine of importance to both public and sectarian education. This doctrine was broad enough to cover both separation of church and state and separation of religion and state. Yet the case is illustrative of what Justice Rutledge described as a great drive to secure public funds for the aid and support of religious schools.

Another great drive, noted by Justice Rutledge, designed to introduce religious instruction into the public schools, appeared for a brief time to have been checked. In the *McCollum* case of 1948, the Court for the first time invalidated either federal or state action as amounting to an establishment of religion. It declared a particular plan for a released time program for religious instruction in the public schools to be unconstitutional. Later, however, in *Zorach v. Clauson*, 1952, the Court upheld a plan of similar purpose but of slightly different and more widely practiced operation. Consequently public schools which feel the need to provide such instruction need only conform to the practice sanctioned.

In the famous cases, [15] and [16], involving requirements that school children must salute the flag, despite their contrary religious convictions, the Court's latest decision on the matter, a decision rendered in the midst of war and of war's demand for national unity, nevertheless reversed its earlier ruling and declared that to require the salute "invades the sphere of intellect and spirit which it is the purpose of the First Amendment of our Constitution to reserve from all official control." Presumably, most teachers, and the present Court at least, will strive to maintain that view.

In turning from religious questions to those involving freedom of speech, the Court has twice ruled on state legislation which subjected teachers to loyalty checks and tests. The decision, by a sharply divided court, in *Adler v. Board of Education*, 1952, upheld New York's Feinberg law which required school authorities (1) to adopt and enforce rules for the removal of teachers found ineligible for loyalty reasons, (2) to keep a list of banned organizations, and (3) to make membership in such organizations prima facie evidence of disloyalty and cause for discharge from employment in the public schools. Later, within the same year, in *Wieman v. Updegraf*, the Court unanimously invalidated the form of loyalty oath imposed by Oklahoma on teachers and others. Because the oath in question made no distinction between knowing affiliation and innocent affiliation with banned organizations, the Court declared that it offended due process of law. In neither the *Adler* case nor the *Wieman* case were loyalty oaths per se under examination. Judging from the decision in the *Wieman* case it is clear, however, that the present Court does not approve of them.

Rights of teachers, of parents, and of private schools in providing children with religious or foreign language instruction which, in the words of the Court, "they think important and we cannot say is harmful," have been affirmed by several decisions, [25], [26], and [27], which appear to be conclusive.

On the other hand, two decisions, [13] and [14], have denied any constitutional right of male students to attend state universities and remain free from the required programs in military training. Similarly, the Court has found that no constitutional rights of a student were violated when he was required to forswear allegiance to a Greek letter fraternity as a condition of admission to university [23]. These three decisions sustaining state legislation also appear conclusive.

Eight cases have brought the "separate but equal" doctrine before the Court from the District of Columbia and states permitting or requiring segregation by race in their schools. The first of these decisions was handed down in 1899. The two latest came together on May 17, 1954, when the Court, declaring that "'separate but equal' has no place in public education," expressly held that segregation by race in the public schools is unconstitutional. Beginning in 1938 and the *Gaines* case, (third of the eight) the Court had, however, grown increasingly critical in its scrutiny of the record presented in order to determine whether equality did, in fact, exist. And in each case that followed the decision was in favor of the Negro citizen pressing the matter.

In certain of the cases reviewed, especially those where religion and race have been involved, the Court has fulfilled well its function as the great stabilizer. Taking all the cases in sum indicates that the Supreme Court, although applying a Constitution which has remained ever silent upon the matter of education has, nevertheless, exercised notable influence upon both the concept and pattern of American education. This has been accomplished through decisions which, either test school legislation against constitutional provisions, or, test acts of school authorities against the rights of individuals. Thus the Court has affected the people and the educational system which ultimately bear responsibility for the maintenance of our functioning social order.

BIBLIOGRAPHY

BOOKS AND PERIODICALS

1. "Action Report." *Time* 64:91-92. Sept. 13, 1954.
2. Ashmore, Harry S. *The Negro and the Schools.* 2nd ed. Chapel Hill: University of North Carolina, 1954.
3. Beard, Charles A. and Beard, Mary. *The Rise of American Civilization.* Rev. ed. New York: The Macmillan Co., 1946. 2 vols. in one.
4. "A Biblical Injunction." *Time* 62:29. Dec. 14, 1953.
5. Bittner, Walton S. and Mallory, Hervey F. *University Teaching by Mail.* New York: The Macmillan Co., 1933.
6. Brown, Samuel Windsor. *The Secularization of American Education as Shown By State Legislation, State Constitutional Provisions and State Supreme Court Decisions.* New York: Columbia University, 1912. (Columbia University. Teachers College Contributions to Education No. 49.)
7. "Burning Issue." *Time* 64:14. Sept. 6, 1954.
8. Carey, Charles H. *A General History of Oregon.* 2 vols. Vol. 2. Portland, Oregon: Metropolitan, 1936.
9. "Come Back." *Time* 60:91. April 24, 1950.
10. Council of State Governments. *The Forty-Eight School Systems.* Chicago, 1949.
11. Craven, Avery, Johnson, Walter, and Dunn, F. Roger. *A Documentary History of the American People.* Boston: Ginn, 1951.
12. Cubberley, Ellwood P. *Public Education in the United States.* Rev. ed. Boston: Houghton Mifflin, 1934.
13. Cubberley, Ellwood P. and Elliott, E. C. *State and County School Administration.* New York: The Macmillan Co., 1915. 2 vols.
14. Cushman, Robert Eugene. *Leading Constitutional Decisions.* 9th ed. New York: Appleton-Century-Crofts, 1950.

15. "Day of the Demagogues." *Time* 64:43. Oct. 25, 1954.

16. Edwards, Newton. *The Courts and the Public Schools*. Chicago: University of Chicago, 1933.

17. Edwards, Newton and Richey, Herman G. *The School in the American Social Order*. Boston: Houghton Mifflin, 1947.

18. "Evasive Action." *Time*. 64:52. Nov. 15, 1954.

19. Farrand, Max (ed.) *The Records of the Federal Convention of 1787*. New Haven: Yale University, 1937. 4 vols.

20. Faulkner, Harold Underwood. *American Political and Social History*. 5th ed. New York: Appleton-Century-Crofts, 1948.

21 *The Federalist*, a commentary on the Constitution of the United States, edited by Henry Cabot Lodge. New York: G. P. Putnam's Sons, 1889.

22. Hamilton, Robert R. and Mort, Paul R. *The Law and Public Education: With Cases*. Chicago: Foundation Press, 1941.

23. Johnson, Charles S. *Patterns of Negro Segregation*. New York: Harper, 1943.

24. Kirkland, Edward C. *A History of American Economic Life*. Rev. ed. New York: Crofts, 1946.

25. Knight, Edgar W. and Hall, Clifton L. *Readings in American Educational History*. New York: Appleton-Century-Crofts, 1951.

26. McLaughlin, Andrew C. *A Constitutional History of the United States*. New York: Appleton-Century, 1935.

27. "Mississippi's Choice." *Time* 65:42. Jan. 3, 1955.

28. Morison, Samuel Eliot and Commager, Henry Steele. *The Growth of the American Republic*. 3d ed. New York: Oxford, 1942. 2 vols.

29. Myrdal, Gunnar. *An American Dilemma*. New York: Harper, 1944. 2 vols.

30. New York *Times*. News section, p. 1. Aug. 31, 1954.

31. New York *Times*. Sec. 4, p. 2E. Sept. 12, 1954.

32. New York *Times*. Sec. 4, p. 6E. Sept. 12, 1954.

33. New York *Times*. News section, p. 32. Sept. 30, 1954.

34. New York *Times*. News section, p. 31. Nov. 4, 1954.

35. *Oregonian* (Portland, Oregon). News section, p. 1. Nov. 28, 1953.

36. *Oregonian* (Portland, Oregon). News section, p. 3. Nov. 28, 1953.

37. *Oregonian* (Portland, Oregon). Editorial section, p. 10. Dec. 6, 1953.

38. "Quiet, Please." *Time* 64:50. Oct. 18, 1954.

39. "Races." *Time* 64:13-14. Sept. 6, 1954.

40. "Racial Flareup." *Time* 64:78-79. Oct. 11, 1954.

41. Remmlein, Madaline Kinter. *School Law*. New York: McGraw-Hill, 1950.

42. Rosenfeld, Harry N. "The Parochial School Bus Case." *Nation's Schools* 39:41-43. April, 1947.

43. Rotnem, Victor W. and Folsom, F. G., Jr. "Recent Restrictions upon Religious Liberty." *American Political Science Review* 36:1053-68. 1942.

44. Seagle, William. "Basic Rights" (book review). *Nation* 159:387. 1944.

45. "The Supreme Court." *Time* 62:15-19. Dec. 21, 1953.

46. Taylor, Howard C. *The Educational Significance of the Early Federal Land Ordinances.* New York: Columbia University, 1922.

47. Tewksbury, Donald G. *The Founding of American Colleges and Universities before the Civil War.* New York: Columbia University, 1932.

48. *U. S. Constitution.* The Constitution of the United States of America, analysis and interpretation; annotations of cases decided by the Supreme Court of the United States to June 30, 1952. Prepared by the Legislative Reference Service, Library of Congress, Edward S. Corwin, ed. Washington: Government Printing Office, 1953. (82d Cong., 2d sess. Senate document no. 170)

49. U. S. President's commission on higher education, *Higher Education for American Democracy.* New York: Harper, 1947. 6 vols. in one.

50. Warren, Charles. *Congress, the Constitution and the Supreme Court.* Boston: Little, Brown, 1925.

51. White, Walter. *A Man Called White.* New York: Viking, 1948.

52. Wildes, Harry Emerson. *Lonely Midas: The Story of Stephen Girard.* New York: Farrar and Rinehart, 1943.

COURT REPORTS

(Note: Where two sources are shown for a numbered citation, the page reference in the text are to the second source cited.)

53. *Adler v. Board of Education,* 342 U. S. 485, 72 Sup. Ct. 380 (1952).

54. *Allen v. Regents of the University System of Georgia.* 304 U. S. 439, 58 Sup. Ct. 980 (1938).

55. *Alston v. School Board of the City of Norfolk,* 112 F. 2d 992 (C.C.A. 4th 1940).

56. *Alston v. School Board of the City of Norfolk,* 311 U. S. 693, 61 Sup. Ct. 75 (1940).

57. *Barron v. Baltimore,* 7 Pet. 243 (U. S. 1833).

58. *Berea College v. Commonwealth of Kentucky,* 211 U. S. 45, 29 Sup. Ct. 33 (1908).

59. *Bolling v. Sharpe,* 347 U. S. 497, 74 Sup. Ct. 693 (1954).

60. *Bradfield v. Roberts,* 175 U. S. 291, 20 Sup. Ct. 121 (1899).

61. *Briggs v. Elliott,* 347 U. S. 483, 74 Sup. Ct. 686 (1954).

62. *Brown v. Board of Education of Topeka* (memorandum), 345 U. S. 972, 73 Sup. Ct. 1114 (1953).

63. *Brown v. Board of Education of Topeka,* 347 U. S. 483, 74 Sup. Ct. 686 (1954).

64. *Burkitt v. School District No. 1,* 195 Ore. 471, 246 P. 2d 566 (1952).

65. *Burstyn v. Wilson,* 343 U. S. 495, 72 Sup. Ct. 777 (1952).

66. *Cantwell v. Connecticut,* 310 U. S. 396, 60 Sup. Ct. 900 (1940).

67. *Carr v. Corning,* 182 F. 2d 14 (App. D. C. 1950).

68, *Chaplinsky v. New Hampshire,* 315 U. S. 568, 62 Sup. Ct. 766 (1942).

69. *Chicago, M. & St. P. Ry. Co. v. Minnesota,* 134 U. S. 418, 10 Sup. Ct. 462 (1890).

70. *Cochran v. Louisiana*, 281 U. S. 370, 50 Sup. Ct. 335 (1930).

71. *Collector v. Day*, 11 Wall. 113 (U. S. 1871).

72. *Cumming v. County Board of Education*, 175 U. S. 528, 24 Sup. Ct. 197 (1899).

73. *Davis v. County School Board*, 347 U. S. 483, 74 Sup. Ct. 686 (1954).

74. *DeJonge v. Oregon*, 299 U. S. 353, 57 Sup. Ct. 255 (1937).

75. *Dodge v. Board of Education*, 302 U. S. 74, 58 Sup. Ct. 98 (1937).

76. *Doremus v. Board of Education*, 342 U. S. 429, 72 Sup. Ct. 394 (1952).

77. *Everson v. Board of Education*, 330 U. S. 1, 67 Sup. Ct. 504 (1947).

78. *Farrington v. Tokushige*, 273 U. S. 284, 47 Sup. Ct. 406 (1927).

79. *Federal Radio Commission v. Nelson Brothers*, 289 U. S. 266, 53 Sup. Ct. 627 (1933).

80. *Fisher v. Hurst*, 333 U. S. 147, 68 Sup. Ct. 389 (1948).

81. *Fiske v. Kansas*, 274 U. S. 380, 47 Sup. Ct. 655 (1927).

82. *Fletcher v. Peck*, 6 Cranch 87 (U. S. 1810).

83. *Freeman v. County School Board*, 82 F. Supp. 167 (D.C.E.D.Va. 1948).

84. *Gabrielli v. Knickerbocker*, 306 U. S. 621, 59 Sup. Ct. 786 (1939).

85. *Garner v. Los Angeles Board of Public Works*, 341 U. S. 716, 71 Sup. Ct. 909 (1951).

86. *Gebhart v. Belton*, 347 U. S. 483, 74 Sup. Ct. 686 (1954).

87. *Gerende v. Board of Supervisors*, 341 U. S. 56, 71 Sup. Ct. 565 (1951).

88. *Gibbons v. Ogden*, 9 Wheat. 1 (U. S. 1824).

89. *Gideons International v. Tudor*, 348 U. S. 816, 75 Sup. Ct. 25 (1954).

90. *Gilbert v. Minnesota*, 254 U. S. 325, 41 Sup. Ct. 125 (1920).

91. *Girouard v. United States*, 328 U. S. 61, 66 Sup. Ct. 826 (1946).

92. *Gitlow v. New York*, 268 U. S. 652 (1925).

93. *Gong Lum v. Rice*, 275 U. S. 78, 48 Sup. Ct. 91 (1927).

94. *Graves v. O'Keefe*, 306 U. S. 466, 59 Sup. Ct. 595 (1939).

95. *Greathouse v. Board of School Commissioners*, 198 Ind. 95, 151 N. E. 411 (1926).

96. *Hall v. DeCuir*, 95 U. S. 485 (1878).

97. *Hamilton v. Regents of the University of California*, 293 U. S. 245, 55 Sup. Ct. 197 (1934).

98. *Head v. University of Missouri*, 19 Wall. 526 (U. S. 1874).

99. *Henderson v. United States*, 339 U. S. 816, 70 Sup. Ct. 843 (1950).

100. *Herring v. State Board of Education*, 303 U. S. 624, 58 Sup. Ct. 752 (1938).

101. *Hurtado v. California*, 110 U. S. 516, 538 (1884).

102. *Illinois ex rel. McCollum v. Board of Education*, 333 U. S. 203, 68 Sup. Ct. 461 (1948).

103. *In re Summers*, 325 U. S. 561, 65 Sup. Ct. 1307 (1945).

104. *Indiana ex rel. Anderson v. Brand*, 303 U. S. 95, 58 Sup. Ct. 43 (1938).

105. *International Text-Book Co. v. Pigg*, 217 U. S. 91, 30 Sup. Ct. 481 (1910).

106. *Jacobson v. Commonwealth of Massachusetts*, 197 U. S. 11, 35 Sup. Ct. 358 (1905).

107. *Johnson v. Deerfield*, 306 U. S. 621, 307 U. S. 650, 59 Sup. Ct. 791 (1939).

108. *Jones v. Opelika*, 316 U. S. 584, 62 Sup. Ct. 1231 (1942).

109. *Leoles v. Landers*, 302 U. S. 656, 58 Sup. Ct. 364 (1937).

110. *McCabe v. Atchison, Topeka and Santa Fe Ry. Co.*, 235 U. S. 151, 35 Sup. Ct. 69 (1914).

111. *McCulloch v. Maryland*, 4 Wheat. 316 (U. S. 1819).

112. *McLaurin v. Oklahoma State Regents*, 339 U. S. 637, 70 Sup. Ct. 851 (1950).

113. *Meyer v. Nebraska*, 262 U. S. 390, 43 Sup. Ct. 625 (1923).

114. *Minersville School District v. Gobitis*, 310 U. S. 586, 60 Sup. Ct. 1011 (1940).

115. *Missouri ex rel. Gaines v. Canada*, 305 U. S. 337, 59 Sup. Ct. 232 (1938).

116. *Mo Hock Ke Lok Po v. Stainback*, 74 F. Supp. 852 (D. C. Hawaii 1947).

117. *Morris v. Williams*, 149 F. 2d 703 (C.C.A. 8th 1945).

118. *Murdock v. Pennsylvania*, 319 U. S. 105, 63 Sup. Ct. 870 (1943).

119. *Mutual Film Corporation v. Hodges*, 236 U. S. 248, 35 Sup. Ct. 393 (1915).

120. *Near v. Minnesota*, 283 U. S. 697, 51 Sup. Ct. 625 (1931).

121. *Ogden v. Saunders*, 12 Wheat. 213 (U. S. 1827).

122. *Palko v. Connecticut*, 302 U. S. 319, 58 Sup. Ct. 149 (1937).

123. *Pearson v. Coale*, 165 Md. 224, 167 A. 54 (1933).

124. *Pearson v. Coale*, 290 U. S. 597, 54 Sup. Ct. 131 (1933).

125. *Pennsylvania College Cases*, 13 Wall. 190 (U. S. 1872).

126. *People ex rel. Cisco v. School Board*, 161 N. Y. 598, 56 N. E. 81 (1900).

127. *Phelps v. Board of Education*, 300 U. S. 319, 57 Sup. Ct. 483 (1937).

128. *Pierce v. Society of Sisters*, 268 U. S. 510, 45 Sup. Ct. 571 (1925).

129. *Plessy v. Ferguson*, 163 U. S. 537, 16 Sup. Ct. 1138 (1896).

130. *Powell v. Alabama*, 287 U. S. 45, 53 Sup. Ct. 55 (1932).

131. *Proprietors of the Charles River Bridge v. Proprietors of the Warren Bridge*, 11 Pet. 420 (U. S. 1837).

132. *Quick Bear v. Leupp*, 210 U. S. 50, 28 Sup. Ct. 690 (1908).

133. *Reynolds v. Board of Education for Dade County, Florida.* 148 F. 2d 754 (C.C.A. 5th 1945).

134. *Reynolds v. United States*, 98 U. S. 178 (1878).

135. *Roberts v. City of Boston*, 5 Cush. 198 (Mass. 1849).

136. *Rosenberg v. Board of Education of the City of New York*, 196 N. Y. Misc. 542, 92 N. Y. Supp. 2d 344 (Sup. Ct. 1949).

137. *Scopes v. State of Tennessee*, 154 Tenn. 105, 289 S. W. 363 (1927).

138. *Scott v. Sandford*, 19 How. 393 (U. S. 1857).

139. *Seton Hall College v. South Orange*, 242 U. S. 100, 37 Sup. Ct. 54 (1916).

140. *Shelley v. Kraemer*, 334 U. S. 1, 68 Sup. Ct. 836 (1948).

141. *Sipuel v. Oklahoma Board of Regents*, 332 U. S. 631, 68 Sup. Ct. 299 (1948).

142. *Slaughterhouse Cases*, 16 Wall. 36 (U. S. 1873).

143. *Springfield Township v. Quick*, 22 How. 56 (U. S. 1859).

144. *Stainback v. Mo Hock Ke Lok Po*, 336 U. S. 368, 69 Sup. Ct. 606 (1949).
145. *Stromberg v. California*, 283 U. S. 359, 51 Sup. Ct. 532 (1931).
146. *Sweatt v. Painter*, 339 U. S. 629, 70 Sup. Ct. 848 (1950).
147. *Terry v. Adams*, 345 U. S. 461, 73 Sup. Ct. 809 (1953).
148. *Trustees for Vincennes University v. State of Indiana*, 14 How. 268 (U. S. 1852).
149. *Trustees of Dartmouth College v. Woodward*, 4 Wheat. 518 (U. S. 1819).
150. *Tudor v. Board of Education*, 14 N. J. 31, 100 A. 2d 857 (1953).
151. *United States v. Paramount Pictures*, 334 U. S. 131, 68 Sup. Ct. 915 (1948).
152. *University v. People*, 99 U. S. 309 (1879).
153. *University of Illinois v. United States*, 289 U. S. 48, 53 Sup. Ct. 509 (1933).
154. *Vidal v. Girard's Executors*, 2 How. 127 (U. S. 1844).
155. *Washington, A. & G. R. R. Co. v. Brown*, 17 Wall. 445 (U. S. 1873).
156. *Washington University v. Rouse*, 8 Wall. 439 (U. S. 1869).
157. *Waugh v. Mississippi University*, 237 U. S. 589, 35 Sup. Ct. 720 (1915).
158. *West Virginia State Board of Education v. Barnette*, 319 U. S. 624, 63 Sup. Ct. 1178 (1943).
159. *Western Union Telegraph Company v. Foster*, 247 U. S. 105, 38 Sup. Ct. 438 (1918).
160. *Wieman v. Updegraf*, 344 U. S. 183, 73 Sup. Ct. 215 (1952).
161. *Wilson v. Abilene Independent School District*, 190 S. W. 2d 406 (Tex. Ct. Civ. App. 1945).
162. *Yu Cong Eng v. Trinidad*, 271 U. S. 500, 525, 46 Sup. Ct. 619 (1926).
163. *Zorach v Clauson*, 343 U. S. 306, 72 Sup. Ct. 679 (1952).
164. *Zucht v. King*, 260 U. S. 174, 43 Sup. Ct. 24 (1922).

APPENDIXES

APPENDIX A—CONSTITUTION OF THE UNITED STATES

Reduced to those portions which have had a bearing on the "education cases."

PREAMBLE

We, the people of the United States, in order to form a more perfect Union, establish justice, insure domestic tranquility, provide for the common defense, promote the general welfare, and secure the blessings of liberty to ourselves and our posterity, do ordain and establish this Constitution for the United States of America.

ARTICLE I

Congress

All legislative powers herein granted shall be vested in a Congress of the United States, which shall consist of a Senate and House of Representatives.

Powers of Congress

Section 8. The Congress shall have power to lay and collect taxes, duties, imposts, and excises, to pay the debts and provide for the common defense and general welfare of the United States; but all duties, imposts and excises shall be uniform throughout the United States . . .

To regulate commerce with foreign nations, and among the several States, and with the Indian tribes . . .

To promote the progress of science and useful arts, by securing for limited times to authors and inventors the exclusive right to their respective writing and discoveries . . .

To constitute tribunals inferior to the Supreme Court . . .

To exercise exclusive legislation in all cases whatsoever, over such district (not exceeding ten miles square) as may, by cession of particular States, and the acceptance of Congress, become the seat of the government of the United States, and to exercise like authority over all places purchased by the consent of the legislature of the State in which the same shall be, for the erection of forts, Magazine, arsenals, dockyards, and other needful buildings;—and

To make all laws which shall be necessary and proper for carrying into execution the foregoing powers, and all other powers vested by this Constitution in the government of the United States, or in any department or officer thereof.

Restrictions on Congress

Section 9. . . . No bill of attainder or *ex post facto* law shall be passed. . . .

Restrictions on the States

Section 10. No State shall . . . pass any bill of attainder, *ex post facto* law, or law impairing the obligation of contracts. . . .

ARTICLE II

The Executive

The Executive power shall be vested in a President of the United States of America. . . .

Section 2. . . . He shall have power, by and with the advice and consent of the Senate, to make treaties, provided two thirds of the Senators present concur; and he shall nominate, and by and with the advice and consent of the Senate, shall appoint ambassadors, other public ministers and consuls, Judges of the Supreme Court and all other officers of the United States, whose appointments are not herein otherwise provided for, and which shall be established by law; but the Congress may by law vest the appointment of such inferior officers as they think proper in the President alone, in the courts of law, or in the head of departments. . . .

Section 3. He shall from time to time give to the Congress information of the state of the Union, and recommend to their consideration such measures as he shall judge necessary and expedient; he may, on extraordinary occasions, convene both houses, or either of them . . . he shall take care that the laws be faithfully executed, and shall commission all the officers of the United States.

ARTICLE III

The Judiciary

The judicial power of the United States shall be vested in one Supreme Court, and in such inferior courts as the Congress may from time to time ordain and establish. The Judges, both of the Supreme and inferior courts, shall hold their offices during good behavior, and shall, at stated times, receive for their services a compensation, which shall not be diminished during their continuance in office.

Section 2. The judicial power shall extend to all cases, in law and equity, arising under this Constitution, the laws of the United States, and treaties made, or which shall be made, under their authority; to all cases affecting ambassadors, other public ministers and consuls; to all cases of admiralty and maritime jurisdiction; to controversies to which the United States shall be a party; to controversies between two or more States; between a State and citizens of another State, between citizens of different States; between citizens of the same State claiming lands under grants of different States, and between a State, or the citizens thereof, and foreign states, citizens or subjects.

In all cases affecting ambassadors, other public ministers and consuls, and those in which a State shall be a party, the Supreme Court shall have original jurisdiction. In all the other cases before mentioned, the Supreme Court shall have appellate jurisdiction; both as to law and fact, with some exceptions, and under such regulations as the Congress shall make. . . .

ARTICLE IV

Section 2. The citizens of each State shall be entitled to all privileges and immunities of citizens in the several States. . . .

Section 3. New States may be admitted by the Congress into this Union . . .

Section 4. The United States shall guarantee to every State in the Union a republican form of government. . . .

ARTICLE V

Amendments

The Congress, whenever two thirds of both houses shall deem it necessary, shall propose amendments to this Constitution, or, on the application of the Legislatures of two thirds of the several States, shall call a convention for proposing amendments, which, in either case, shall be valid to all intents and purposes, as part of this Constitution, when ratified by the Legislatures of three fourths of the several States, or by conventions in three fourths thereof, as the one or the other mode of ratification may be proposed by the Congress. . . .

ARTICLE VI

This Constitution, and the laws of the United States which shall be made in pursuance thereof; and all treaties made, or which shall be made, under the authority of the United States, shall be the supreme law of the land, and the judges in every State shall be bound thereby, anything in the Constitution or laws of any State to the contrary notwithstanding.

The Senators and Representatives before mentioned, and the members of the several State Legislatures, and all executive and judicial officers, both of the United States and of the several States, shall be bound by oath or affirmation to support this Constitution; but no religious test shall ever be required as a qualification to any office or public trust under the United States.

AMENDMENTS TO THE CONSTITUTION

ARTICLE I

Congress shall make no law respecting an establishment of religion, or prohibiting the free exercise thereof; or abridging the freedom of speech, or of the press; or the right of the people peaceably to assemble, and to petition the Government for a redress of grievances.

ARTICLE V

No person shall be held to answer for a capital, or other infamous crime, unless on a presentment or indictment of a Grand Jury, except in cases arising in the land or naval forces, or in the militia, when in actual service in time of war or public danger; nor shall any person be subject for the same offense to be twice put in jeopardy of life and limb; nor shall be compelled in any criminal case to be a witness against himself, not be deprived of life, liberty, or property, without due process of law; nor shall private property be taken for public use, without just compensation.

ARTICLE IX

The enumeration in the Constitution of certain rights shall not be construed to deny or disparage others retained by the people.

ARTICLE X

The powers not delegated to the United States by the Constitution, nor prohibited by it to the States, are reserved to the States respectively, or to the people.

ARTICLE XIV

All persons born or naturalized in the United States, and subject to the jurisdiction thereof, are citizens of the United States and of the State wherein they reside. No State shall make or enforce any law which shall abridge the privileges or immunities of citizens of the United States; nor shall any State deprive any person of life, liberty, or property without due process of law; nor deny to any person within its jurisdiction the equal protection of the laws.

APPENDIX B—HOW THE SUPREME COURT FUNCTIONS

THE JUSTICES

The Constitution and the statutes impose no requirements as to professional background or other experience upon Supreme Court Justices, but all those appointed have served at one time or another in some aspect of the legal profession. About half of them occupied judicial positions before their appointment. Many have had long political or administrative experience. A few, notably Justice Frankfurter on the present Court, have had experience as teachers, largely at the college and university level.

The Justices, upon first donning their judicial robes, are supposed to divest themselves of partisanship forever after. The tempering of the need for partisanship after appointment has conduced to a kind of impartiality of judgment that has led some observers to declare democracy too much slowed. Other observers have insisted that "the Supreme Court follows the election returns."

PROCEDURE IN THE SUPREME COURT

The Supreme Court deals largely with cases taken on appeal from lower courts. During two weeks of each month between early October and late May the Justices hear arguments on cases. Counsel for each party must present briefs prior to the oral argument. Currently (1954), oral argument is usually limited to one hour for each side. No witnesses appear, all questioning being of counsel by the Justices. The Supreme Court *Rules* also prescribe the contents of briefs within relatively fixed forms.

HOW THE SUPREME COURT TAKES CASES FROM LOWER COURTS (1954)

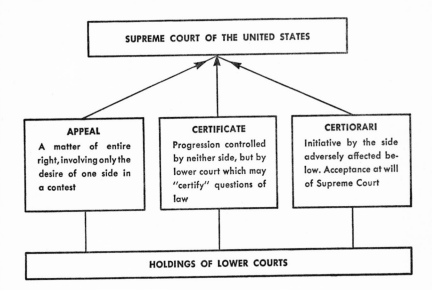

Fig. 3

Following the arguments the Justices devote two more weeks of each month to study of cases. On Saturdays they enter "conference" and discuss the cases. The Chief Justice's opinion is stated first; thence, moving downward in order of seniority each Justice states his opinion in turn, after which they all vote, but reversing the previous order so that the Chief Justice becomes the last. If the Court is "divided" and the Chief Justice finds himself with the minority, the responsibility for writing, or of assigning the writing, of the Court's opinion thereby devolves upon the senior associate Justice remaining with the majority. The opinion of the majority is called the "majority opinion" or the "opinion of the Court." It may take months to write. Any Justice agreeing with the majority opinion, but whose reasons differ, may write a "concurring opinion." Any Justice disagreeing with the majority may record his judgment and reasons in a "dissenting opinion." Three days of each month during the term are "Decision Mondays."

JURISDICTION

The Supreme Court enjoys both original and appellate jurisdiction by virtue of both the Constitution and congressional acts.

ORIGINAL

Article III of the Constitution confers upon the Supreme Court certain powers, as a court of first instance, extending, among other cases, to "those in which a State shall be a party. . . ."

APPELLATE

This power is likewise conferred by Article III, wherein the appellate jurisdiction of the Supreme Court is in accordance "with such exceptions and under such regulations as the Congress shall make." This, in effect, brings within the purview of the Supreme Court certain cases that have been, or are being, decided in lower courts as prescribed by the "Judicial Code" emanating from Congress.

THE JUDICIAL CODE AND PROVISIONS FOR REVIEW

Included within the *United States Code*, a compilation of general and "permanent" federal laws in force on January 3, 1941, is a part (Title 28) called the "Judicial Code and the Judiciary." This is a codification of statutes governing the federal judicial system on January 1, 1912. It, and the larger codification embracing it, has, of course, been much revised and amended. This Judicial Code establishes the appellate jurisdiction of the Supreme Court.

Under it cases may be directed to the Supreme Court in three ways: By appeal, by certificate, and by writ of certiorari.

Appeal

Appeal as a term pertaining to cases reaching the Supreme Court is more technical than in the usage connected with courts in general. Here it describes a matter of entire right and involves only the desire of one side in a contest. The Court exercises no discretionary power over entertaining the case.

Certificate

Certificate differs from appeal in that the lower court, and neither party to a contest, controls the progression to the Supreme Court. The lower court "certifies" for decision by the higher court certain questions of law pertinent to a case before the lower court.

Writ of Certiorari

Writ of Certiorari, like certificate, but unlike appeal, is entirely subject to court control, but in this instance the control is by the higher court. The initiative, however, lies with the side of a suit adversely affected by a lower court's decision and which wishes to petition the higher court for a writ of certiorari, in order "to be informed more fully." If the higher court decides to grant the petition, it issues the writ to the lower court, which is then required to forward the record of the case.

COURTS SUBJECT TO THE SUPREME COURT'S APPELLATE JURISDICTION

Cases may reach the Supreme Court through: Those federal courts, "constitutional courts," established under Article III of the Constitution; certain other federal courts, "legislative courts," created by congressional action in accordance with powers derived from Article I; and from certain state courts.

Constitutional Courts

Constitutional Courts involved in this study include Federal District Courts and the Court of Appeals (until recently designated the Circuit Court of Appeals).

HOW CASES MAY MOVE TOWARD THE SUPREME COURT

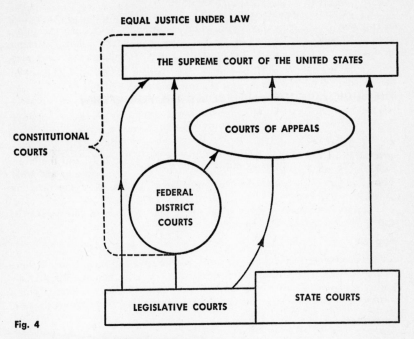

Fig. 4

THE FEDERAL DISTRICT COURTS

The Judicial Code affords direct appeal from these courts to the Supreme Court in limited types of cases. Pertinent here are the following: Suits involving the constitutionality of an act of Congress; suits to enjoin enforcement of orders of the Interstate Commerce Commission; and suits to enjoin enforcement of state statutes or the orders of state administrative boards.

THE COURT OF APPEALS

This court may review all cases in contests not specified to proceed directly from the Federal District Court to the Supreme Court. It may, upon entertaining a case, certify questions to the Supreme Court, or the Supreme Court may issue a writ of certiorari to it upon approving a petition to that effect from the party adversely affected by a decision of the circuit court. In addition, in all cases where the Court of Appeals decides in favor of the party insisting that a state statute is allegedly repugnant to the Constitution, or to the laws and treaties made under the Constitution, an appeal to the Supreme Court may be made by the side of the contest relying upon the state statute.

COURTS OF THE DISTRICT OF COLUMBIA

(Until 1933 these were regarded as legislative courts, but in that year the Supreme Court of the United States changed these courts to the classification of constitutional courts.)

Legislative Courts

Legislative Courts involved in this study include the Customs Courts and, before 1933, the Courts of the District of Columbia.

State Courts

The Judicial Code empowers the Supreme Court to review, upon appeal, the decision of the highest state court possessing jurisdiction over the contest. This will not always be the state supreme court, even in those states where the state supreme court is the "highest" court. Decisions of state courts which the Supreme Court will take on appeal are those in which: The validity of a treaty or statute of the United States is at issue and was not sustained by the decision of the lower court; or the question as to whether a state statute is repugnant to the Constitution, or to the treaties and laws made under it, was decided in the affirmative by the lower court. The Supreme Court of the United States may exercise its prerogative of issuing a writ of certiorari in cases involving the foregoing, and it may also issue such writs where any right, title, or privilege under the Constitution, treaties, or federal statutes was the issue of a petition by either party to a suit.